HIGH

ALASKA

HIGH
ALASKA

A HISTORICAL GUIDE

TO

DENALI · MOUNT FORAKER & MOUNT HUNTER

JONATHAN WATERMAN

Route Photographs By Bradford Washburn

THE AMERICAN ALPINE CLUB
NEW YORK

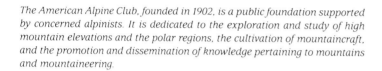

The American Alpine Club, founded in 1902, is a public foundation supported by concerned alpinists. It is dedicated to the exploration and study of high mountain elevations and the polar regions, the cultivation of mountaincraft, and the promotion and dissemination of knowledge pertaining to mountains and mountaineering.

© Jonathan Waterman 1988

First Hardcover Edition 1988
First Paperback Edition 1989

Library of Congress Catalog Card Number 88-72045
ISBN 0-930410-32-7 (Cloth)
ISBN 0-930410-41-6 (Paper)

Manufactured in the United States of America

BOOK DESIGN BY CAROL MALCOLM/CM DESIGN

PUBLISHED BY
THE AMERICAN ALPINE CLUB, INC.
113 EAST 90TH STREET
NEW YORK, NEW YORK 10128-1589
U.S.A.

To the Spirits of

Denali

Sultana &

Begguya

The High One, The Woman, and the Child

Credits

BLACK AND WHITE PHOTOGRAPH SOURCES ARE LISTED below. Page number locations follow the names of the photographers and photograph collections. All route photographs used in the book are by Bradford Washburn.

PHOTOGRAPHERS:

James Balog: *85*
Bryan Becker: *182–83, 184*
Gary Bocarde: *318*
Jim Hale: *91*
Alan Kearney: *333, 369*
Michael Kennedy: *296–97, 326*
Werner R. Landry: *293*
Peter Lev: *204, 205*
Patrick Morrow: *102–3*
Chris Noble: *52*
Brian Okonek: *41, 323, 361*
Glenn Randall: *137, 252–53*
Roger Robinson: *48, 129, 319*
Doug Scott: *176–77*
Jack Tackle: *140–41*
John Thackray: *96*
Les Viereck: *130*
Jonathan Waterman: *54, 88, 168, 331*

PHOTOGRAPH COLLECTIONS:

The American Alpine Club: *131, 132, 170–71*
Catacomb Ridge Expedition: *208*
Charles S. Houston, M.D.:   *249*
Charlie Sassara: *97*
Bradford Washburn: *86*
Guy Waterman: *365*

Acknowledgments

S CORES OF MEN AND WOMEN SHAPED THE HISTORY OF these mountains, shared their stories with me, and permitted me to view their photographs. I am grateful to them all.

My sincere thanks are extended to those who could make their cameras talk when words would fail: James Balog, Brian Becker, Gary Bocarde, Jim Hale, Charles S. Houston, Alan Kearney, Michael Kennedy, Werner R. Landry, Peter Lev, Patrick Morrow, Chris Noble, Brian Okonek, Dave Parkhurst, Glenn Randall, Roger Robinson, Charlie Sassara, Doug Scott, Jack Tackle, John Thackray, Gray Thompson, Les Viereck, and Bradford Washburn.

I am indebted to: Brian Okonek, who has spent many years in the Alaska Range and guided me and many others through its intricacies; Guy and Laura Waterman for their perfectionist passion for writing and mountains; Bradford Washburn for his generosity, and his expertise of Mount McKinley, the name he prefers over Denali; Kim Heakox for his encouragement with the manuscript and his commiseration with me about our shared craft; Bob Seibert, Roger Robinson, Scott Gill, and Ralph Moore, all of the Talkeetna Ranger Station, whom I badgered with obscure questions; Ned Lewis and Roy Kligfield for their translations of Japanese and Italian texts; and Michael Kennedy, who has climbed the most elegant routes on the three great peaks of the Alaska Range.

I am grateful to Bradford Washburn and the Museum of Science in Boston for their kind cooperation regarding the use of the route photographs and map in this book. The aerial photographs—the finest of Alaska's mountains—were taken by Washburn over a period of forty years.

The Washburn photographs may be viewed at the Museum of Science and the Talkeetna Ranger Station. The Washburn photographs used in this book have been donated to the ranger station by the publisher and added to the collection there. For the convenience of those who wish to purchase prints from the Museum of Science (see Appendix), the order numbers are shown with each photograph. For those who desire perspectives not shown in this work, many other high-quality photographs are also available from the museum.

CONTENTS

INTRODUCTION
10

DENALI

PART·1

CHAPTER 1
THE NORTHERN ROUTES

Early Exploration and Attempts
39

Muldrow Glacier
46

Pioneer Ridge
50

Wickersham Wall: Canadian Route
51

Wickersham Wall: Harvard Route
55

Route Guides & Firsts
58

Map
80

CHAPTER 2
THE WESTERN ROUTES

West Buttress
83

Northwest Buttress
92

West Rib
95

West Rim
102

Route Guides & Firsts
104

Map
124

CHAPTER 3
THE SOUTH BUTTRESS

1954 Route
127

Southeast Spur
131

Ramp Route
135

Reality Ridge
136

Isis Face
138

Ridge of No Return
140

Route Guides & Firsts
144

Map
164

CHAPTER 4
THE SOUTH FACE

Cassin Ridge
167

American Direct
172

Milan Krišsak Memorial
178

Southwest Face
180

Czech Direct
184

Route Guides & Firsts
186

Map
200

CHAPTER 5
THE EAST BUTTRESS

1963 Route
203

Catacomb Ridge
206

Traleika Spur
209

Route Guides & Firsts
212

Map
222

MOUNT FORAKER PART·II

MOUNT HUNTER PART·III

CHAPTER 6
THE NORTHERN ROUTES
▲

Northwest Ridge
247

Archangel Ridge
250

Highway of Diamonds
253

Route Guides & Firsts
256

Map
264

CHAPTER 7
THE EASTERN ROUTES
▲

Southeast Ridge
267

Northeast Ridge
269

East Face
273

Route Guides & Firsts
276

Map
286

CHAPTER 8
THE SOUTHERN ROUTES
▲

Talkeetna Ridge
289

French Ridge
291

Infinite Spur
294

Southwest Ridge
298

Route Guides & Firsts
300

Map
310

CHAPTER 9
THE NORTHERN ROUTES
▲

West Ridge
317

East Ridge
320

Northeast Ridge
322

Kennedy–Lowe
324

North Buttress
328

Diamond Arête—East Face
332

Route Guides & Firsts
336

Map
356

CHAPTER 10
THE SOUTHERN ROUTES
▲

South Ridge
359

Southeast Ridge
362

Southeast Spur
363

Southwest Ridge
368

Route Guides & Firsts
372

Map
386

APPENDIX
389

BIBLIOGRAPHY
397

INTRODUCTION

W HILE LIVING CLOSE TO THESE MOUNTAINS, I WAS often struck by the remarkable people who frequented the Alaska Range. Many of them return again and again. I have witnessed climbers, like prospectors of an earlier era, who staked their fortunes, sacrificed their careers, and left their loved ones to climb these peaks. Some reach the summit and some do not. Some get frostbitten, rescued, or even killed. But more than a few come out after a significant climb with a new gleam in their eyes, as if they, too, had struck gold. Here, then, are the stories of climbers made wealthy by their new routes.

In recent years, there has been an explosion in climbing activity on Denali, Mount Foraker, and Mount Hunter. Information about the routes on these peaks and, more important, the mountaineers themselves, has never been compiled in a single volume. This book is a history of the first ascents of and significant later routes on the three greatest peaks in the Alaska Range.

Denali, Mount Foraker, and Mount Hunter are treated collectively in this work because they are the most frequently climbed peaks in the Alaska Range and present similar challenges in terms of arctic cold, altitude, crevasse and avalanche hazard, and time commitment. These are the three big ones—the Haydn, Mozart, and Beethoven of classic Alaskan mountaineering.

In discussing new routes, I have included the climbers' previous mountaineering histories, which should help the reader determine the level of experience needed for these climbs. I have discovered that many of those who made the first ascents then went on to make significant ascents around the world, an accomplishment due, in part, to their apprenticeship in the Alaska Range.

I have telephoned, corresponded with, or met many of these mountaineers outside of the Alaska Range. Better still, I have climbed and skied with, rescued (and been rescued by) others. As not all of their stories were forthcoming, I often had to rely on extensive research and literature searches to fill the blanks. Because of the peripatetic nature of the game, many were out on expeditions, had moved to new addresses, couldn't speak English, had not published an account of their climbs, or, sadly, would never return from their last mountain. Nonetheless, I have sought out their stories, their triumphs and tragedies, their laughter, and their spirit with an eager ear.

This book is written in the spirit of the pioneers, the Fred Beckeys and the Bradford Washburns, who have shown others the way. I have tried to breathe their lives into these pages, because, wherever we climb in these magnificent mountains, we are indebted to them.

Somehow, it almost seems dangerous to unveil these harsh, yet sublime mountains. Will inexperienced climbers, who otherwise might not come, get in over their heads? Or degrade the range environmentally? To the first, I can only reply that the Alaska Range can be a deadly place, even for the most experienced alpinist. And in terms of environmental impact, I believe that any mountaineer who spends even a week in the shadow of these lovely giants should be so strongly influenced as to leave no trace of human passage.

To the original native population, these mountains were truly awesome. When they pointed at Denali, Sultana, and Begguya—the three peaks that dominate the Alaska Range—they could only have exclaimed in terms of disbelief, reverence, and respect. These mountains demand no less from us.

Structure of the Book

The dual intention of this book is to provide a history of the ascents of Denali, Mount Foraker and Mount Hunter, as well as to serve as a mountaineering guide. A further and important perspective is provided by historical, scenic, and route-delineated photographs.

In view of the ever-variable and highly subjective route conditions in the Alaska Range, the book cannot, however, provide completely accurate topographical information. Nor can it be a substitute for good judgment and knowledge won from experience in the cold at high altitude. In the words of Terry and Renny Russell: "Adventure is not in the guidebook / And beauty is not on the map / Seek and ye shall find."

The naming of routes is an erratic practice in the Alaska Range. I have deferred to the most popular or more recent names, despite those given in published accounts. For example, Riccardo Cassin named his route on Denali the "South Buttress," but, for years, climbers have called it the "Cassin." Often, when a route is not given a name, it is simply referred to by its compass orientation, or the name shown on the Washburn map.

Routes are listed in their chronological order of ascent. Howev-

er, variations, or prominent faces and buttresses (e.g., Denali's South Face or South Buttress), are ordered chronologically within their own sections to show the historical evolution of a particular mountain feature, and for easy interpretation of route, map, and photographic information.

▲ The Route Guide ▲

Approaches are a prime consideration, for they can be both time consuming and dangerous. In an effort to preserve the wilderness integrity within the more remote parts of Denali National Park and Preserve, flight landings or airdrops are prohibited inside the old (Mount McKinley) park boundaries. Climbers on the south side most commonly approach via airplane from the 7,200-foot Southeast Fork of the Kahiltna Glacier, or the 5,600-foot level on the Ruth Glacier. North side climbers walk in from Wonder Lake, or the western park boundary.

Mileage is given from the nearest landing strip (or Wonder Lake) to the base of the climb; in some cases, the base might be located a mile from the climb, so climbers can observe avalanche activity. The easiest approach to the base of each climb is given, regardless of the first-ascent party's approach. Air or dog-sled transportation can be arranged with various approach services (see Appendix).

Total Time includes the approach, climb, and descent, and will vary for each ascent depending on weather, snow conditions, and party strength. These times, which are based upon minimal load relaying without fixed ropes or siege tactics, should be considered approximations only. Prior acclimatization (climbing high on an easier route, then dropping back down to the intended climb) is essential for true alpine-style ascents of the more difficult routes on Denali and Mount Foraker.

Climbing Miles are measured from the base, or bergschrund, to the highest peak of each mountain.

Vertical Gain of Route is the difference between the summit and base elevations and does not include the approach. Considerable ups and downs on long ridges are noted.

Alaska Grade is based upon Boyd N. Everett, Jr.'s 1966 paper, "The Organization of an Alaskan Expedition." A grading system that is unique to Alaska is needed because of the severe storms, the cold, the altitude, and the extensive cornicing. Conditions can change radically from day to day, which accounts for dramatic and, often, subjective appraisals of actual difficulty. A 5.8 climb in Yosemite Valley might feel like a 5.10 while carrying a heavy pack high on Denali under adverse conditions.

The highest grade on these three peaks is an Alaska Grade 6 (not to be confused with the UIAA Grade VI), which is reserved for the most severe climbs (e.g., Mount Hunter's Southeast Spur and Diamond Arête, Mount Foraker's French Ridge, and Denali's Southwest Face). The Cassin Ridge on Denali and Mount Foraker's Talkeetna Ridge are rated Grade 5 because they offer sustained and difficult climbing, while, because of lesser technical difficulties, providing the option of retreat (as opposed to Grade 6).

The Alaska grading system is also a means of comparing one climb with another. The West Buttress and Muldrow Glacier routes on Denali receive a Grade 2, while one of Mount Foraker's easiest routes, the West Ridge, is a Grade 3+ (the + is added to denote a slightly higher level of difficulty). The Canadian Route on Denali's huge Wickersham Wall is only a Grade 3, for there are no technical difficulties, but speed and avalanche-awareness are needed. Cornice problems and technical climbing difficulties interspersed with broad easy terrain (such as are found on Denali's Southeast Spur, Mount Foraker's Archangel Ridge, and Mount Hunter's Southeast Ridge) all rate a Grade 4.

In summary, each ascending grade has all the elements of the previous grades. Grade 1 is an easy glacier route (not found on Denali, Mount Foraker or Mount Hunter); Grade 2 is moderate, with no technical difficulties aside from knife-edges, high altitude, and weather problems; Grade 3 is moderate-to-hard, a mildly technical climb with occasional cornicing and short steep sections; Grade 4 is hard-to-difficult, and involves more sustained climbing; Grade 5 is difficult, with sustained technical climbing requiring a high level of commitment and scant bivouac sites; and Grade 6 is severe, with poor retreat options (generally long, corniced ridges), hanging bivouacs subjected to spindrift avalanches, or offering the highest standards of sustained technical climbing for over four thousand feet. (See Appendix for hardware suggestions according to the Alaska Grade of each route.)

Difficulties, Dangers, Ratings often provide the angle of the snow and ice and pertinent avalanche problems. The Yosemite Decimal System rating is given (when known); but, again, the tremendous variability in snow and ice conditions, the storms, and the mixed climbing will all conspire against such ratings.

Camps are elevations at which climbers pitched tents or bivouacked. These campsite elevations are intended to show where earlier parties have camped and should only be used as a general guideline for future ascents. On the steeper routes, it is often difficult to determine the elevation of the first-ascent party's bivouac; moreover, it is common for a ledge to be chopped almost anywhere. Detailed descriptions are sometimes provided following the elevation.

References include journals, books, periodicals, maps, and other information that will be of assistance to the climber for each particular route, but are not intended as a comprehensive bibliography. In many cases, information sources have been conversations or letters, which have not been cited. Because of frequent references to *The American Alpine Journal* and the *Alpine Journal*, the abbreviations *AAJ* and *AJ* are used.

Some first-ascent teams left detailed expedition reports and route topos with the Park Service. These are available upon request at the Talkeetna Ranger Station for climbers to read. For Mount Foraker and Mount Hunter's southern routes, the United States Geographical Survey (USGS) maps (see Appendix) are listed by their quadrangle (e.g., Talkeetna D-3); the Washburn map will not cover these routes. The USGS maps will not be needed for either Denali or the northern routes on Mount Hunter; these are covered by the Washburn map.

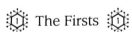 The Firsts

Climbers' surnames and the dates they reached the highest peak of each mountain (Denali's South Peak, Mount Foraker's North Peak, and Mount Hunter's North Peak) are given. Parenthetically enclosed names are those of the expedition's climbing members who did not reach the high point. If the highest peak was not reached by the expedition, the highest point attained is listed before the date.

Ascent indicates the first party known to have climbed the route; it is possible, although highly improbable, that there have been earlier, unrecorded ascents of several routes.

Alpine Style is a pure, yet terribly committing practice on these peaks. Fixing ropes or relaying loads above the base of the climb does not constitute an alpine-style ascent. Each climb was carefully reviewed to insure that it met these criteria. However, some allowances have been made for fixing the climbing ropes a few pitches above the bergschrund, retreating and trying again, unrequested rescues after the climb was completed, or stocking food and acclimatizing high on another route.

Winter is defined by ascents completed between December 21 and March 21. Although winter conditions are often encountered during April climbs, they are not true winter ascents because of the lack of continuous cold and the lengthened daylight hours.

Solo ascents include those by climbers who did not rope into a partner, or share food or tentage.

Ski Descents name the first persons to have skied from the peak to the base.

Variations are made after the first ascent of a route, utilizing a major portion of it. Variations can avoid difficulties, add difficulties, or add a safer twist to the original route.

Sérac sunrise at 15,000 feet.
JONATHAN WATERMAN

The north side of Denali.
JONATHAN WATERMAN

Denali from Turtle Hill, above the McKinley River.
BRIAN OKONEK

Denali from 12,700 feet on Mount Crosson at 3 A.M.
BRIAN OKONEK

Skiing the lower portion of the Canadian Route on Denali's Wickersham Wall.
CHRIS NOBLE

Denali from the north.
JONATHAN WATERMAN

On the West Buttress of Denali at 16,400 feet.
JIM HALE

Rappelling over séracs on Denali's South Buttress.
CHRIS NOBLE

Belay cornice traverse, the Southeast Spur on Denali.
BOYD N. EVERETT, JR. COLLECTION/AAC

On the American Direct Route, South Face of Denali.
GRAY THOMPSON

Roger Mear peering into a bergschrund camp on Denali.
JONATHAN WATERMAN

PART·1

DENALI

PART·1

AT 20,320 FEET, DENali is the highest mountain in North America. Its lower North Peak is 19,470 feet high. Because of Denali's height and position just south of the Arctic Circle, it is arguably the coldest mountain on earth. All other 20,000-foot peaks are spread between latitude 43° north and 32° south of the equator; Denali lies at latitude 63°04' north. Surpassing 20,000 feet of free-standing height, Denali is one of the world's highest peaks rising out of relatively flat environs.

It was first sighted in 1794 by George Vancouver, who reported two stupendous mountains in the distance, crowned with snow and apparently detached from each other. In 1834 a Russian expedition attempted a more in-depth exploration, but little ground was gained.

At this point, the mountain had many names. The people living closest to the mountain, in the interior, had long called it *Denali,* "the high one." In the Susitna region, it was called *Doleyka;* around Cook Inlet, it was *Traleika;* the Russians called it *Bulshaia Gora* and *Tenada.* Its first English name was Densmore's Mountain, after a prospector. Early Fairbanks residents referred to its dual summits as the Churchill Peaks.

It took a Princeton man, William Dickey, who was also a prospector, to finally make a name stick. In 1897, he wrote to the

New York Sun, "We name our great peak Mt. McKinley, after William McKinley of Ohio, who had been nominated for the presidency, and that fact was the first news we received on our way out of that wonderful wilderness."

Naming the mountain after the political candidate of his choice was a logical move for a gold prospector, for William McKinley supported the gold standard as a basis for the economy. Prior to naming the mountain, Dickey had also spent several days with some obnoxious silver prospectors, who were, naturally, rabid champions of the silver standard.

Dickey had met the natives of the Cook Inlet area, but he did not seem to sympathize with their ambiguities and lackluster indigenous customs. One cannot help but feel that if Dickey had met the fierce interior Indians he referred to as "the Apaches of the North," he might have had more appreciation for their reverence of the mountain and passed the name *Denali* on to the *New York Sun.*

Over seven hundred mountaineers attempt to climb Denali every year by way of its two dozen routes. The West Buttress is the most frequently climbed route; the Muldrow Glacier, the West Rib and the Cassin routes are next in order of popularity. Yet, it is rare to cross ropes with another party on another route.

The arctic weather conditions, high altitude, and avalanche and crevasse hazards make Denali the most hazardous of the three great peaks in the Alaska Range. There have been fifty-one deaths and hundreds of rescues on the mountain. Cold and altitude seem to be the primary factors contributing to accidents. Frostbite is common. Denali is a difficult mountain—only half of those who attempt to reach its summit succeed.

CHAPTER 1

THE NORTHERN ROUTES

Early Exploration and Attempts
Muldrow Glacier
Pioneer Ridge
Wickersham Wall: Canadian Route
Wickersham Wall: Harvard Route

Early Exploration and Attempts

I N 1896, WILLIAM DICKEY CARRIED OUT ROUGH SURVEYS of the mountain, finding it to be over 20,000 feet. In 1898, Robert Muldrow and George Eldrige's surveys deemed the mountain to be 20,464 feet.

The first extensive survey and exploration of Denali's environs was undertaken in 1902 by Alfred H. Brooks, a geologist with the U.S. Geological Survey. He measured the mountain at 20,300 feet (Bradford Washburn's conclusive 1947 survey was 20,320 feet). Brooks' nine-man party traveled 80 miles in 105 days; they started from Cook Inlet, crossed Rainy Pass, then traced Denali's north side, eventually exiting to the Yukon River.

Brooks drew the first useful map of the area, which was used widely by explorers, climbers and prospectors. An article by Brooks and D. L. Reaburn, "Plan for Climbing Mt. McKinley," appeared in the January 1903 *National Geographic Magazine*. In it, Brooks suggested approaching from the north and wintering over before the climb.

Judge James Wickersham of Fairbanks (who had read Brooks' article) made the first attempt to climb Denali in 1903. Approaching via the present-day Peters Glacier, Wickersham and his four mutinous partners (some of whom would attempt to leave during the climb, others during the float homeward) cringed beneath the enormous north face. Later it was named the Wickersham Wall.

Judge Wickersham wrote in his diary that

> Immense masses of snow and ice high on the mountainside broke loose with the report of a cannon. With rapidly accelerating speed they shot down the ice encrusted slope, gathering momentum every second…gathering other masses…& finally strike the glacier with the roar of a hundred great guns, cover the medial moraine & throw a great sheet far up on the opposite mountain wall.

Initiating the timeless tone and mood that over a dozen other climbers would match during future efforts on the fourteen-thousand-foot wall, Wickersham wrote:

> One feels his insignificance in the presence of such a stupendous catastrophe which he cannot control nor from which he could possibly escape if within its path. It sent a shiver of fear down my back & warned us to keep clear of the avalanche's path—& we will.

In an extraordinarily bold attempt, Wickersham's team reached 8,100 feet on the Jeffrey Spur (named for George Jeffrey, a court stenographer and a member of the team). "Glare ice" and a "spur as sharp as a house roof rapidly rising to where it was nearly perpendicular," as well as constant snow slides, forced a retreat.

This route was first climbed in 1963. In recent literature, parties have been fond of paraphrasing Wickersham's appraisal of the wall as an impossible climb. Yet, in the clear handwriting of Wickersham's diary, one can read: "…Stevens agreed with me that no one man could reach the summit in the present condition of the mountain…constant warm conditions of two or three days past—that hundreds of slides are coming down in every direction."

Like the other pioneers on Denali, Wickersham recognized both the boundaries of the possible and the safety of his own team. Given the primitive equipment and scanty knowledge with which the pioneers climbed, no modern-day climber would attempt or succeed on anything bolder than those routes pioneered by Wickersham, Frederick A. Cook, Belmore Browne, Herschel C. Parker and Merl LaVoy, the Sourdoughs, and Harry P. Karstens and Hudson Stuck. These men set the standards.

In 1903, Dr. Frederick A. Cook and five partners completed the first circumnavigation of the mountain. To put this feat in perspective, one can regard Galen Rowell's circumnavigation of 1978. The members of both teams were among the most accomplished explorers of their day. Although neither party reached the summit, both expeditions were recorded in books: Robert Dunn's *The Shameless Diary of an Explorer* and Rowell's *High and Wild*. The difference was that, in 1903, Cook's team covered hundreds of miles of unknown territory, the mountain had never been climbed, and they had no air support.

Starting at Cook Inlet (named after Captain Cook), they crossed the Alaska Range west of the Kichatna Spires, encountering horrible difficulties with their horses, then traversed the tundra foothills to the north of Mounts Dall, Russell and Foraker.

Cook and his party made a determined attempt to climb the scantly charted Denali. After two months (Rowell's shorter circumnavigation took nineteen days), Cook and Dunn found Wickersham's abandoned camp on the Peters Glacier. They continued to the Northwest Buttress and started climbing. They reached ten thousand feet and bivouacked.

Robert Dunn (who later made the first ascent of Mount Wrangell) wrote about the next day:

> We were checkmated by steepness at 11,300 feet….But remember this: also with scarce two weeks provisions below on which to

reach the coast, and winter coming....I don't think the slope we did climb would have worried an experienced mountaineer, who might succeed another time.

The party continued out through completely uncharted country, past Mounts Brooks and Mather, coaxing their horses over a steep pass near Mount Pendleton and building a raft to descend the rugged Chulitna and Susitna rivers.

Cook had been to the Arctic three times and to the Antarctic once. Following his successful circumnavigation, he held an unblemished record of exploration. It is speculated that his need

Frederick Cook's "Fake Peak" (indicated by the arrow) as seen from Mount Dickey ▶

for sponsorship to get to the North Pole drove him, three years later, to claim a fraudulent ascent of Denali.

In June 1906, Cook returned to Alaska with seven others and successfully explored the southern approaches to Denali in a huge twenty-five-horsepower motorboat, the *Bulshaia* (the Russian name for Denali). The Yetna River drainages and Mystic Pass approaches were impenetrable. They turned their focus to the southeastern approach, named the Takosha ("land of no trees") Mountains and decided that the Ruth Glacier was the only feasible approach. Running short of time, the expedition returned to Cook Inlet in August.

The expedition members, including Belmore Browne and Herschel C. Parker, either caught a steamer back to the States, or carried on with other business in Alaska. On a last-minute impulse, Cook set out with his assistant horse packer, Edward N. Barrill. After boating up the Susitna, Chulitna and Tokositna rivers, the two men set out through the alders to the Ruth Glacier (named after Cook's stepdaughter, Ruth Hunt).

In a two-week round-trip dash, Cook claimed to have made the summit by gaining the East Buttress and traversing to Karstens Ridge (an arduous feat today and nigh impossible in Cook's day, particularly given the short time and the pair's limited mountaineering background for such a technical route). Newspapers around the country blazoned the headline: *McKinley Is Conquered*. Three years later, Barrill published an affidavit stating that he and Cook never got higher than ten thousand feet.

After Cook's expedition, Brooks, the renowned geologist and early explorer of the Denali area, collected two and a half dollars from a friend and man of the cloth in the Yukon. Brooks had bet that Cook would not make it from the south. His friend's name was Hudson Stuck.

In a Fairbanks bar, in a year of Denali wagering, Tom Lloyd bet Bill McPhee two cents that he was not too old (he was forty-nine) and heavy to climb Denali. McPhee offered him five hundred dollars to make the ascent and prove to the "tribe of Cheechacos" that no man had ever set foot upon Denali's summit. Most Alaskans of the day were driven to a frenzy by the fraudulent claims of Cook, one of the Cheechaco Easterners, the "bunch of bespectacled highbrows."

Two more Alaskan pioneers threw in a thousand dollars and Lloyd deliberately escaped Fairbanks as other sponsors were sidling up to him. Lloyd outfitted his team in China with less equipment than an Eastern expedition would take for one day. (Cook's two expeditions had been sponsored by *Harper's Magazine* at a cost of twenty-eight thousand dollars).

Lloyd had recruited a Swede, Peter Anderson (47), Billy Taylor (27), and Charles McGonagall (40). All were unassuming miners, hardened "sourdoughs," who had gazed up at Denali countless times while working their gold claims in Kantishna. None of them had ever climbed a mountain. They left in December with four horses and a team of sled dogs.

By February 27, they had occupied their first camp beneath the Muldrow Glacier. They spent another month establishing themselves at an eleven-thousand-foot camp, beneath what would later be called Karstens Ridge.

After one attempt, in which they came close to reaching the North Summit (which was undoubtedly to their advantage in terms of acclimatization), the three miners packed Thermoses and doughnuts and set out for the North Peak on April 3, 1910, thinking it was the highest and "toughest." Lloyd was not fit enough to join them.

They wore creepers and hefted alpine poles, which, when carried properly, prevented them from falling in crevasses. Dragging and carrying a fourteen-foot limbed spruce tree, they marched up the knife-edge ridge. They cut across the Harper Glacier to the steep couloir (later named the Sourdough Couloir) and climbed it.

At about 19,000 feet, they planted the pole in some rocks. Taylor and Anderson continued along the narrow ridge (now known as the Pioneer Ridge) to the North Summit, 19,470 feet. It was thirty below and the altitude made Taylor feel "light-like. You had to watch yourself or your feet would come up quick."

The Sourdoughs would have easily seen the South Peak, two miles away, nearly nine hundred feet higher. If they had wanted to get to the highest point, they must have felt some level of disappointment, for from that vantage point no climber would fail to realize that the South Peak is higher.

Nonetheless, it was an incredible achievement. To date, no one has come close to repeating their eighteen-hour trip from the Muldrow Glacier to the North Summit and back. These men unknowingly matched the fast-and-light standards which only highly trained alpinists would apply more than a half century later. Their nonchalance, and lack of ropes or climbing experience, made their climb all the more remarkable.

Unfortunately, Lloyd fraudulently claimed to have made both the North and South summits, and boasted up a storm back in Fairbanks. In typical workingman fashion, Anderson, Taylor and McGonagall stayed in Kantishna to work their claims.

Lloyd sent word that he needed pictures to prove their ascent. According to McGonagall, who was interviewed by Francis P.

Farquhar in 1948, "…Pete, Bill and I went back up and took some more pictures at the place between the two peaks where you can look over to Foraker." They had reached Denali Pass, 18,200 feet, moving continuously from the timber, without camping for three days.

By the time they returned to Fairbanks in June, Lloyd's boasting and the further lack of photographs (the Sourdoughs had little experience with cameras) had completely discredited their climb. No one believed their stories. Three years later, however, during the first ascent of the South Summit, the Sourdough flagpole was spotted through binoculars, although previous and subsequent parties never saw it. Over the years, people gradually came to accept the Sourdough ascent.

In the summer following the Sourdough climb, two separate expeditions arrived on the Ruth Glacier, attempting to repeat Cook's route, or, at least, investigate his claim.

On July 12, representatives of the Mazamas (a mountaineering club out of Portland) reached an altitude of 5,500 feet in the Sheldon Amphitheater. Before turning back, they made the first ascent of Mount Barrille (7,650 feet).

Herschel Parker and Belmore Browne returned, with a photographer, Merl LaVoy. These men became prominent players in the history of Denali. With five others, they spent the entire summer on the Ruth. In a serious attempt to reach the summit of Denali, they reached 10,300 feet on the Northwest Fork of the Ruth Glacier. Because of difficulties in continuing up Cook's claimed route across the East Buttress, these eight strong men turned back after a month's effort, convinced that Cook and Barrill could not have climbed the route in less than two weeks.

Their suspicions were confirmed when they climbed the Fake Peak (5,360 feet) in the Sheldon Amphitheater. Near the summit, they took photographs which perfectly matched Cook's Denali "summit photograph."

But Cook had ardent and loyal supporters. Controversy swirled around North America's greatest peak into the 1940s and 1950s, until climbers grew familiar with Denali. Over the course of two summers, Bradford Washburn and H. Adams Carter would photograph Fake Peak and conduct an elaborate investigation. Washburn would accurately map and photograph Denali from the air. As the veils of the unknown were lifted from the Alaska Range, Cook's claim became transparent.

On March 30, 1912, an expedition sponsored by *The Fairbanks Daily Times* could not find the crucial pass, named McPhee by the Sourdoughs, but renamed McGonagall by Hudson Stuck. They detoured to 8,000 feet on the Peters Glacier and climbed

to 9,240 feet on the Pioneer Ridge. To date, the entire length of this route has not been repeated.

Three months later, Parker, Browne and LaVoy were back. The men had the mountain in their blood. They had tried to show the world that Cook had not reached the top and, now, they played their final hand, trying to claim the summit in an honorable manner.

In two and a half months, covering over three hundred miles from Seward, they approached the mountain by dogsled. From Mile 295 on the railroad, they crossed the Chulitna River and went up the West Fork Glacier, over Anderson Pass and down onto the Muldrow Glacier. For three weeks they rested and lived off the abundant herds of caribou and sheep. When spring came, they began their ascent.

On June 6, Mount Katmai erupted (unbeknownst to the climbers) and spewed its ash from over 350 miles away. Later, they noticed grit in their teapot and cups and assumed that nearby rock cliffs were being crumbled by the glacier.

They made their summit attempt on June 29 from the Harper Glacier. A storm lashed out at them 300 feet from the top. They tried to take shelter in snow holes. Finally, after crawling 330 feet on his hands and knees to within 660 feet of the summit (less than 100 vertical feet), Browne shouted, "The game's up; we've got to get down!" On a good day, it is only a twelve-minute stroll from this spot to the top.

Had they spent one more day trying to finish the last few feet, the trio would surely have perished. The day they descended to Cache Creek, the Muldrow Glacier was devastated by an enormous earthquake.

They tried again two days later, but they were spent. Browne speculated that their forced diet of fatty pemmican (they had run out of other food) was not conducive to acclimatization and had produced an adverse effect.

Browne knew it would be their last attempt on Denali. Although they had become impassioned with the mountain and it had a hold on their lives, it never occurred to them to claim they had reached the summit, as Cook had done.

Browne wrote about the summit attempt: "As I brushed the frost from my glasses and squinted upward through the stinging snow I saw a sight that will haunt me to my dying day. *The slope above me was no longer steep!* That was all I could see." Modern-day mountaineers, who have turned around on the summit ridge in similar storms, just a few feet shy, would do well to remember the timeless honor of Parker, Browne and LaVoy.

Muldrow Glacier

THE MULDROW GLACIER ROUTE BEGINS AT McGONA-gall Pass, nineteen miles from the Wonder Lake trailhead. After passing two icefalls, the glacier dead-ends at the huge Harper Icefall, which is circumvented by Karstens Ridge. The most popular route continues up the Harper Glacier to Denali Pass, intersecting with the West Buttress route, then climbing more steeply on an ill-defined ridge to the 19,600-foot plateau and the summit.

Harry P. Karstens, the "Seventy-Mile Kid," had tried his hand at placer mining, but was too restless and energetic for that type of stooped-over and confining work. He found his true calling out on the trail, mushing dogs and delivering mail over great distances, living the wide-open-and-fifty-below adventure of Alaska.

From 1906 to 1908, Karstens guided Charles Sheldon on the north side of Denali. Sheldon, whose writings and political lobbying were largely responsible for the creation of Mount McKinley National Park ten years later, wrote about his guide: "He is a tall, stalwart man, well-poised, frank, and strictly honorable, and peculiarly fitted by youth and experience for explorations in little-known regions."

Karstens spent long hours out on the tundra, studying the mountain through binoculars and working out his key (and namesake) ridge to the upper basin. He tried to convince Sheldon to join him, but Sheldon was not a mountain climber and refused.

Meanwhile, the Episcopal Archdeacon of the Yukon, Hudson Stuck, remarked, "I would rather climb that mountain than discover the richest gold mine in Alaska." Born in England, this man of the cloth had climbed in his home country, in Canada and in Colorado. In 1907, he had reached the summit of Mount Rainier.

The forty-nine-year-old Stuck had long known about the Seventy-Mile Kid, then thirty-five, and was more than willing to effect a partnership with him, despite Karstens' complete lack of climbing experience. Stuck would put together a team, get the supplies and provide transportation, if Karstens could provide the leadership on the mountain. Karstens jumped at the offer.

Stuck recruited two twenty-one-year-olds, Walter Harper, along with his dog and boat driver, and Robert G. Tatum, who hailed from Tennessee and was staying in the Nenana Mission. By a striking coincidence, Harper's father, Arthur, had entered the

first overland record of sighting Denali as "a great ice mountain" in 1878.

On a shoestring budget compared to those of his predecessors, and a more paltry sum than any modern-day expedition could hope to climb Denali with, Stuck assembled the entire expedition for less than a thousand dollars.

By mid-May, they had mushed into the Muldrow Glacier. They were beset by storms, but Stuck didn't seem to mind, for he was happy tutoring Harper in the tent. Four to six hours a day, with the canvas walls flapping a staccato beat, the half-native gleefully took lessons in physics, math, geology and English.

The earthquake of the previous year had severely altered the key ridge, which Browne and the Sourdoughs had waltzed up in a few days. The Seventy-Mile Kid and Harper toiled for three weeks, hewing a staircase, while Stuck and Tatum ferried loads up the twisted and sérac-jumbled ridge. Fixed ropes were not a component of such early ascents.

Finally, Tatum and Karstens were seen waving at the top of the ridge and the way above was clear. The party then proceeded to make five camps on the Harper Glacier. By the time they were at their eighteen-thousand foot camp, they had spent forty-eight days on the mountain. They should have been superbly acclimatized.

However, according to Stuck's *The Ascent of Denali*, everyone but Harper was turning sleeplessly in his caribou and down. They spent the evening before the summit attempt huddled around the stove in a tight tent.

It is likely that they suffered from acute mountain sickness, brought on by their diet of high fat and protein, which fits logically with Stuck's descriptions of the summit day: "We were rather a sorry company. Karstens still had internal pains. Tatum and I had severe headaches."

Karstens wrote in his diary,

> I had one of the most severe headaches. If it were not the final climb I should have stayed in camp but being…such a promising day I managed to pull through. I put Walter in lead and kept him there all day with never a change. I took second place on the rope so I could direct Walter.

In an act befitting the native name of the mountain, young Walter Harper, native blood coursing strongly through his veins, was the first ever to set foot on Denali's summit. It was June 7, 1913. When the more senior archdeacon joined Harper, he passed out.

When Stuck came to, in the interest of science, he set up an instrument tent. The temperature was 7°F. It took him a pains-

On the Harper Glacier at 18,000 feet ◄

taking half hour to set up and read the barometer at 13,617 inches. The aneroid read 20,300 feet.

With the primitive camera of the day, they took summit photos and nearly froze their fingers. The photographs were triple-exposed, barely discernible.

One can read into Stuck's account that this was the literal and metaphoric high point of their lives. Karstens would spend the rest of his years in the shadow of Denali, as the first superintendent of the park, then as a businessman in Fairbanks. Stuck would seek out other adventures on dogsleds in the Arctic, accompanied by Harper, authoring three books before he died in 1920. Tatum became a reverend in one of Stuck's missions. Harper would die a tragic death on a ferryboat in 1918, while bound for medical school with his newlywed wife, in an attempt to finish the education that Stuck had initiated on the mountain. He had been planning to climb Mount Foraker.

Those precious moments on the summit, before and after they said a hymn around an American flag, would follow each man eternally. Stuck wrote fondly of those moments:

> There was no pride of conquest, no trace of that exultation of victory some enjoy upon the first ascent of a lofty peak, no gloating over good fortune that had hoisted us a few hundred feet higher than others who had struggled and been discomfited…rather a privileged communion with the high places of the earth had been granted.

After Stuck's successful ascent in 1913, a Philadelphia lawyer (who was to testify before a congressional committee investigating the Mount McKinley controversy) wrote:

> Lloyd denies Cook. Browne denies Cook and Lloyd. Stuck denies Cook and Lloyd, and while not denying Browne, repeats over and over that Browne did not reach the top. There is a perfect epidemic of denials. So much so that it would be more accurate to nickname the peak Mt. Denial, instead of Mt. Denali.

North and South Peaks—Airplane Support

The Muldrow Glacier route was not repeated until 1932, an important year on Denali. Alfred Lindley, Harry Liek, Grant Pearson and Erling Strom became the first climbers to use skis, and the first to climb both the North and South Peaks. The North Peak was climbed from Denali Pass.

That same year, Allen Carpé and Theodore Koven (who would both die in crevasse falls) were landed on the Muldrow Glacier by an airplane, which would become an integral tool to every first ascent on Denali.

Denali Pass Variation

In 1947, a team led by Bradford Washburn made the soon-to-be-popular variation of the 1913 route, to Denali Pass, thence finishing along the ridge and across the 19,600-foot plateau. Barbara Washburn then became the first woman to stand on the top of North America. (This variation would also coincide with Washburn's West Buttress route, done in 1951.)

As an interesting historical note, Belmore Browne's son, George, reached the summit with the 1947 party (the fourth ascent of Denali). The principal advantage of this ridge variation is that it allows one to watch the weather moving in from the west and south—for it was a sudden, unforeseen storm that stopped Belmore Browne in 1912, on the blind-sided Northeastern finish, one hundred feet from the top.

Solo

In May 1982, Tom Griffith soloed the Muldrow Glacier route. This was a risky venture, for the first two icefalls are considerably crevassed and Griffith had no means of preventing himself from falling in. (Naomi Uemura, Dave Johnston and Charlie Porter used pole and sled systems for their West Buttress and Cassin Ridge solos.) Griffith did make the summit, a bold and historical achievement.

The Pioneer Ridge

THE PIONEER RIDGE BEGINS AT GUNSIGHT PASS AS A serrated knife-edge, studded with rock pinnacles. Along its latter half, it becomes a more moderate snow and ice ridge, dividing the Wickersham Wall and the Harper Glacier. When it finally reaches the 19,470-foot North Peak, the ridge gains 13,000 feet along its eleven-mile length.

This route was attempted in 1912 by Ralph Cairns' expedition; they could not find McGonagall Pass and ended up on the Peters Glacier. Gaining the ridge via Gunsight Pass, Cairns reached 9,240 feet, where further progress was blocked by pinnacles. Two years earlier, the Sourdoughs climbed the North Peak by utilizing the last 1,200 feet of this razored ridge.

It was not until 1961 that the upper half of the route was completed by Canadian and German climbers who were attracted to a new route, instead of the well-known West Buttress or the unsettled Muldrow Glacier.

Adolf Baur, Donald Lyon, Larry Fowler, Dietrich Haumann and Sev Heiberg set off from Wonder Lake with ninety-five-pound packs and arrived at McGonagall Pass two days later. The long ridge reared up in front of them, startling them, curling only once along its otherwise direct eleven-mile course to the peak. But they didn't have the time to climb the entire ridge, and it looked difficult, so they cut up to the Flatiron Spur. (To date, no one has completed the entire ridge.)

After an airdrop of supplies, the team moved their gear up to 12,500 feet, and dug a snow cave on the ridge above the Flatiron. From there , they climbed on the west side of the sharp ridge crest, postholing across steep snowfields to Taylor Spur. The avalanche potential made them uneasy.

Above fifteen thousand feet, they encountered a sharp knife-edge and snow-covered loose rocks. A day-long storm stopped them. Then they belayed up snow and ice to their seventeen-thousand-foot camp, dropping off the windy ridge to make better time on the snow and ice below.

High winds were a continual problem at this high, exposed site, and during the first two nights, both tents were either broken or buried. A snow cave saved them as the storm grew stronger, yet most of the climbers suffered frostbitten fingers and toes.

When the storm abated, they battled upwards in a headwind. They found a protected col for a quick lunch at eighteen thousand feet; here they estimated the temperature at −20°F. In only four hours from the cave, they reached the North Summit in the late afternoon of July 23.

Weary and licking their wounds, the party balanced down the ridge and trudged out on their barely recognizable glacier route. They got to the McKinley River four days after reaching the summit.

With the customary "trailhead fever" which beckons many footsore and hungry climbers on the north side, the team elected to cross the river during its highest, midafternoon cycle. Haumann started across. Suddenly, weighted by his waistbelt and heavy pack, his feet were knocked from under him in midstream. He was swept downriver. Baur and Fowler ran down and saved his life. They found a shallower crossing and reached the trailhead that evening, twenty-three days after they had left.

Wickersham Wall
Canadian Route

ONE OF THE LARGEST MOUNTAIN FACES IN THE WORLD, the Wickersham Wall rises 14,000 feet from the 5,400-foot Peters Glacier to the 19,470-foot North Peak. This four-mile-wide, north-facing wall is bordered by the Pioneer Ridge on the north and the Northwest Buttress on the south. Although the wall is rimmed with hanging glaciers, there is a spur ridge on the west side of the wall which is the Canadian Route.

In *The American Alpine Journal 1962*, Bradford Washburn wrote an article entitled "Opportunities on Mount McKinley," one of many articles that would inspire Denali climbers. A snaking black line, marked with camps and even an arrow to show an

avalanche slope at 11,500 feet, traces the western edge of the Wickersham Wall on Washburn's photograph.

Indeed, the year before, while inside their tent at 11,500 feet, Warren Bleser and his team rode out an avalanche for seventy feet to the brink of a cliff. Their other supply tent was avalanched off the mountain. The team beat a hasty retreat.

Hans Gmoser, who would later develop helicopter skiing, put together a team of five guides from Canada, plus two Americans. He filmed the expedition in order to promote alpine skiing in connection with mountaineering. The expedition was sponsored by a Toronto newspaper and Head skis.

Hans Schwarz, Gunther Prinz, Pat Boswell, Dietrich Raubach, Leo Grillmair, Hank Kaufmann, Torn Spencer and Gmoser arrived at the base of the wall on June 1, 1963.

Although Gmoser was aware of the possibility of the direct route (see Harvard Route), his team chose the western route, for they did not think the other was safe.

After receiving an airdrop, they waited out a storm that left one and one half feet of new snow. Avalanches roared down most of the wall. They decided to spend as little time as possible on the route.

One night, it snowed four inches, which compelled the team to move even faster, up out of the avalanche zone, to the ridge at 16,600 feet.

Climbers at approximately 13,000 feet on the Canadian Route of the Wickersham Wall ▼

Working like demons, and skiing back down to pick up loads, the team climbed from 7,000 to 18,100 feet in seven days. This rapid style of climbing was a logical solution to the avalanche dangers. There are no real technical difficulties on the route, so, initially, speed was no problem for the Canadians.

The Sourdoughs had done their climb quickly in 1910. In the sixties, "fast and light" was becoming an ideal in alpinism. However, the Canadians, unlike the Sourdoughs, were not "carrying high and sleeping low." They had pushed themselves brutally, making high camps, then ferrying loads back up. In 1963, little was known about acclimatization.

On June 13, with Spencer and Kaufmann "extremely sick and in serious condition," the other six raced a storm to the North Summit. Prinz, Schwarz and Gmoser made it.

By the next day the storm was raging. Gmoser made an attempt to get the sick pair down. They descended only two hundred yards. By the morning of June 15, seven feet of snow covered their tents.

The next day, by what Gmoser termed a miracle, they were able to get Kaufmann and Spencer down to 16,600 feet, but they had become separated from the rest of the party. At this point, according to Spencer, everyone but Schwarz and Gmoser was sick. Raubach could not speak and was paralyzed on one side by what appeared to be a stroke (probably cerebral edema).

Fortunately, the weather cleared and the party was able to evacuate itself down to the West Buttress. As they started down the West Buttress, another storm came up, but the team finally found a note of enjoyment, wedeling down the mountain in deep powder.

Variations—Alpine Style

Two variations were added to this route in 1983. Chris Noble's second alpine-style ascent team—vying for the first ski descent of the Wickersham—cut directly up an icefall to the top of the Jeffrey Glacier (named after Judge Wickersham's court stenographer and expedition member) which minimizes exposure to hanging glaciers on the wall.

On their ninth day of climbing (including two rest days), Noble and Kelly McKean started to the North Summit, while Evelyn Lees (sick from the rapid ascent) and Rick Wyatt decided to descend to their high camp; Lees slipped and fell 1,000 feet, unable to self-arrest because her ice ax was strapped to her pack. She broke her wrist and they suspected that her hip was fractured. The ski descent was abandoned. Wyatt, Noble, and McKean evacuated her to 14,300 feet on the West Buttress.

*Storm clouds over Denali and
Mount Huntington* ◄

Later that year, Gary Speer, Tim Gage, and Markus Hutnak climbed another variation on the Canadian Route. They followed the ramplike Jeffrey Glacier to 7,000 feet, then cut west, below the small icefall to Jeffrey Point, which offered a bit more protection from avalanches than the 1963 route At 15,500 feet, they avoided finishing on the Northwest Buttress by cutting directly to 18,500 feet.

Although they fixed ropes, this team was completely self-sufficient. The year before, they had attempted the route and left a cache at the base. Noble's team found the cache, assumed it was abandoned and took whatever they could use. Although nothing valuable was taken, Speer's accusations, then Noble's rebuttal, spiced the letters section of *Climbing* magazine. (None of the three ascents reached the South Peak.)

Wickersham Wall
Harvard Route

O N THE EAST SIDE OF THE GLACIER-RIMMED WICKERSHAM Wall, there is a slightly protected wrinkle. This, the Harvard Route, is the longer, more difficult and dangerous of the two routes up this oft-photographed, fourteen-thousand-foot wall. It forms a direct line to the North Summit. As of 1987, only the Harvard climbers have touched it. In mid-June 1963, a crew of Harvard tigers, Hank Abrons, Peter Carman, Chris Goetze, John Graham, Don Jensen, Dick Millikan, and Dave Roberts, arrived at McKinley Park Headquarters. Goetze, at twenty-three, was the oldest.

Despite their youth and relative lack of expeditionary experience, they were a very strong group. The Harvard Mountaineering Club's climbers were among the best in the country. Hank Abrons, the titular leader amongst a tight-knit band of friends "who would have enjoyed being anywhere together," had distinguished himself on the first ascent of the Southeast Spur of Denali the year before. He had also climbed Mount Waddington in 1961 with Millikan and Goetze, who had spent the summer of 1962 in the Tetons, climbing the hardest routes to be found; it was this pair who set the boisterous tone and helped establish the team's morale.

The youngest members, Roberts and Jensen, twenty years old and green to Alaska, would forge an unforgettable route up Mount Huntington's West Face three years later. Roberts would return for ten seasons in Alaska, carving a legacy of difficult routes, and, eventually, relating his Alaskan experiences as one of North America's preeminent mountaineering journalists.

However, that day in McKinley Park, the tourists and hotel employees paid little attention to these poorly-dressed East Coast college students, sporting homemade equipment. The stars of the day were the Canadians, impeccably dressed in European guide clothing, fresh from their impressive first ascent on the other side of the wall. In front of the chagrined Harvard climbers, the Canadians were invited to a free feast at the hotel. A hotel employee mistakenly conceded to the Harvard team that he'd feed them, *if* they could make it up the Wickersham.

Seven days later, with the help of an airdrop (the customary tactic of the era, banned in 1964), the seven climbers established themselves at the base of their route. The Canadian route was visible several miles up the Peters Glacier.

Recalling the climb for this book, Roberts wrote:

> The avalanches that came down either side of the spur that defined our route were pretty damned spectacular—still by far the biggest I've ever seen. Here our blithe inexperience helped out, for a few years later I would have known enough to be daunted by them. In particular, when we pitched a camp on the edge of the icefall right below the rock spur where the technical difficulties of our route began, we were doing something really stupid.
>
> One night small rocks drilled holes in our tents; in the daytime, a huge boulder bounced directly over John Graham's head as he stood outside the tent. We just thought this was part of the game, whooped it up, even slept all right. Same reaction when we discovered much higher that we'd set up camp directly over a huge crevasse; somebody peeing discovered the abyss.

The team alternated leads, pairing off the more experienced climbers with the less experienced. All of the technical climbing was below twelve thousand feet. There were difficult steps of steep ice, sugar snow, and occasional Class 5 and aid moves on rotten schist. They fixed ropes on two fifths of the route and, at one camp, rigged a pulley system and hauled a thousand pounds of gear.

In the May 1965 issue of *Harvard Mountaineering,* Millikan painted a typical scene at their seventh camp, at 14,500 feet.

> John is sprawled out in the snow trying to down a whole loaf of logan bread so he can start on the bag of candy bars in front of him. Dave is swilling from a great bucket of Wyler's lemonade. Cardboard boxes lie scattered all around the tents, crudely torn open, their contents strewn around in the snow. Pete is methodically going through the remains, collecting lemon drops and stuffing them in his loot bag. Hank, oblivious to the lack of couth around him, is twenty feet up an overhanging ice wall, dangling from an ice screw which seems to be slowly pulling out on him. Pete attempts to show that with four ice axes he can do as well as Hank with his fancy pitons and slings and lands on his back in the snow.

At their ninth camp, they were hit by a storm that lasted for five days. They sat it out safely in Goetze's ingenious "bomb-shelter" tents, just above the layer of clouds. However, their pilot, Don Sheldon, grew concerned. When he flew by, he could only see their tracks, disappearing into huge avalanche piles.

Sheldon initiated an intensive aerial search by mentioning his concern to a reporter. While the Harvard climbers lay bored and thinking about food in their sleeping bags, the search planes canvassed the mountain beneath them. *The Huntly–Brinkley News*

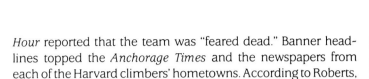

Hour reported that the team was "feared dead." Banner headlines topped the *Anchorage Times* and the newspapers from each of the Harvard climbers' hometowns. According to Roberts, his mother pasted clippings about him in a ghoulish scrapbook.

Up above the Wickersham, Sheldon finally broke through the clouds and spotted the Harvard team. As suddenly as the search had begun, it was called off. (One of the search pilots would later mail the impoverished team a bill for five hundred dollars; the team's spiritual advisor and former colleague, Bradford Washburn, told them not to pay as the search had not been requested by any of the climbers.)

On July 16, they reached the North Summit in a gale. Carman fell off the narrow summit ridge because he couldn't see his feet, but was held in the middle of a three-man rope.

Staggering down to a flat spot, they piled into a tent. That night's dinner pot was knocked over onto Jensen's sleeping bag. Curses filled the tent, but the cook prevailed and scraped stew, hair and lint back into the pot. It was reheated and served, tasting of kerosene. Jensen slept cold for the next few nights.

The next day the weather cleared. They met Dave Johnston, J. Vincent Hoeman, Thomas Choate and Cliff Ells, doing the first traverse of the Muldrow Glacier to the West Buttress. In a feat uncommon for Denali's north-side routes, the Harvard party continued to the South Peak on July 19. Johnston and Hoeman pitched camp on the summit and both parties witnessed a ninety-three-percent solar eclipse. The temperature dropped from −5°F to −25°F.

The Harvard team descended the West Buttress to Kahiltna Pass, then down the Peters Glacier, through the Tluna Icefall, having several scares with crevasses. In typical eager retreating form, the team had a near-drowning—the closest call of the trip—while crossing the McKinley River. Roberts wrote:

> It took a huge amount of hard work, but was not excessive technically. It seemed a very social climb; we may have been hungry and cold, but we never got lonely, and I don't remember being as scared as I ought to have been. Thus it took me the next two years, on Deborah and Huntington, to learn the "deeper" virtues of Alaskan expeditioneering—to answer the challenge of which required the kind of obsessive commitment under constant strain that was Don Jensen's great forte.

More than a month after they started, the ragged, smelly crew returned to the hotel. They looked like bums as they reminded the reluctant hoteliers, who later tried to hand them a bill, of their promised free meal. They were ushered to a far corner of the restaurant, where they ate a tremendous quantity of food.

Denali

THE NORTHERN ROUTES

1	*McGonagall Pass*	8	*North Peak*
2	*Muldrow Glacier*	9	*South Peak*
3	*Pioneer Ridge*	10	*Harper Glacier*
4	*Gunsight Pass*	11	*Traleika Glacier*
5	*Wickersham Wall*	12	*Traleika Spur*
6	*Harvard Route*	13	*Unclimbed*
7	*Canadian Route*		

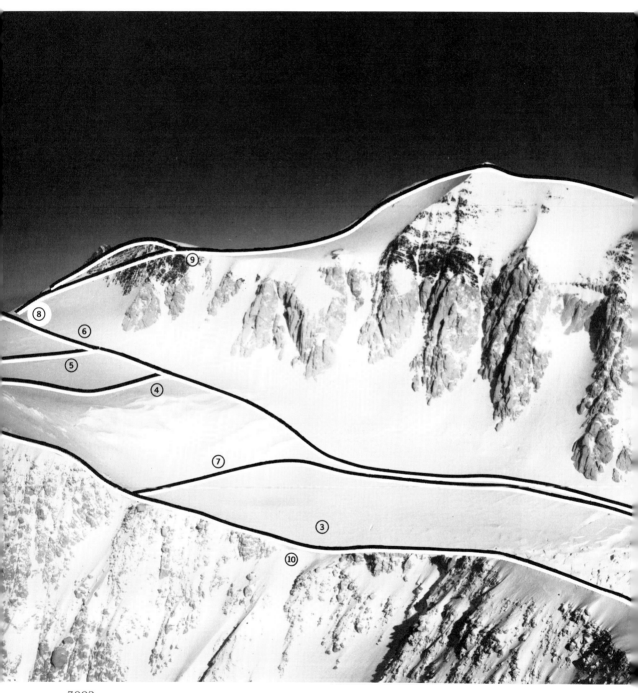

3082

1	*1910 Sourdough Couloir*	7	*1932 Route*
2	*Pioneer Ridge*	8	*Denali Pass*
3	*Harper Glacier*	9	*North Peak Routes*
4	*1913 Route*	10	*Northeast Ridge*
5	*1912 Route*	11	*Unclimbed*
6	*1947 Variation*		

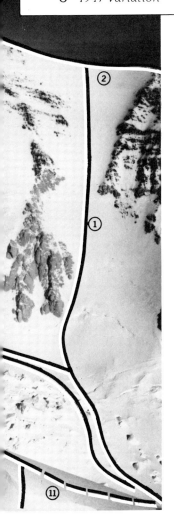

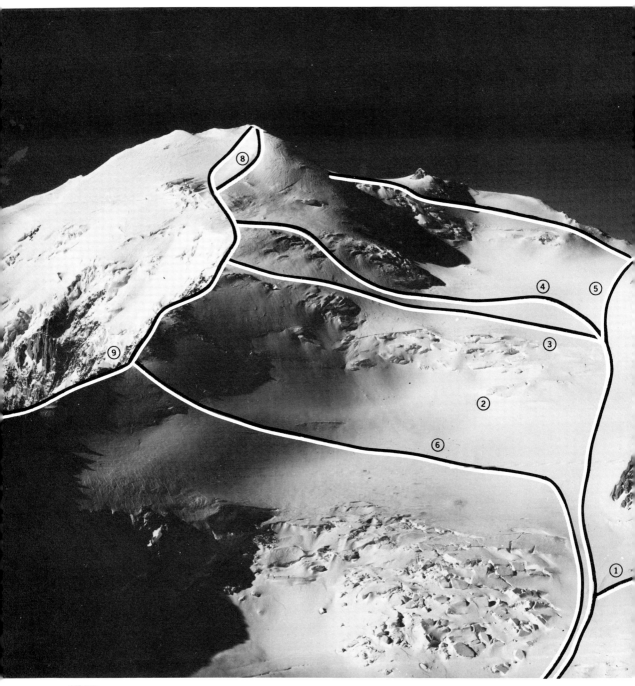

3278

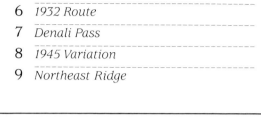

1   *1910 Sourdough Couloir*

2   *Harper Glacier*

3   *1913 Route*

4   *1912 Route*

5   *1947 Variation*

6   *1932 Route*

7   *Denali Pass*

8   *1945 Variation*

9   *Northeast Ridge*

▲ 1 *Karstens Ridge*
2 *Harper Glacier*
3 *Denali Pass*
4 *Sourdough Couloir*
5 *Pioneer Ridge*
6 *1932 Route*
7 *Northeast Ridge*
8 *Unclimbed*

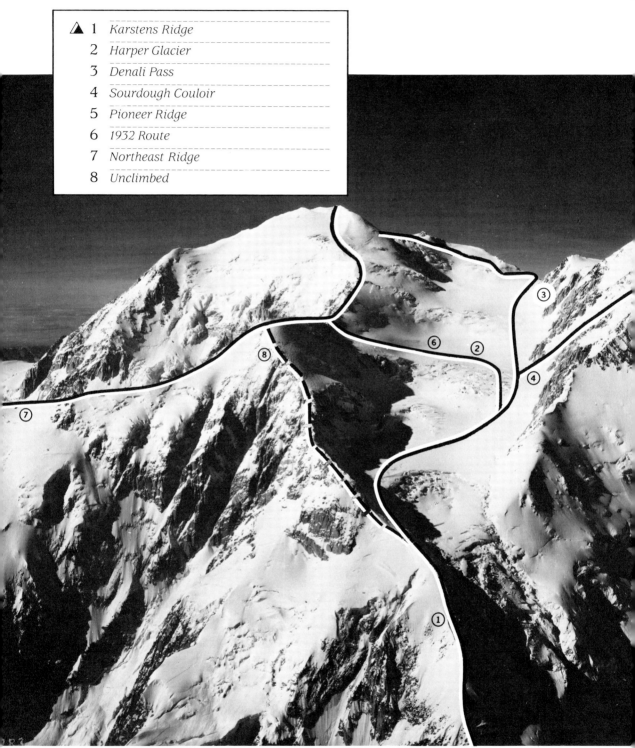

3283

Route Guide

***A**pproach:* 19 miles from 2,100-foot Wonder Lake trailhead, cross the McKinley River (sometimes the most objectively dangerous part of the expedition) and continue to the Glacier via Cache Creek and the 5,720-foot McGonagall Pass. Before Wonder Lake Road is plowed free (usually in May), start from Kantishna, 3 miles from the Wonder Lake trailhead.

***T**otal Time:* 14–28 days.

***C**limbing Miles:* 18.

***V**ertical Gain of Route:* 14,600 feet.

***A**laska Grade:* 2.

***D**ifficulties, Dangers, Rating:* Travel and camp with heed to hanging glaciers which rim Mounts Tatum, Carpé and Koven. Karstens Ridge has 30- to 40-degree snow and ice.

***C**amps:* Avoid fecal-contaminated McGonagall Pass; 5,700; 6,600; 8,100; 9,600; Karstens Ridge: 11,000, 12,100; 14,900; 16,800.

***R**eferences:* 1933, 1948, 1980 (approach map) AAJ; Summer 1985 Alaska Journal; Conquest of Denali, *Browne;* The Pioneer Years, *Moore;* Hall of the Mountain King, *Snyder;* White Winds, *Wilcox.*

Firsts

***A**scent:* June 7, 1913; Karstens, Stuck, Harper, Tatum. North Peak: April 3, 1910; Anderson, Taylor, (McGonagall, Lloyd).

***A**lpine Style:* North Peak: April 3, 1910; Anderson, Taylor, (McGonagall, Lloyd).

***S**olo:* May 23, 1982; Griffith.

***V**ariation:* Via Denali Pass: June 6, 1947; B. & B. Washburn, Browne, Hackett, Lange, Deeke, Craig, Gale, (Pearson).

MULDROW GLACIER

	1	*Traleika Glacier, West Fork*
	2	*Denali Pass*
▲	3	*Karstens Ridge, Muldrow Glacier Route*
	4	*Unclimbed*

5814

▲ 1 *Pioneer Ridge*
2 *Flatiron*
3 *Muldrow Glacier*
4 *Unclimbed*

3540

Route Guide

A*pproach:* 23 miles from 2,100-foot Wonder Lake trailhead, cross the McKinley River (sometimes the most objectively dangerous part of the expedition) and Cache Creek to McGonagall Pass, then along glacier to 6,650-foot Gunsight Pass; or continue 6 miles along glacier to Flatiron. Before Wonder Lake Road is plowed free (usually in May), start from Kantishna, 3 miles from the Wonder Lake trailhead.

T*otal Time:* 14–28 days.

C*limbing Miles:* 11 (or 5 via Flatiron).

V*ertical Gain of Route:* North Summit: 12,900 feet. South Summit: 13,800 feet.

A*laska Grade:* 4 (5 from Gunsight Pass).

D*ifficulties, Dangers, Rating:* Travel and camp with heed to hanging glaciers which rim Mounts Tatum, Carpé and Koven. Up to 70-degree snow and ice; Class 5 rock pinnacles (Gunsight Pass start)

C*amps:* Avoid fecal-contaminated McGonagall Pass; 5,700; 8,100; 9,600; 12,500 (ridge above Flatiron); 15,070; 17,000.

R*eferences:* 1962, 1980 (approach map) AAJ.

Firsts

A*scent:* North Peak: July 23, 1961; Baur, Lyon, Fowler, Haumann, Heiberg. South Peak: June 22, 1971; Ullin, Sloan, Cole, Foster, Mucke.

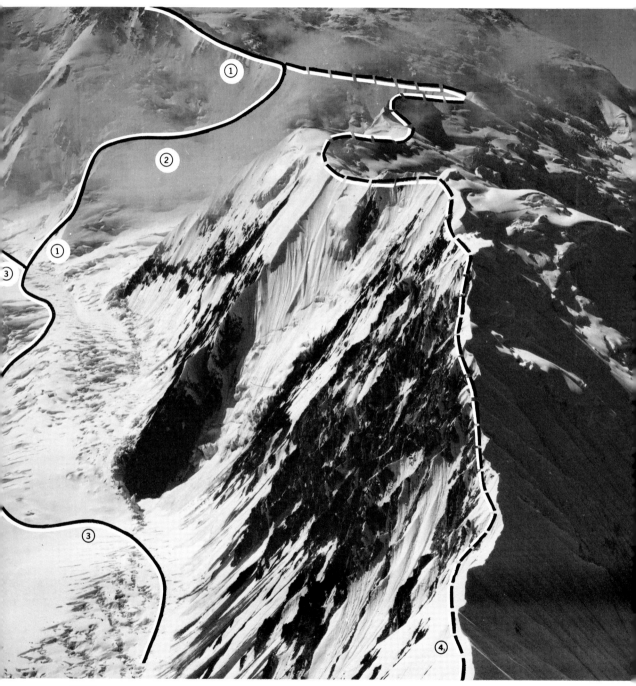

5802

▲ 1 *Pioneer Ridge*

2 *Flatiron*

3 *Muldrow Glacier*

4 *Unclimbed*

Route Guide

Approach: *15 miles from the 7,200-foot Kahiltna Southeast Fork landing strip via Kahiltna Pass, to Peters Glacier, around Northwest side of Tluna Icefall, to the 6,000-foot base; in 1986 the Peters Glacier surged and dropped several hundred feet, rendering it nearly impassable for several years.*

Total Time: *12-24 days.*

Climbing Miles: *10 (North Peak: 7).*

Vertical Gain of Route: *14,300 feet (North Peak: 13,400 feet).*

Alaska Grade: *3.*

Difficulties, Dangers, Rating: *10- to 45-degree snow and ice climbing with little technical terrain; timing, speed and strategically chosen campsites are crucial factors, for the first half of route is exposed to hanging glaciers and the second half is dangerous after snowstorms.*

Camps: *7,200 area (on or against Jeffery Point ridge); 10,000; 12,500; 15,500; 16,600 (intersection of Northwest Buttress).*

References: *1964, 1984, AAJ; November 1983 Climbing; January 1984 Powder.*

Firsts

Ascent: *North Peak: June 13, 1963; Prinz, Schwarz, Gmoser, (Boswell, Raubach, Grillmair, Kaufmann, Spencer).*

Alpine Style: *North Peak: May 18, 1983; Nobel, McKlean, (Lees, Wyatt).*

Variations: *Direct start, North Peak: May 18, 1983; Noble, McKlean, (Lees, Wyatt). Direct finish, North Peak: June 15, 1983; Speer, Gage, Hutnak.*

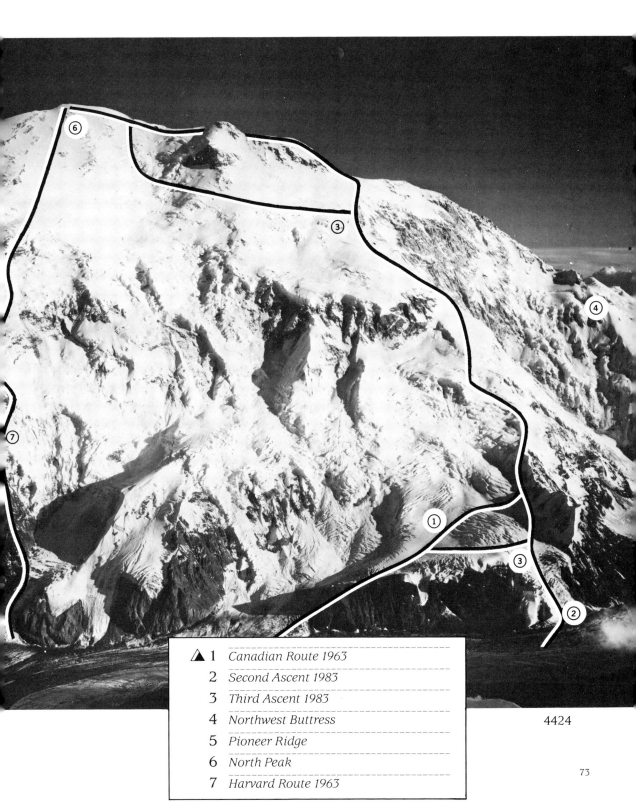

▲ 1 *Canadian Route 1963*
2 *Second Ascent 1983*
3 *Third Ascent 1983*
4 *Northwest Buttress*
5 *Pioneer Ridge*
6 *North Peak*
7 *Harvard Route 1963*

4424

4413

▲ 1 *Canadian Route 1963*

2 *Third Ascent 1983*

3 *Northwest Buttress*

4 *North Peak*

5 *Harvard Route*

▲ 1 *Harvard Route*

4826

Route Guide

A*pproach:* 17 miles from 7,200-foot Southeast Fork of Kahiltna landing strip via Kahilta Pass, to Peters Glacier, around Northwest side of Tluna Icefall, to the 5,400-foot base. In 1986 the Peters Glacier surged and dropped several hundred feet, rendering it nearly impassable for several years.

T*otal Time:* 13-25 days.

C*limbing Miles:* 7 (North Peak: 4).

V*ertical Gain of Route:* 14,900 feet (North Peak: 14,000 feet).

A*laska Grade:* 4+.

D*ifficulties, Dangers, Rating:* An acclimatized team on an alpine-style ascent—with proper timing, speed and strategically chosen campsites—may minimize inherent avalanche and rockfall danger; start up icefall onto a faint spur which averages 50 degrees, with near vertical steps (5.5, A1); the upper, sérac-studded wall is 30 degrees.

C*amps:* 6,900; 8,100; 9,200; 14,500; 16,100; 17,400.

R*eferences:* 1964 AAJ; May 1965 Harvard Mountaineering; Expedition Report, Talkeetna Ranger Station; April 1984 Climbing.

Firsts

A*scent:* July 19, 1963; Abrons, Carman, Goetze, Graham, Jensen, Millikan, Roberts; (North Peak: July 16, 1963).

▲ 1 *Harvard Route*

2 *Pioneer Ridge*

3 *Northwest Buttress*

5951

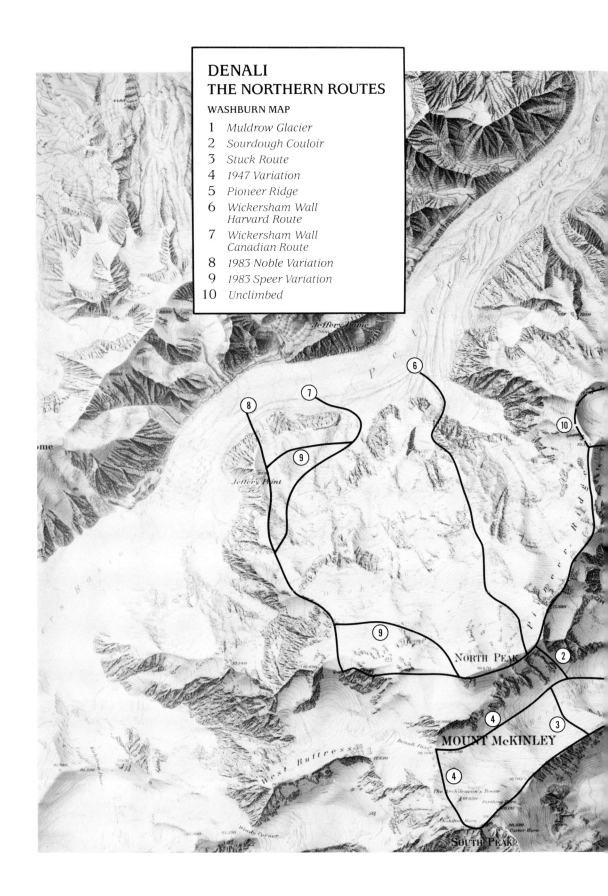

DENALI
THE NORTHERN ROUTES

WASHBURN MAP

1 *Muldrow Glacier*
2 *Sourdough Couloir*
3 *Stuck Route*
4 *1947 Variation*
5 *Pioneer Ridge*
6 *Wickersham Wall*
   Harvard Route
7 *Wickersham Wall*
   Canadian Route
8 *1983 Noble Variation*
9 *1983 Speer Variation*
10 *Unclimbed*

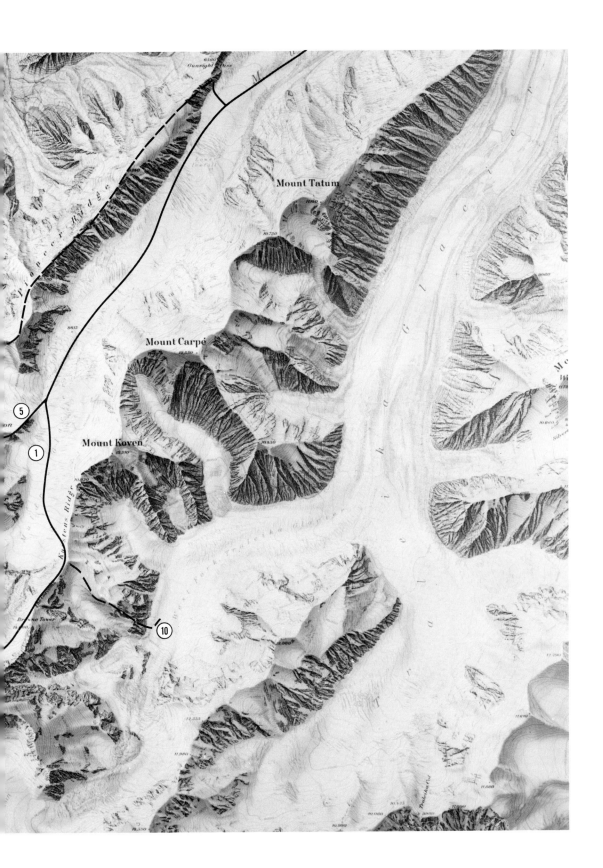

CHAPTER 2

THE WESTERN ROUTES

West Buttress
Northwest Buttress
West Rib
West Rim

West Buttress

THE WEST BUTTRESS ROUTE FOLLOWS THE WINDING Kahiltna Glacier up a series of low-angled headwalls to the large 14,300-foot basin. Above this is a 2,000-foot climb up onto the buttress itself. Once on the narrow buttress crest, the vista of the Alaska Range and the surrounding tundra is one of the most magnificent in North America.

From 17,200 feet, there is a moderately steep and ascending traverse to Denali Pass, where the route intersects with the 1947 Muldrow variation. Short headwalls are climbed to the 19,600-foot plateau, which presents a half mile of plodding to the final summit ridge.

Bradford Washburn recommended this route in *The American Alpine Journal 1947* as the easiest, quickest, safest way up Denali, provided there was air support. Until then, everyone was content to do the Muldrow; no one wanted to spend the money to come all the way to Alaska and take a chance on not succeeding, Washburn wrote.

The West Buttress would revolutionize Denali-climbing in years to come. As the mountain grew popular in the sixties and seventies, this route would consistently attract over seventy-five percent of Denali's climbers.

Washburn's name became synonymous with Denali. He encouraged virtually every first ascent on the mountain. His commitment as Director of the Boston Museum of Science would not allow him to climb actively, so, based upon numerous photographic flights made for the National Geographic Society and the museum, he wrote detailed photo analyses and safety-oriented recommendations for new routes on the mountain. These were published in *The American Alpine Journal*, *Appalachia*, and *The Mountain World*.

Yet Washburn was no paper tiger. As a younger man, he had made many first ascents in the Alps. Before his career with the museum got into full swing, he made Alaskan first ascents of Mounts Bertha and Sanford, the impressive North Ridge of Mount Hayes, and Mounts Silverthrone, Deception, Lucania, Steele, Crillon and Marcus Baker.

In 1950, when a team of Colorado climbers wrote and asked Washburn for photographs of the West Buttress, Washburn asked if he could join them on their climb. The Colorado climbers could hardly say no. Washburn invited Jim Gale. Bill Hackett wrote and asked if he could come along; both were partners from earlier Muldrow trips.

The Colorado climbers were Dr. Henry Buchtel, Dr. John Ambler, Dr. Melvin Griffiths, and Jerry More. Barry Bishop (later to distinguish himself on Mount Everest in 1963) of Cincinnati was one of the originators of the trip.

Terris Moore, who had been on the mountain, agreed to fly the team in and out. He had perfected the art of glacier flying (years after doing the first ascent of 16,227-foot Mount Sanford with Washburn, he landed his airplane on the summit) and would eventually sell his rights to the wheel ski—an invention essential for countless Denali ascents. Moore, then the president of the University of Alaska, had done the shattering first ascents of Mount Fairweather in Alaska (1931) and Minya Konka in China (1932). He would later write an important book, *Mt. McKinley: The Pioneer Climbs*.

The objectives of Washburn's expedition were to do a thorough geologic assessment and to complete surveying work for the Museum of Science map of the mountain. (This detailed map, invaluable to the Alaska Range climber, would become Washburn's *magnum opus* on Denali.)

On June 18, 1951, Moore ferried Washburn, Gale, Buchtel and Hackett from Chelatna Lake to 7,650 feet on the Kahiltna Glacier. The trio proceeded to 10,000 feet and received a military airdrop of 2,570 pounds of various equipment and food. They made the first ascent of Kahiltna Dome (12,525 feet) and did extensive surveying from there.

Meanwhile, the rest of the team crept up the Peters Glacier from Wonder Lake, collecting geologic samples. More and Bishop made the first ascent of Peters Dome (10,600 feet) and left a surveying station on top for Washburn. They climbed over Kahiltna Pass and met Washburn on June 30.

On July 4, Washburn, Hackett and Gale started up Denali, while the remaining members finished their geological work and acted as a support team. Washburn named the 13,200 foot area Windy Corner, after the ninety-mile-per-hour winds he encountered there.

Washburn carried six hundred feet of fixed rope for the crux of the climb from fifteen thousand to seventeen thousand feet. Up to the bergschrund, they exhausted themselves, plowing, then shoveling, a three-foot-wide, two hundred-yard-long trench in loose snow. Above the bergschrund, they found hard blue ice which required twenty or thirty "hard whacks" for each step.

Once on the ridge crest, they continued fixing rope up to

seventeen thousand feet. On July 10, the four climbers finished
the ascent of the western side of the mountain. At Denali Pass
they found a minimum-register thermometer they had cached
in 1947; it read −59°F. Four and a half hours later, they became
the first of thousands of climbers to reach the summit via the
West Buttress route. Buchtel, More, Bishop, Ambler and Griffiths
reached the summit several days later.

Always eager in his role as the vicarious and inspiring mountaineer, Washburn concluded in *The American Alpine Journal
1952,* "Now that McKinley's western ridge has been climbed, the
Alaska Range offers, in particular, two outstanding pioneer
ascents: the north wall of the North Peak, still a magnificent
possiblity, and the western ridge of Mount Hunter."

First Winter Ascent

In late January 1967, an eight-man international team flew
into the Kahiltna Glacier to attempt the first winter ascent of
Denali. Several days later, Jacques Batkin (who made the first

The lower Kahiltna Glacier; the dark bands are glacial rock moraines, and the white sections are ice ▼

ascent of Mount Huntington) died in a crevasse fall. The team was disheartened, but felt Batkin would have wanted them to continue.

On February 28, Dave Johnston, Art Davidson and Ray Genet made the summit. During the descent, they were trapped at Denali Pass for six days in an awful windstorm, with little to eat and drink. The temperature dropped to −148°F with the wind-chill factor. Their fierce will to live brought them back down alive, but frostbitten. It was a remarkable, timeless achievement.

Genet became a successful guide on Denali and later died while descending from the summit of Mount Everest. Davidson, who had devoted himself to climbing Alaskan mountains with an intense flourish, wrote a book about the ascent, *Minus 148: The Winter Ascent of Mt. McKinley*. In 1966, he climbed some first ascents in the southern Alaska Range and in 1968 he returned to the West Buttress with the Arctic Institute of Biology.

Johnston lives at the base of Denali, his dining room window framing the mountain. He has quietly amassed an incredible number of first ascents in the Alaska Range and is still actively climbing. In the winter of 1986, he tried to solo the West Buttress, walking all the way from his cabin, forty-five miles distant, but turned around at Windy Corner after freezing his toes.

Bradford Washburn harnessed into position for aerial photography ▲

Ski Descent

On July 5, 1970, the forty-eight-year-old Tsuyoshi Ueki, a Japanese ski team demonstrator, became the first to ski the entire West Buttress route. The descent was filmed for a Japanese television special.

Solo

In the summer of 1970, Mount McKinley National Park received an application from a twenty-nine-year-old Japanese, Naomi Uemura, who wanted to be the first to solo Denali.

In 1952, stringent climbing regulations had been put into effect for Denali climbers, one of which prevented solo climbing. But in 1970, most of those regulations were dropped, including that requiring "permission to climb." Climbers were only asked to carry a radio and submit registrations. Uemura had chosen his time well.

On July 31, the park superintendent replied to Uemura's letter.

> We have your application to make a solo climb of Mt. McKinley. You have a great deal of climbing experience and I'm sure [you] realize the risks involved in climbing a [mountain] such as McKinley alone. We cannot authorize you do so.

The superintendent went on to recommend that Uemura contact Ray Genet in Talkeetna for assistance. The Park Service played a bluff, but Uemura held four aces. He wrote back:

> I wish to climb Mt. McKinley, the highest in North America, this summer. I was lucky enough to be able to stand on the top of Everest as a member of the Japanese Mt. Everest team. On the world-highest peak, I chose Mt. McKinley as my next goal.

The letter went on to say that he wanted to climb the highest peak on every continent. His application listed his solo ascents of Aconcagua, Mounts Kilimanjaro and Kenya, Mont Blanc, Mount Sanford (in the nearby Wrangell Mountains) and the Matterhorn.

> I myself don't understand why I climb. But I climbed, and I need no justification. What I feel very strongly now is that I've been looking for something completely new through these experiences. I feel myself like a 100-meter runner who is doing his best to cut just 0.1 second off the world record.
> Would you please be kind enough to help me?

He arrived in Talkeetna in mid-August and was given a salmon, salmon eggs, and bread, which lasted him for ten days on Denali. Such simple, high-fat food would become Uemura's trademark on his long solo trips. He climbed the mountain in eight and a half days, reaching the summit on August 26, 1970.

History will remember Uemura for his incredible solo achievements, but the remarkable thing about him was his sincere modesty and unassuming nature. Another part of his greatness lay in his deep interest in everyone he met. He was tremendously acclaimed in Japan, revered by thousands, much like an American sports hero. His adventure books were read by all Japanese schoolchildren.

Uemura continued climbing, but he also became interested in grander adventures. At the headwaters of the Amazon River, he built a raft out of jungle wood and floated to the ocean. He mushed a dog team from Greenland to the western coast of Alaska. He became the first man to solo to the North Pole, barely escaping a mauling by a polar bear.

Finally, he received the funding to climb to the top of the seventh continent, the Vinson Massif in Antarctica. However, he chose to return to Denali and make the first winter solo climb, perhaps as training for Antarctica.

He arrived in Talkeetna in January 1984, the darkest, most bitter part of the Alaskan winter. On Denali, based on his time spent with the indigenous Greenlanders, Uemura ate raw caribou and seal fat, a difficult food for acclimatization.

Uemura started climbing the West Buttress on February 1,

At 16,800 feet on the West Buttress ◄

with a spruce pole dangling from his waist, in case he fell into a crevasse. He left his 17,200-foot camp and reached the summit on February 12 (the Japanese and American flags sewn by his wife were found there two months later). It was both his forty-third birthday and the day of his death. He descended from the summit in increasingly raw conditions. A support plane passed by, unable to see Uemura and buffeted by strong winds. Reportedly, he was heard to say over his radio, "I am lost."

Despite extensive searches over the next three months, his body was never recovered. His untouched camp was found at 17,200 feet. He carried no shovel on his summit climb and it is presumed that he died from altitude sickness, hypothermia, or a fall.

A year later, a wealthy Texan, Dick Bass, was the first to complete over a period of a few years what Uemura had spent decades of his life dreaming of and working toward. Bass

tenaciously returned to Mount Everest several times until he succeeded.

Messner Couloir Variation

This route was formerly named the Hourglass Couloir, then the Saudan Couloir. It is a 5,000-foot couloir which cuts directly from the 14,300-foot West Buttress basin to Archdeacon's Tower. The angle in the narrowest section approaches fifty degrees and, like many of the routes on Denali, its difficulty depends upon the ever-variable snow and ice conditions.

In 1972, Swiss extreme skier Sylvain Saudan arrived on the West Buttress with a support team, intending to climb to the summit and ski the couloir. He later made extravagant claims to have skied from the summit, but several witnesses verified that he was too tired to reach the summit, so he strapped on his skis at 19,500 feet and skied the couloir—an impressive feat.

On June 6, 1976, Reinhold Messner and Oswald Oelz arrived at the landing strip and climbed to the 14,300-foot camp in several days. After waiting nearly a week to acclimatize, this dynamic duo tandem-soloed the couloir on June 13. Messner carried only an ice ax and a movie camera. It took Messner eight hours to reach the summit; Oelz took ten. They descended the route within three hours. (In 1980, Messner's rival, Peter Habeler, glissaded this couloir in forty-five minutes during a rescue.)

Most climbers who have completed the couloir agree that the West Rib finish is a far more pleasurable and varied route to the summit. The Messner Couloir involves monotonous, seemingly endless step-kicking for five thousand feet.

McClods Rib Variation

On June 10, 1977, Bugs McKeith soloed this mixed rock rib, just to the north of the Messner Couloir; the average angle of the rib is about the same as the Messner Couloir: forty-five degrees. A week before, McKeith had reached the summit via a new variation on the West Rib, on the upper Southwest Face, called Clod Face.

Probing with a bamboo wand, he gingerly worked his way through an icefall at the base of the route and climbed over several bergschrunds. Moving quickly, he frontpointed up snow and ice, up to sixty-five degrees in steepness. He found occasional easy rock climbing.

When he reached the 19,600-foot plateau, he fell sound asleep in the sunshine. He was awoken by a friend, Jon Jones, carrying a

dartboard to the summit, where he scored seventy, beating McKeith's previous summit score of thirty. After his nap, McKeith descended from the plateau, reaching his 14,300-foot camp twelve hours after he had left.

Upper West Buttress Direct Variation

In early June of 1980, Duane Muetzel, Ken Graff, Neal Beidleman and Granger Banks arrived at the 12,300-foot West Buttress basin. They had just completed the third ascent of Mount Foraker's Sultana Ridge and, after bivouacking at 17,200 feet, they were well acclimatized.

They left the normal West Buttress route at 12,500 feet and climbed diagonally up and right toward the 16,030-foot-high summit of the buttress. With full packs, they climbed low-angled ice, occasionally up to sixty degrees, and some 5.7 rock. They reached the intersection of the standard West Buttress route after sixteen hours of climbing. The following day, they climbed to the summit, lingering for a moment next to a pair of frozen German climbers at 19,650 feet.

On May 27, 1982, Bruce Hickox and Sabine Von Glinski climbed up the prominent couloir, closest to Windy Corner, as seen from the 12,500-foot basin. They found blue ice up to sixty degrees, then good step-kicking. After about 800 feet, they wandered up through boulders and fourth-class rock. They camped on the ridge at 16,000 feet and descended the next day via the fixed ropes. Descending to their lower camp for more supplies, they finished climbing the normal West Buttress route and summited nine days later.

Denali guide Michael Covington had safely led his clients through numerous epics on the West Buttress, the Cassin Ridge, the West Rib and the South Buttress.

On June 24, he arrived at the bottom of the West Buttress Direct with his clients, Bill Holton and Stan Olsen. They did a slight variation on the 1980 route, calling it Thunder Ridge, after the tremendous thunder and lightning storms they saw. Their tent would have blown away in a severe windstorm if they had not spun an elaborate cocoon of climbing rope around it.

On May 10, 1984, Doug VanEtton and Martin Schmidt traversed north from the 12,200-foot level, into a large forty-five-degree gully which drops to the Peters Glacier. They bivouacked that night on a tiny platform beneath a rock band, 1,000 feet below the 16,030-foot summit.

The next day they climbed to the West Buttress summit and walked to the fixed ropes at 16,200 feet. They descended to the

14,300-foot camp and reached the summit several days later via the upper West Rib. It is rumored that the Japanese may have climbed this route, although no one has tried the avalanche-menaced start from the Peters Glacier.

Dennen's Gully Variation

At the same time that Covington, Olsen and Holton were on their climb, a young Englishman, Barney Dennen, set out from the 14,300-foot West Buttress camp. He began soloing a 2,000-foot, forty-five- to sixty-degree ice gully, directly north of camp. A sudden, severe storm blew in. After seven hours, he reached the crest of the West Buttress.

On the Kahiltna Glacier ▲

While walking on whited-out cornices toward the standard West Buttress route, he collapsed a cornice and fell 500 feet. He dug a cave with his bare fingers and shivered through a miserable and stormy night. The next day, with terribly frostbitten fingers, he limped back to 14,300 feet. All of his fingers were eventually amputated.

Northwest Buttress

P

ERHAPS IT IS BECAUSE THE NORTHWEST BUTTRESS leads to the North Peak instead of the higher South Peak that this moderately difficult ridge is seldom climbed. However, it is a classic Alaskan route because it offers the full spectrum of climbing: snow and ice cornices, a knife-edge ridge, couloirs, frost-fractured schist towers and pink-speckled granite. Last, but not least, it has an awe-inspiring view down the biggest wall in the world and across the vast Alaskan tundra.

The first ascent (1954) was conceived during meetings of the University of Alaska Alpine Club in Fairbanks and was based on Bradford Washburn's detailed description in *The American Alpine Journal 1947*. That year, the Fairbanks members would simultaneously climb both the Northwest and South buttresses of Denali.

Following the lead of Stuck and the Sourdoughs, Alaskan climbers would continue to be one of the most prominent and consistent forces in the Alaska Range for the next three decades. This could be due, in part, to their proximity to the mountains and their propensity for arctic weather.

The Fairbanks contingent, Donald McLean and Charles Wilson, enlisted Captain Bill Hackett and Henry Meybohm. Meybohm was a ski instructor from Germany, living in Anchorage.

The thirty-five-year-old Hackett had already taken part in the 1947 Muldrow Glacier ascent with Washburn, testing various cold weather gear for the military. He would also return with Washburn and do the first ascent of the West Buttress in 1951. Hackett was responsible for inviting Fred Beckey, whom he had befriended in the army. After the Northwest Buttress climb, Beckey and Meybohm would continue climbing with the characteristic Beckey fervor and knock off first ascents of Mounts Deborah and Hunter.

Hackett was an unusual man, successfully integrating mountaineering and military careers. In World War II, he was a leader of a forty-seven man platoon in Italy that saw all but nine men wounded or killed. When he completed the Northwest Buttress, the zenith (but not the end) of his Alaskan career, he would be the first man to have reached the highest mountains on five continents, a record that would stand uncontested for twenty years.

On the Northwest Buttress, the team planned to test vapor-barrier sleeping pads and down-filled, "walk-around" sleeping robes for the United States Air Force. And contrary to popular belief about climbing in the fifties, the foresightful Beckey had stiff boot soles and frontpoints for ice climbing.

On May 2, 1954, the five men landed twenty miles from the Peters Glacier, just north of Mount Foraker. Within three days, they were established at the foot of the Northwest Buttress.

When their airdrop pilot buzzed right over their heads, they thought it strange that he didn't return. Out of sight of their base camp, a sudden down-draft forced the plane down onto the glacier, where it overturned. An hour later, much to everyone's surprise, the pilot and passenger sheepishly strolled into camp. They were "rescued" three days later by the Air Force. This experience provided a prime incentive for the National Park Service to ban airdrops in 1964.

The climbers began work in earnest, chopping steps and fixing ropes up a couloir on the northern side of the ridge, across a plateau; from here they followed a coxcomb section of the ridge, occasionally straddling it like a horse. They established Camp 1 at 10,500 feet, just below Frederick A. Cook's 1903 high point.

Beckey found the high-profiled Logan tents to be "spooky" in the wind, so with his usual restless energy, he set to digging a snow cave for shelter. Because of the protected nature of this spot on the ridge, they only used it for storage.

On May 13, Beckey and McLean climbed unroped on frozen and rotten schist, placing fixed ropes to the top of a pyramid at 12,500 feet. Another pyramid was circumvented by traversing into a cirque. They chopped steps for six hours, up a couloir out of the cirque, watching the ice chips skitter 6,000 feet to the Tluna Icefall. They regained the buttress at 14,200 feet.

Camp 2 was established in the cirque and loads were carried in framepacks which Beckey described as digging into his shoulders. Those were the days of canvas and Goldline ropes and "Goodyear" boots. And ice climbers had arms like lumberjacks; routes which can now be dispensed so quickly with frontpoints were laboriously chopped with steps from top to bottom, despite Beckey's presence.

At the 15,000-foot level on the ridge, Beckey stroked his fingers over beautiful pink granite. In a fitting gesture, for Beckey would become the most prolific mountaineer in North America, he hammered in the first rock pitons on North America's highest peak. Ropes were fixed and Camp 3 was established at 14,800 feet, beneath these cliffs.

Beckey led his party to the next camp, at 15,600 feet, in just a few hours. Camps were made at 17,400 feet, then again at 18,500 feet in a matter of a few days. As three of the climbers contracted acute mountain sickness from climbing so rapidly, McLean injected them with a hormone known for its value in stress conditions.

On May 27, at 7:30 P.M., they reached the North Summit; it was a threatening day, and Beckey continually looked askance at the deteriorating weather. They retreated to their high camp at 18,500 feet, hoping, eventually, to get a shot at the South Summit.

After four days of storm, their fuel ran out. They rappelled the rock cliffs with a long rope. Six feet of snow covered their steps in the thirteen-thousand-foot cirque, where they were forced to shovel their way back to the windblown ridge.

Down, but not yet out of danger, Hackett nearly drowned in a river crossing. At Wonder Lake, as a final, sad blow to end an enjoyable expedition, they were informed that Elton Thayer had died while descending from the ascent of the South Buttress. In the fifties, there were very few climbers and a death within this close-knit community was an irrevocable and devastating loss.

Variations

In 1982, two members of Gary Bocarde's guided Mountain Trip team completed the second ascent of this route. They made a variation on the start by climbing the couloir on the south side of the buttress. Other variations were made which avoided the coxcomb by traversing under it and by climbing around on snow and ice to avoid various sections of rock.

In 1984, Vern Tejas (who made the first winter ascent of Mount Hunter in 1980) and John Schweider became the first climbers to reach both the North and South Peaks. Tejas climbed the route with Footfangs strapped to his floppy bunny boots.

West Rib

THE WEST RIB HAS BECOME POPULAR FOR SEVERAL REAsons. It provides a relatively direct route to the South Summit, and it is safe, with the exception of the approach. It has fine campsites and its moderately angled snow and ice slopes offer an enjoyable, yet not too technically difficult, challenge.

The climb was conceived in the Log Cabin Bar in Jackson, Wyoming, where Pete Sinclair, Jake Breitenbach, Barry Corbet (Dartmouth Mountaineering Club members) and Bill Buckingham were celebrating the second and complete ascent of Mount Moran's South Buttress. Good climbers are generally aware of big unclimbed routes, the plums of the day, and all four had seen the Washburn photographs of the routes on Denali's South Face in a recent issue of *The Mountain World*. Someone proposed a toast, "Let's do the South Face of McKinley next summer!" They clinked their beer mugs and were committed.

Given its location next to the Cassin Ridge, the significance of the West Rib is often overlooked. The first ascent of the West Rib was the cover story in *The American Alpine Journal 1960* and was mentioned in the Sports section of the July 13, 1959 *Time Magazine*.

Breitenbach had the only big mountain experience of the team, having climbed the West Buttress a few years earlier. Sinclair had never been on a glacier before, while Corbet and Buckingham had a fair amount of experience in the Tetons and in Canada. Their average age was twenty-three.

On June 7, 1959, Don Sheldon flew the four climbers in. Their equipment consisted of steel carabiners, 7/16-inch rope, the ubiquitous, floppy bunny boots, ten-point crampons, twenty soft iron pitons, and ice screws that looked like corkscrews. Their innovative sleeping pads were made out of fiber glass house insulation; the latter worked well until the inevitable contact with crampons rendered them soggy sponges.

ABC Radio had loaned them a miniaturized recorder for making a series of recordings for future broadcasts. They were to take it all the way to the summit, and, if the recordings were suitable, they would be paid for their efforts. They became so occupied with the mountain itself, as well as being microphone-shy and unable to take themselves seriously, that, in the end, the recordings were not deemed what America wanted to hear.

*Jonathan Waterman in a couloir
on the West Rib route* ◄

They did, however, record some hit tunes from the Talkeetna Fairview jukebox, which provided them with hours of entertainment on the mountain. Thus, while they had no radios, this first small recorder-accompanied ascent of Denali was decades ahead of its time.

After nearly trying the Cassin, they made two false starts up messy sections on the West Rib. Finally, they found the prominent snow-ice couloir on the eastern side of the rib. Within several days, they had chopped steps, fixed all of their rope and ferried their loads up to an uncomfortable and cramped Concentration Camp. The food seemed barely palatable, the clouds seemed to constantly threaten storms, they were appalled by the smell of one another's feet and, most of all, they were scared by

*Charlie Sassara during winter
ascent of the West Rib* ▶

the route above them.

They had a heart-stopping moment, stepping through a cornice and looking down three thousand feet to the glacier. They were further disheartened with they discovered that the difficulties above did not ease getting to the "domes."

Buckingham wrote: "After two days of rather freaked-out dithering about, there was a growing sentiment to bag it—we were all spooked by the cramped, exposed, eerie aerie where we were camped, staring at those evil glassy domes…"

Then, in a stroke of boldness, Corbet and Buckingham quickly went down and pulled up the fixed ropes, before Breitenbach might object. They fixed ropes up over both domes, to 13,900 feet and a beautiful flat spot, Paradise Camp. They had chopped

a stairway of approximately five thousand steps to get there. That evening their confidence and morale soared.

Sinclair wrote in the 1960 *Dartmouth Mountaineering Club Journal:* "Such moments are times for giving thanks that you are not one of those people who go through an entire lifetime without climbing a mountain."

With few delays, the team moved steadily up the mountain. They arrived, exhausted, at Camp Fatigue (14,800 feet). Above this camp, they would easily be able to traverse down onto the West Buttress. Everything was working. The weather had been perfect for ten days and they hurried on, convinced it could not last forever. They pitched Balcony Camp at 16,900 feet. On their summit day, they scrambled up rocks and followed a shallow couloir from 18,000 feet to the 19,600-foot plateau. They all lay in the snow exhausted and a bit altitude-sick from their rapid ascent. After an hour or more, Corbet started wandering toward the summit, followed by Sinclair, then Breitenbach.

Buckingham got to his feet half an hour later and was surprised to see the remaining distance to the top diminish rather easily.

> I was bemused as I passed a number of small vomit stains in the snow, but every slight undulation in the summit plateau required an enormous effort.

He reached the summit ridge just as the others were starting down, but in a gesture of camaraderie, which was symbolic of the spirit of this climb, they accompanied him back to the top. He gasped,

> Do you realize, do you know what we've done? Four hackers—we've made a great ascent…
>
> It was a superb summit day—not a breath of wind, but the view was only a sea of clouds with scattered, towering columns of cumulus, the North Peak being the only mountain visible. We were most fortunate in having had remarkably fine weather for the entire expedition.

Corbet and Sinclair traced their steps back to Balcony Camp, efficiently setting up rappels, while Breitenbach and Buckingham followed numbly. In the morning, they woke up under two feet of new snow on the tents, the first bad weather in two weeks.

The descent in a whiteout was difficult. At 12,900 feet, Breitenbach fell into a crevasse and hung upside down above a seemingly bottomless abyss. Fortunately, the only loss was a down jacket and two rolls of summit film.

Twenty-seven years later, Buckingham wrote:

> We were an exceedingly well-matched and compatible team, and the expedition was pervaded from beginning to end by a spirit of

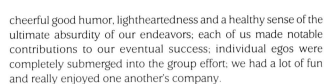

cheerful good humor, lightheartedness and a healthy sense of the ultimate absurdity of our endeavors; each of us made notable contributions to our eventual success; individual egos were completely submerged into the group effort; we had a lot of fun and really enjoyed one another's company.

The bonds formed on our expedition were strong and lasting, marred only by the tragedies of later years, Jake's death on Everest and Barry's paraplegia resulting from a helicopter accident while filming a ski movie.

Corbet wrote a profound testimony to the spirit of the West Rib, eulogizing Breitenbach in *The American Alpine Journal 1964:*

> …Jake scribed the future through his friends, which imprint will survive. His friends will recognize the epitaph Jake always wanted– Long live the crew.

West of the West Rib Variation

In 1972, James Wickwire, Alex Bertulis, Robert Schaller, M.D., Tom Stewart, Charlie Raymond and Leif-Norman Patterson came to Denali with the intention of climbing the Cassin Ridge alpine style. They underestimated the icy conditions on the Cassin and retreated from thirteen thousand feet.

Schaller had taken a small fall and hurt his knee, but he refused to turn back and continued climbing. After the trip, he learned that he had broken his tibia.

Their variation on the West Rib traversed above a hanging glacier, avoiding the rib's initial crux couloir. The terrain was easy, but threatened by hanging-glacier avalanches, and they quickly reached a broad snow shoulder at 14,200 feet. They bivouacked in a shallow crevasse, in down jackets and half-sleeping bags. They traveled without tents, as if Denali were a smaller mountain. Nonetheless, no one was frostbitten, thanks to good weather.

Their second day was spent climbing to the east of the rib proper, up a soft avalanche slope, some ice, then some rock scrambling to a ledge at 16,800 feet and another cold bivouac.

Wickwire wrote about the summit in his diary:

> Leif and Charlie soon left for the summit…I decided to wait alone for Rob, Tom and Alex. Rob…had a lot of guts coming up there with his bad knee. Tom…walked along the very ridge crest and teetered a couple of times toward the abyss of the South Face. We were all unroped. He passed it off as a joke, but I still wonder whether it was the effect of the altitude. Alex…was in great pain from his back, but worse, he looked exhausted. His eyes were hollow; I have never seen him look so bad.

Their summit day took them twenty-four hours. However, climbing Denali in three days without prior acclimatization and with minimal gear is neither enjoyable nor safe. Bertulis concluded in *The American Alpine Journal 1973* that they had underestimated the unpredictable mountain and were very fortunate.

Western Direct Start Variation

In early June 1972, a team of Japanese women ferried loads to 9,500 feet on the Northeast Fork. Michiko Sekita, Nobue Yajima, Mitsuko Toyama, Sachiko Watanabe and Sueko Inoue spent a week fixing 2,000 feet of rope up a deep-cut ice couloir on the west side of the West Rib. They rejoined the original route at 13,000 feet.

Yajima, Toyama and Watanabe reached the summit on June 29, but were overcome by a storm and fell during their descent. Ray Genet found their bodies at the fifteen-thousand-foot level.

Southwestern Direct Start Variation

In 1977, the Hosei University Alpine Club from Japan added a difficult start up a mixed couloir on the southwest side of the rib, south of the 1972 Japanese women's variation, also joining the original West Rib route at thirteen thousand feet.

Clod Face Variation

In 1977, Bugs McKeith, Jon Jones, Eckhart Grassman (later killed on Mount Edith Cavell), and Allan Derbyshire departed from their camp at the junction of the Northeast Fork. They called their team CLOD (Calgary leftovers on Denali), because they never got invited to take Calgary Mountain Club trips.

After a few days, they reached the 13,900-foot camp on the West Rib and started their variation, traversing east onto the upper Southwest Face. They climbed over a steep rock rib at 15,000 feet and continued up to a snow slope that was broken only by a large rock. They chopped out tent platforms.

The next day, they left their tents and carried only bivouac gear. They climbed under a steep granite wall and dug a snow cave at 17,200 feet.

On June 3, their summit day, as they soloed up a steep couloir, a military plane buzzed back and forth, simulating the roar of an avalanche, scaring them badly each time it passed. The exposure was incredible: McKeith wrote in the 1978 *Canadian Alpine Journal* that he would have fallen 8,000 feet if he had slipped. The

couloir brought them to the 19,600-foot plateau, one half mile from the summit.

Once on the summit, McKeith (who would lose his life several years later when a cornice collapsed beneath him on Mount Assiniboine's summit) pulled out a square of red cloth with a dart board printed on it. There, at 20,320 feet, he threw darts at his cloth in the snow, not quite able to best his high score.

The most popular variation on the West Rib is commonly done by traversing over from 14,300 feet on the West Buttress. This was first completed by Akio Shoji, Masaaki Hatakeyama and Teruzo Nakamura in 1975. Although there are a few crevasses, the traverse has no technical difficulties.

Solo

In 1977, a four-man German party started up the Kahiltna Glacier to climb the Cassin. However, the team split and Ruprecht Kammerlander completed the first solo of the West Rib.

Third Winter Ascent

On February 28, 1983, Charles Sassara, Robert Frank, Steve Teller, and Chris Hraback arrived at ten thousand feet on the Northeast Fork of the Kahiltna. On March 4, they loaded eight days of food in their packs and began climbing.

At three in the morning on March 11, Hraback, Sassara and Frank started from their eighteen-thousand-foot camp to the summit, leaving the rope behind to save weight. Hraback became exhausted and turned back to camp. By eleven that morning, Sassara and Frank reached the summit.

Tired and cold, they walked back down to 19,600 feet and began frontpointing down the route. Suddenly, Frank yelled, "Falling!" and knocked Sassara off his feet; Sassara managed to self-arrest after 100 feet, but Frank fell head over heels for over 7,000 feet. Sassara, who was understandably numbed, resisted the urge to let go and follow his friend. After composing himself, he climbed down past Frank's camera bag, a glove, some blood, and pieces of flesh and bone.

As of 1987, three of the four "successful" winter ascents have involved deaths. Denali in winter is a harsh mistress.

West Rim

THE WEST RIM OFFERS 4,000 FEET OF AIRY CLIMBING ON a sharp ridge, which culminates just beneath Windy Corner, at 13,600 feet on the West Buttress route. A variety of routes can be followed from there to the summit.

In 1977, an unusual competition was enacted when Alex Bertulis asked Reilly Moss to accompany a Soviet expedition to Denali. Bertulis, who was familiar with the mountain after making his 1972 variation on the West Rib, filled Moss' ear with a new route possibility—the West Rim. In May, Moss teamed up with Mike Helms and they accompanied the Soviets to the Northeast Fork of the Kahiltna.

In a scene typical of Denali's international flavor, the Russian and American teams were joined at the junction of the Northeast Fork by a Canadian team, CLOD. At that point, Helms mentioned to the Canadians, Bernhard Ehmann and Patrick Morrow, that he planned a first ascent of the nearby West Rim, which was very enticing from their vantage point. Morrow and Ehmann immediately adopted this idea as their own and moved their camp to the base of the route at 9,500 feet. The Russians prepared to climb the Cassin Ridge and the West Rib. The remaining members of the CLOD team prepared to do a new variation on the upper Southwest Face.

The next morning, Helms and Moss steamed by the Canadian camp. The trailbreaking was arduous in three feet of new snow; Moss said he went to a tremendous postholing effort for eight hundred feet, sometimes up to his chest. They stopped and camped for the night.

In the morning, Ehmann and Morrow came ripping by the Americans, still sleeping in their tent, recovering from the previous day. The Canadians were carrying a spartan three days' worth of food and moving fast after an effortless jaunt up the Americans' plowed trench.

Moss said he was "rather miffed" at the time. He and Helms had no intention of trying to catch them and preferred to simply move at their own pace, for they weren't traveling nearly as light as the Canadians.

Morrow hoped the Americans would join them, to share trailbreaking and climb the route together. It would be six days until they saw one another again.

Ehmann and Morrow then plowed up fifteen more pitches, bivouacking at eleven thousand feet. Shortly thereafter, the Americans became separated from the Canadians in a storm halfway up the route. Morrow and Ehmann moved like lightning and spent a second night in a bergschrund, two pitches below the top.

After the storm, two thirds of the way up the route, Moss did the most spectacular climbing of his life, straddling a two-pitch-long knife-edge which dropped thousands of feet on either side. After exactly one rope length, there was a lone rock horn to belay from. Morrow also thought this had been the crux of the route.

Morrow and Ehmann climbed out of their snow hole on the third day, and Ehmann led up sixty-degree ice, shouting down that this was his first time ice climbing—Morrow got nervous.

They finished the route after two pitches, trudged over to the 14,300-foot camp, then descended the West Buttress to their 8,000-foot camp for more food. Three days later, they arrived back at the West Buttress camp at 14,300 feet. From there, they climbed up to the West Rib, camped and made what was probably the first ascent of the 3,000-foot, thirty-five-degree snow couloir, to the west of the West Rib, known as the Orient Express (down which three different parties of Japanese and Korean climbers have fallen). They thought they were climbing the Messner Couloir.

On June 9, 1977, after Morrow had nearly skewered Ehmann in an argument about their pace, they rejoiced together on the summit at sunset.

Moss and Helms had been slowed by a snowstorm and spent seven days on the West Rim. When they reached the West Buttress, they descended and met up with the successful Russians at base camp. Moss was so taken by the Russian climbers, he enrolled in a Russian language class and climbed in the Pamirs the following summer. In 1980, Helms returned and climbed the Cassin Ridge, where he played a part in the rescue of Simon McCartney (see Southwest Face). In 1985, Morrow would become the second person to climb the highest peaks on each of the seven continents; Denali had been his first.

*Traversing from the West Rib into
the Orient Express* ◄

DENALI

THE WESTERN ROUTES

⑬

1	Kahiltna Glacier	8	Orient Express
2	Kahiltna Glacier, Northeast Fork	9	West Rib Cutoff
3	West Rim	10	Windy Corner
4	West Rib	11	West Buttress Direct Routes
5	Cassin Ridge	12	Denali Pass
6	West Buttress	13	Northwest Buttress
7	Messner Couloir	14	Unclimbed

7267

▲ 1	West Buttress	9	North Peak
2	Messner Couloir	10	South Peak
3	West Rib Cutoff	11	West Buttress Direct 1980
4	West Rib	12	Thunder Ridge 1982
5	Orient Express	13	Upper Peters Glacier Couloir 1984
6	Rescue Gully	14	West Buttress Direct 1982
7	McClods Rib	15	Windy Corner
8	Denali Pass	16	Basin, 14,300 Feet

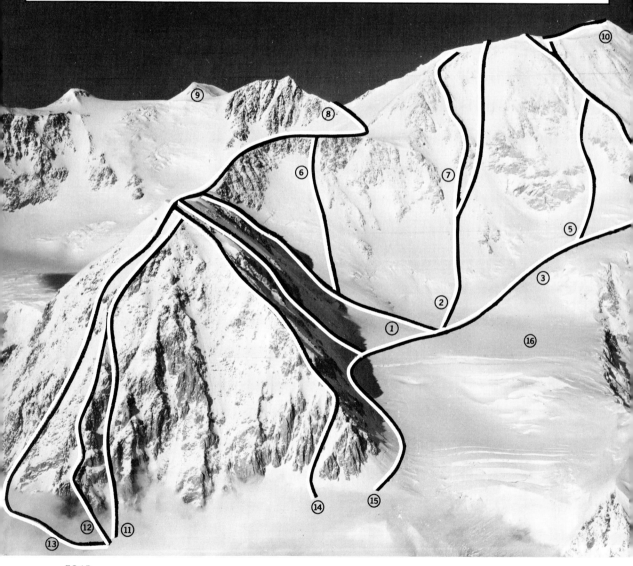

5962

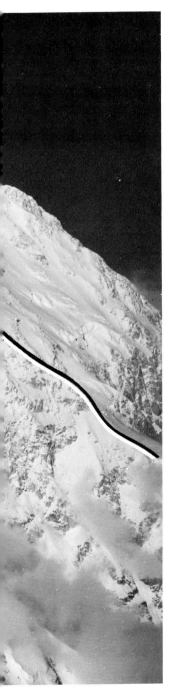

Route Guide

Approach: *Start from the 7,200-foot Southeast Fork of the Kahiltna landing strip.*

Total Time: *10-24 days .*

Climbing Miles: *17.*

Vertical Gain of Route: *13,100 feet.*

Alaska Grade: *2.*

Difficulties, Dangers, Rating: *There is a 40- to 50-degree snow and ice headwall from 15,000 to 16,000 feet; numerous crevasse falls, altitude sickness and Denali Pass falls (without ice axes) belie the route's easy reputation.*

Camps: *7,200; 7,600; 8,900; 10,900; 12,900 (in bergschrund to avoid wind and avalanches); 14,300; 16,200; 17,200.*

References: *1952* AAJ; *May-June 1982* Climbing; Minus 148°, *Davidson; 1984* Ascent; Surviving Denali, *Waterman.*

Firsts

Ascent: *July 10, 13, 14, 1951; Washburn, Hackett, Gale, Buchtel, Ambler, Griffiths, More, Bishop.*

Alpine Style: *May 17, 1960; J. & L. Whittaker, Schoening, Day.*

Winter: *February 28, 1967; Johnston, Davidson, Genet, (Blomberg, Nishimae, Batkin, Wickman, Edwards).*

Solo: *August 26, 1970; Uemura.*

Ski descent: *July 5, 1970; Ueki.*

Variations: *Messner Couloir: June 13, 1976; Messner, Oelz. West Buttress Direct–North: June 1980; Muetzel, Graff, Beidleman, Banks. West Buttress Direct–South: May 27, 1982; Hickox, Von Glinski. Upper Peters Couloir: May 14, 1984; VanEtton, Schmidt.*

WEST BUTTRESS

▲ 1   *West Buttress*

2   *Kahiltna Pass*

3   *Windy Corner*

4   *Northwest Buttress*

5   *Peters Glacier*

6   *Unclimbed*

⑤

2365

WEST BUTTRESS

▲ 1   *West Buttress*

2   *West Buttress Direct 1980*

3   *West Buttress Direct 1982*

4   *Thunder Ridge 1982*

5   *Upper Peters Couloir 1984*

6   *McClods Rib*

7   *Messner Couloir*

8   *Denali Pass*

9   *Northwest Buttress*

10   *West Rib*

11   *Unclimbed*

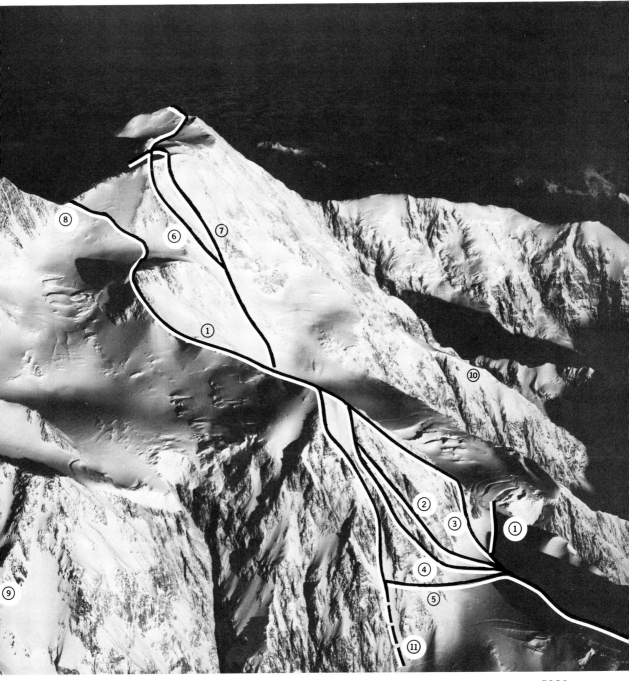

5098

111

4407

Route Guide

Approach: *10 miles from the 7,200-foot Southeast Fork of the Kahiltna, via the 10,000-foot Kahiltna Pass, to the 7,700-foot base.*

Total Time: *12–24 days.*

Climbing Miles: *9 (North Peak: 6).*

Vertical Gain of Route: *12,600 feet (North Peak: 11,900 feet).*

Alaska Grade: *4.*

Difficulties, Dangers, Rating: *Occasional mixed climbing through the two rock pyramids; snow and ice up to 65 degrees; low Class 5 rock climbing on rotten schist and frost-shattered granite.*

Camps: *10,200; 11,000; 12,500; 14,200; 15,600; 16,600; 17,400; 18,500.*

References: *1955, 1984, AAJ.*

Firsts

Ascent: *North Peak: May 27, 1954; Wilson, McClean, Hackett, Beckey, Meybohm.*

Variations: *Southern Couloir start and North Peak: May 14, 1982; Rehmer, Snyder, (Bocarde, Stolpman, Novey, Shrimpton). North and South peaks: May 15 and 17, 1983; Tejas, Schwieder.*

▲ 1   *Northwest Buttress 1954*

2   *1982 Variation*

3   *Peters Glacier*

4   *Canadian Route*

5   *Wickersham Wall*

6   *Upper Peters Couloir 1984*

7   *Kahiltna Pass*

8   *Peters Dome*

9   *Unclimbed*

▲ 1   *Northwest Buttress*

5958

2367

▲ 1   *Northwest Buttress*
  2   *Unclimbed*

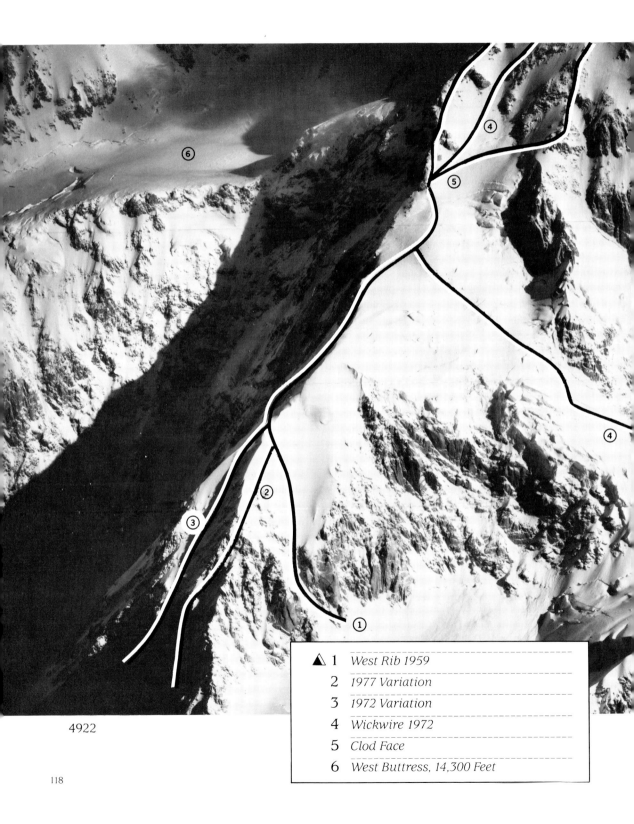

4922

▲ 1	West Rib 1959
2	1977 Variation
3	1972 Variation
4	Wickwire 1972
5	Clod Face
6	West Buttress, 14,300 Feet

Route Guide

A*pproach:* 11 miles from the 7,200-foot Southeast Fork of the Kahiltna landing strip, via Northeast Fork to 11,100 feet; travel quickly and camp with heed to hanging-glacier activity.

T*otal Time:* 14-24 days .

C*limbing Miles:* 3.

V*ertical Gain of Route:* 9,200 feet.

A*laska Grade:* 4.

D*ifficulties, Dangers, Rating:* 40- to 50-degree snow and ice from 11,100 to 13,300 feet (initial couloir); short sections of up to 60-degree ice.

C*amps:* 13,300; 13,900; 15,200; 15,900; 16,900 (Balcony Camp).

R*eferences:* 1960, 1978, (Clod Face), 1984 (winter ascent) AAJ; 1978 Canadian Alpine Journal.

Firsts

A*scent:* June 19, 1959; Sinclair, Breitenbach, Corbet, Buckingham.

A*lpine Style:* West of the West Rib: June 25, 1972; Bertulis, Wickwire, Schaller, Patterson, Raymond, Stewart.

W*inter:* March 11, 1983; Sassara, Frank, (Hraback, Teller).

S*olo:* 1977; Kammerlander.

V*ariations:* West of the West Rib: June 25, 1972; Bertulis, Wickwire, Schaller, Patterson, Raymond, Stewart. Western Direct Start: June 29, 1972; Yajima, Toyama, Watanabe, (Sekita, Inoue). Southwestern Direct start: 1977; Hosei University Alpine Club. West Rib from 14,300 on West Buttress: August 8, 1975; Shoji, Hatakeyama, Nakamura. Clod Face: June 3, 1977; McKeith, Grassman, Jones, Derbyshire.

4781

▲ 1   *West Rib*

2   *Wickwire 1972*

3   *Clod Face Variation*

4   *Southwest Face*

5   *Cassin Ridge*

6   *Orient Express*

7   *West Buttress Finish*

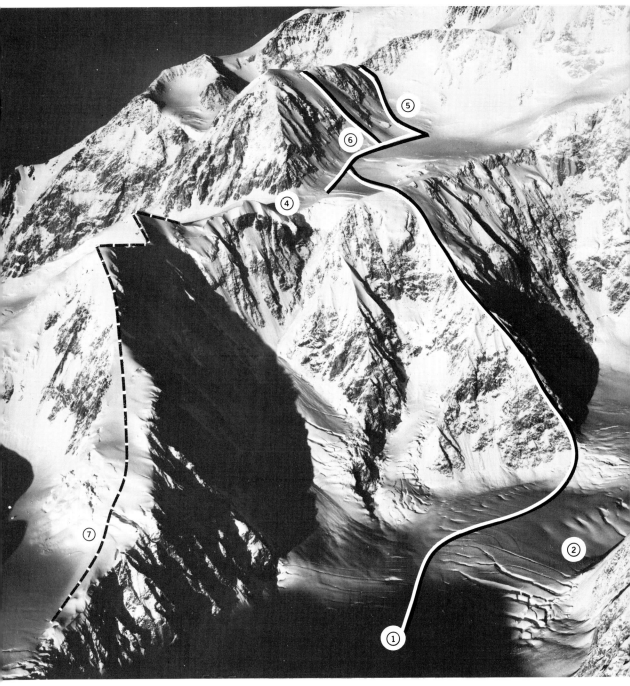

5035

 # Route Guide

Approach: *8 miles from the 7,200-foot Southeast Fork of the Kahiltna landing strip to the 9,500-foot base on the Northeast Fork of the Kahiltna Glacier; travel and camp with heed to hanging glaciers in Northeast Fork.*

Total Time: *10–24 days .*

Climbing Miles: *1 (to 14,300 feet).*

Vertical Gain of Route: *4,000 feet.*

Alaska Grade: *4.*

Difficulties, Dangers, Rating: *Up to 70-degree ice and a knife-edged ridge.*

Camps: *10,300; 11,000; 13,300 (bergschrund).*

References: *1979 AAJ; 1979 Canadian Alpine Journal; Beyond Everest, Morrow.*

 # Firsts

Ascent: *June 9, 1977; Ehmann, Morrow.*

Alpine Style: *June 9, 1977; Ehmann, Morrow.*

▲ 1	West Rim
2	Kahiltna Glacier, Northeast Fork
3	West Rib
4	Windy Corner
5	West Buttress
6	Dennen's Gully
7	Unclimbed

DENALI
THE WESTERN ROUTES

WASHBURN MAP

1 *Northwest Buttress*
2 *1982 Bocarde Variation*
3 *West Buttress*
4 *Messner Couloir*
5 *McClods Rib*
6 *Orient Express*
7 *West Rib*
8 *1977 Southwest Variation*
9 *1972 Western Variation*
10 *1972 Wickwire Variation*
11 *Clod Face Variation*
12 *West Rim*
13 *Hickox Variation*
14 *1980 West Buttress Direct*
15 *Thunder Ridge Variation*
16 *Upper Peters Couloir*
17 *Unclimbed*

Kahiltna Dome

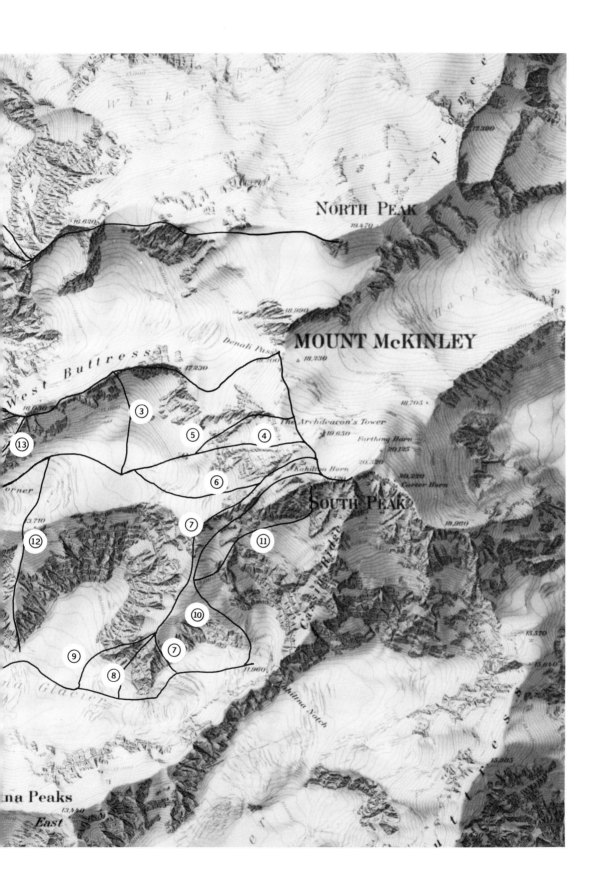

CHAPTER 3

THE SOUTH BUTTRESS

1954 Route
Southeast Spur
Ramp Route
Reality Ridge
Isis Face
Ridge of No Return

1954 Route

THIS MASSIVE BUTTRESS IS THE MOST PROMINENT FEA-
ture of Denali's southern side. It curls down in a long leg
and, several miles away from the peak, crests above fifteen
thousand feet five times. Six different major routes cut up onto
the South Buttress proper; two of them (Isis Face and Ridge of No
Return) have been climbed only to the top of the buttress, rather
than to Denali's summit. The entire buttress has never been
done from the Southeast Fork of the Kahiltna.

The American Alpine Journal 1955 carried an article entitled
"The First Traverse of Mt. McKinley." Beneath this bold print,
there was a subtitle: "A First Ascent of the South Buttress." So, the
significance of the climb was both in accomplishing the first
traverse of the mountain and in doing a new route.

Elton Thayer was ambitious, but he climbed for spiritual reasons,
to commune with nature and the mountains. He had done notable
first ascents of King Peak (Mount Logan) and Mount Hess.

While working as a ranger in Mount McKinley National Park,
the mountain beckoned him. In the summer of 1953, his fourth
year as a ranger, he put together a team for the unclimbed South
Buttress. Morton Wood had attempted Denali in 1947 and was
ready to settle a score, for he had gotten altitude sickness. Les
Viereck had reconnoitered Mount Drum in the Wrangell Mountains with Thayer, and George Argus had spent a summer on the
Juneau Ice Cap.

During the winter, at an Alaska Alpine Club meeting in Fairbanks,
Thayer discussed his proposed climb with Don McLean and
Buck Wilson of the Northwest Buttress team. Thayer would leave
first. Their climbs would be first ascents, statements of the Alaskan
climbers' mettle in their own backyards, just like the Sourdoughs
and Stuck.

Before Thayer left, he received Bradford Washburn's detailed
analysis of the South Buttress route, later published in the June
1954 issue of *Appalachia*. He carried the advance manuscript
with him on the climb.

On April 17, these four good friends began slogging with seven-
ty-pound packs from the Alaska Railroad stop of Curry (north of
Talkeetna) to the Ruth Glacier. Nowadays, climbers who fly in to
seven thousand feet often forget the hardships of the pioneers'

overland approaches. The bushwhacking was unforgiving, particularly with their huge packs catching on alders and the danger of lurking bears. The Susitna and Chulitna river crossings were hazardous at best, and improbable if the "ice was out." Finally, the sticky spring snow had to be kicked off their snowshoes, nearly every step, for fifty miles.

Argus and Viereck were both on leave from the army. Viereck was a military game warden who had great difficulty getting away, because his boss had been caught stealing money from game licenses. Viereck had told them that he was going away for "the weekend." Somehow, like Argus, Viereck got a thirty-day leave.

On April 23, they received an airdrop in the Great Gorge of the Ruth Glacier, from Wood's wife, Ginny. They proceeded by leap-frogging their camps upward. By the end of the month, they had climbed onto the South Buttress via an 11,800-foot pass, which separates the West Fork of the Ruth and the East Fork of the Kahiltna.

They carried four hundred feet of fixed rope, twelve ice pitons and circular tube pickets, and two tiny cotton tents which Thayer's wife, Bernice, had sewn. They were also forced to carry their huge trail snowshoes.

The four climbers were so compatible during this demanding six-week climb that they seldom disagreed with one another, and then only when they were tired. Thayer's leadership was only a formality, for the team worked together like magic. They grew close.

While the lead climber chopped steps up the ice (measured at forty-six to fifty degrees), the rear climbers were barraged by ice chips. One day they spent five hours chopping steps just a hundred yards. They called this one-thousand-foot section the "Lotsa Face."

From May 6 to 8, they sat out a storm, the only bad weather for the rest of the trip. Two days of step-chopping blew in; they rechopped.

Farther along the ridge crest, the cornices hung sixty to eighty feet over the Kahiltna Glacier. The climbing was impassible on either side. They found an eerie tunnel, through which they walked, crawled and pushed their packs for a very long distance.

Eventually, they fell behind schedule, so they stopped leapfrogging and began moving alpine style, with ninety-pound packs. When they topped the 15,700-foot crest of the buttress and gazed down the north side, they knew they could make the traverse. In fact, they had to make it. Reversing the Lotsa Face, the myriad of avalanche-prone slopes, the now-torrid rivers and

the thickets of alders was no longer an option. Underneath monster packs, they marched across the 14,500-foot basin, east of the summit.

At the 17,200-foot camp, where they merged with the Northeast (or upper Karstens) Ridge, they were elated. They had made it. And they would not have to carry their packs any higher.

The next day, May 15, they strolled to the summit. Their weeks of toil on the buttress had thoroughly acclimatized them, so they hardly noticed the altitude.

But by May 16, both Viereck and Argus were AWOL from the army—they had gone beyond their thirty-day leave. In somewhat of a hurry to get home and staggering under their awkward, heavy loads, they started down the Harper Glacier.

Thirty-three years later, Viereck would reflect that the ensuing accident "may have been caused by overconfidence because Wood had been on this part of the mountain before and we were on our way down."

Traveling as a rope of four, with Thayer in the rear, they belayed one another down fresh snow on Karstens Ridge. Suddenly,

Denali as seen from a camp on Mount Crosson at sunrise ▼

Thayer slipped, their belays pulled out and the whole team slid toward the Muldrow. They stopped eight hundred feet later. Thayer was dead, hanging over a sérac, his back broken in the fall. Argus had a broken hip.

After an interminable week of waiting for Argus' condition to improve, or for Ginny Wood to fly by and check on them, they painstakingly lowered Argus to a safer camp. Leaving Argus with all of the food, Viereck and Wood started out.

In two days, they arrived at the McKinley River Bar Cabin, famished. They quickly found food, stocked the previous summer by a young Denali-struck ranger on his rounds. It was an old Alaskan tradition to keep firewood and food stocked in wilderness cabins in case of an emergency. Young Ranger Elton Thayer could not make it off the mountain, but he had helped his friends, even after death.

A week after Viereck and Wood had left Argus, the rescue party walked up to his tent. Argus cheerfully invited them in for a cup of tea. He was flown out by helicopter, the first helicopter rescue of many to follow.

Argus was listed by the army as "missing in action." Viereck, after suffering a superior officer's attempt to "stick him with charges," was let off his AWOL status by a sympathetic commanding officer.

Wood wrote in *The American Alpine Journal,*

> I would never encourage anyone to climb the mountain by this route, as it is not, in my opinion, either safe or practical...Not often can four people live together so intimately under such trying conditions as this trip imposed without ever experiencing the slightest frictions or personality conflict. I have never climbed with a more compatible or congenial group than ours.

The loss of a friend and the painful, guarded realization of their own mortality haunt the team members even thirty-three years later. None of the men went on any more major expeditions. Viereck found it hard to recall the good parts of the trip, for the nightmare ending had blackened it all. Argus recovered, although his hip and knees still give him trouble.

In Thayer's obituary in *The American Alpine Journal 1955,* Alston Paige lamented that the people who didn't know Thayer, but were inspired by his character, might forget him; but none of his climbing partners would. However, this situation changed in the seventies and now everyone will remember him. They will read his name on the map, on the high country on Denali's eastern side—where four friends celebrated their good fortune in not having to retrace their footsteps. This area was named Thayer Basin.

On the crest of the South Buttress ▲

Boyd N. Everett, Jr. on the Southeast Spur ►

▲
Southeast Spur

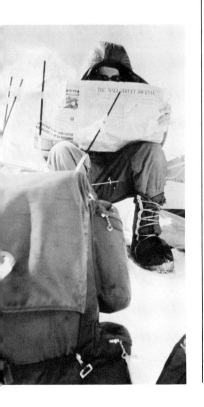

BRANCHING OFF THE SOUTH BUTTRESS, THE SOUTHEAST Spur is a long, indirect route that consists of a myriad of ice walls, cornices, avalanche slopes, and crevasses. Like most routes of the sixties, it was climbed with 2,400 feet of fixed rope. The route has been overlooked (and unrepeated) because it does not offer the pure simplistic lines of the South Face. However, the ice climbing difficulties (there is no rock) and eight miles of climbing make this route quite difficult.

The route was attempted in 1958, by a strong six-man team that included Denali veterans Bill Hackett and Jake Breitenbach. They reached approximately eleven thousand feet, where they were turned back by rotten and steep ice.

Several winters later, at a party in his spartan apartment in New York City, Boyd N. Everett, Jr. planted the seed for the 1962 Southeast Spur expedition. Four of his New York friends were signed on: Sam Silverstein, Chris Wren, Sam Cochrane, and Charles Hollister, all in their mid-to-late twenties.

Everett was twenty-eight years old and an accomplished stock analyst on Wall Street. Few of his Wall Street associates would suspect that this precise man, who dressed in conservative business suits, was quietly initiating huge climbing expeditions. He would become a peerless organizer of climbers and equipment, a Chris Bonington of Alaskan expeditions. Although not a technically gifted rock climber, he had stamina and could chop steps with the best ice climbers of the day. The Southeast Spur would mark the beginning of Everett's realization of his potential.

At the last minute, on the eve of the trip, Everett invited twenty-one-year-old Hank Abrons to join the expedition. His active encouragement of the development of young climbers would be, perhaps, Everett's greatest contribution to mountaineering. After his death in the Himalaya eight years later, a portion of his estate was given to The American Alpine Club's Mountaineering Fellowship Fund, which assists young, expeditionary climbers.

On June 2, in Talkeetna, Everett wore neatly pressed mountain pants and clutched a briefcase, setting himself and his impatient New York partners up for ridicule among the local sourdoughs. The team paced the streets for seven days waiting for the weather to clear before they could fly in. The locals called them the

Boyd Everett, Jr. Expedition, with an emphasis on *Junior*. Three-to-one odds were bet against them.

They started climbing on June 10. One windy night, Abrons and Wren witnessed the wall of their poorly made tent disappear with a horrifying *rip!* Where there had once been a tent wall, they could stare out at Denali's summit, streaming white in the wind. They quickly dug a snow cave.

Their first major obstacle was the "Arrow," a straight line of huge cornices above a steep ice face. (This is also the name of a Shawangunks climb that Everett was fond of.) Cochrane solved the problem on June 15, chopping steps up the ice face directly to the cornices, then delicately cutting a hole through a huge cornice roof with an ice saw. The team tunneled through behind him.

Further contortions were performed on a steep chute and a rotten ice wall. The climbers regularly fell into crevasses. Everett collapsed a huge cornice, his heart pounding madly as tons of ice thundered down to the glacier. The expedition considered abandoning the route because of the numerous unforeseen technical difficulties and objective dangers.

But they continued. Everett was undaunted. On June 17, Abrons led a twenty-foot overhanging ice wall with three hours of chopping and a snow picket.

Cochrane took the crux pitch; he rappelled off a picket to rotten snow overlying sixty-five-degree ice and packed the wet snow into steps for fifty feet. Next, he tunneled through a corniced corner and traversed fifty feet on incredibly hollow snow and, with his shovel, dug a three-foot trench to the top. It took an entire day to both lead and carry loads over this one pitch at 10,700 feet.

The most dangerous section of the route was at 10,800 feet. "The Fluting" involved a long traverse underneath cornices and séracs. Between trips across this area, they watched a sérac trigger an avalanche, which was four hundred feet wide and four feet deep, down their route.

Although it snowed on and off for the next eight days, no more technical difficulties were encountered between the Fluting and the end of the Southeast Spur. Wren described trailbreaking in this section as "wading waist deep in cold oatmeal." On June 26, they made a camp at 13,800 feet; they had nine days of food.

The team decided that its best hopes lay in sending Everett and Cochrane to the summit, so they all set off on June 27 and established a camp at 15,600 feet, on top of the South Buttress. As four of the team descended to 13,800 feet, there was an incident remarkably similar to the 1954 South Buttress tragedy.

◄ *The Southeast Spur*

Abrons, who was last on the rope, fell, pulling Wren off. The rope caught over a sérac and Hollister caught Abrons after he had fallen a hundred feet. Miraculously, no one was hurt.

The next day, Everett and Cochrane followed Thayer's route for half a mile on the crest of the buttress, then cut up new ground on the upper Southeast Face, via a forty-five-degree snow couloir that led above sixteen thousand feet. They camped on a small snowpatch at seventeen thousand feet.

As Cochrane's air mattress had deflated the night before, he experienced a second night of cold and lumpy sleep. In the morning, a malfunctioning stove resulted in a breakfast of cold pea soup and dried fruit.

They skirted all technical difficulties, and in seven hours reached the nineteen-thousand-foot summit plateau. Here, for five hours, they were repeatedly knocked down by the wind and forced to crawl across patches of ice. The wind, which was blowing at fifty to sixty miles per hour, came straight into their faces until they reached the summit.

They took three pictures and left the names of the expedition members and a bottle of dirt from Central Park. The Talkeetna skeptics had lost their bet against this bespectacled New York broker-turned-mountain-climber. The two left within minutes.

Shaking with exhaustion after seven hours without a rest, Everett and Cochrane both took Empirin and Dexedrine. Shortly after this, Cochrane fell two hundred feet before Everett was able to catch him with an ax belay. He was unhurt. They reached seventeen thousand feet after eighteen hours of continuous moving. Because their time had run out, the team was forced to descend without another summit attempt. They reached base camp in three days.

The following year, 1963, Abrons would return to Denali, leading a group of Harvard climbers on a first ascent of the Wickersham Wall. In 1966, Everett's friends were pleased to read his brilliant expedition treatise, "The Organization of an Alaskan Expedition." This timeless report would be photocopied hundreds of times and would inspire countless Alaskan expeditions. In 1967, Everett returned to Denali, masterminding a three-pronged expedition to the Cassin, the American Direct, and the South Buttress.

Ramp Route

THIS ROUTE IS A LOGICAL CUTOFF TO THE LOGISTICALLY cumbersome South Buttress route. It has enjoyed a moderate amount of popularity in recent years, for it provides a quick and relatively uncrowded alternative to the West Buttress. However, there is some avalanche activity, particularly after big snowfalls, on both the glacial approach and the ramp up to 15,600 feet.

On June 25, 1965, Masatsugu Kajiura, Katsuhiko Kaburagi, Hisazumi Nakamura, Dr. Yoshihito Tsukazaki, Art Davidson and Shiro Nishimae arrived at eleven thousand feet on the East Fork of the Kahiltna. Their plan was to attempt the South Face, but this was abandoned after watching numerous avalanches sweep the route. They focused their attention on the snow ramp leading up to the South Buttress.

Nishimae, who had climbed a new route on Mount St. Elias the year before, had been attending college in Anchorage where he had met Art Davidson. The two would also team up in 1967 to make the difficult first winter ascent of Denali, recounted in Davidson's epic book, *Minus 148°: The Winter Ascent of Mt. McKinley*. Davidson became close to the Japanese, despite the language barrier. He learned pidgin Japanese; unlike other Japanese language initiates who learned such common questions as "where is the bus?" Davidson would become an expert at phrases like: "ice, hard climbing, beautiful peak, belay please."

` The American's name appeared on the Japanese climbing prospectus as "Aruper" Davidson. At first, Davidson had been happy about the food list they had sent, which included chops and steaks. Once on the mountain, however, after nearly a week of eating seaweed and rice, Davidson felt somewhat ill and malnourished. He asked his foreign partners where the chops and steaks were. They replied that there had been a mistake on the menu; it was supposed to read *chopsticks*.

The team placed a camp at the bottom of the ramp, neatly crossed an avalanche chute, and made another camp just beneath a sérac at 15,000 feet. By July 1, they established another camp on Thayer's South Buttress route, at 15,570 feet. Davidson had become ill with stomach problems, unable to keep up his strength on Japanese food. He descended to base camp.

Meanwhile, a top-secret CIA expedition helicoptered in, landing close to the unseen Japanese base camp. Davidson, layered in his battleworn and threadbare woolens, strolled over from camp and introduced himself; the slickly-garbed CIA team was shocked. Finally, someone commented that the lone climber "must live up here." The climbers all laughed.

No records of this CIA climb exist in any of the literature or the Park Service files, yet someone had to authorize the helicopter landing, normally prohibited within park boundaries. This expedition was filled with many of the top American climbers of the day, outfitted to the teeth in shiny new down parkas, standing beside huge wooden crates of equipment. The team hoped to climb the South Face as training for equally clandestine climbs that would take place on India's Nanda Devi in 1965, 1966 and 1967, where a plutonium nuclear sensing device was lost and avalanched into a major watershed. A second device was eventually planted on Nanda Kote.

On July 2, the Japanese climbed Boyd N. Everett, Jr.'s 1962 Southeast Spur finish and bivouacked at eighteen thousand feet. Kajiura, Nakamura, and Nishimae reached the summit the next morning, on a calm and clear day, above a sea of clouds.

The team took a brief stab at the incredibly dangerous eastern icefall of Mount Foraker before leaving the Alaska Range. The secretly cloaked CIA spent weeks on the mountain, but rumors have it that they failed.

▲

Reality Ridge

FOR SIX THOUSAND FEET, THIS ROUTE RISES FROM THE West Fork of the Ruth Glacier until it merges with the 1962 Route at 13,100 feet. The climbing difficulties are similar to those on the 1962 Route; however, there is rock climbing. The rotten, ball-bearing snow conditions might be avoided by an early May ascent.

Peter Metcalf visited Bradford Washburn, studied his Denali photographs and uncovered this new route. Metcalf was joined by Lincoln Stoller, Angus Thuermer and Henry Florschutz. Though young, Stoller, Florschutz and Metcalf were all veterans of a new route on Mount Fairweather in 1973.

On June 18, 1975, Cliff Hudson flew Metcalf's group into the Ruth Glacier. Apparently, Hudson had seen the route and, worried about the young climbers' fate, demanded round-trip payment just as the plane left the ground. Metcalf awkwardly signed fifteen traveler's checks on his lap, as Denali loomed bigger and bigger beyond the propeller.

In *The American Alpine Journal 1976,* Metcalf wrote:

> When the plane turned the corner of the West Fork, a queasy feeling hit my stomach. Steep walls and fluted ridges rose up at unbelievable angles in numerous thousand-foot sweeps. All were plastered by huge hanging glaciers, menacing cornices and weird snow formations. I was mentally and physically overwhelmed by what I saw. It was hard to find courage and strength when confronting such an awesome adversary for the first time.

On Reality Ridge ▼

At first, they floundered up to their necks in unconsolidated snow; then, donning their snowshoes, they swam upward. They quickly discovered, as Everett had, that moving at night was the only solution.

After two storms, the team began to make progress. They had set up their first camp on the flat ridge crest. Two climbers fixed ropes, while two carried loads. Battling bottomless snow on top of water ice, they straddled knife-edges, frontpointed beneath cornices, and dropped in and out of little cols.

They dug a snow cave at 11,100 feet in a col. Moving up to their fourth camp at 12,190 feet, the climbing eased, although it was spectacular and exposed. They perched their camp on top of a hanging glacier that completely overhung the east side.

The final thousand feet of the ridge was a series of flutings and cornices, easily traveresed on the west side. Stoller finished off a short eighty-five-degree ice pitch. On July 9, they reached the 13,100-foot crest of the Southeast Spur. The technical difficulties ended.

The team moved across Thayer Basin, up the original South Buttress route and around the north side of the summit cone. They traversed down to the 17,200-foot West Buttress camp, aghast at the crowds. Thuermer reached the summit on July 24.

Seven years later, Metcalf returned to Reality Ridge with Glenn Randall. This duo, who would put up several new impressive routes in the Alaska Range, climbed the route alpine style, reaching the summit in ten days from the Ruth Glacier. Thuermer would return with Randall for a first ascent of Mount Huntington's Southeast Ridge in 1978.

▲

Isis Face

THE ISIS FACE IS AN ELEGANT AND DIFFICULT ICE ARÊTE, which is nearly a face, rising steeply out of the northern toe of the West Fork of the Ruth Glacier. It is sandwiched between the Southeast Spur and the Ridge of No Return.

The route stands as a tribute to Jack Tackle's perseverance and imagination. In 1977, Tackle and Ken Currens had climbed Mount Waddington; then, in 1978, Tackle did two first ascents in the St. Elias Range. He knew that he wanted to do an unclimbed route

on Denali. He consulted Washburn and, through a process of elimination, found a photograph of the Southeast Face of the South Buttress. He was hooked.

Tackle would name the route after a Bob Dylan song. There were striking similarities between his climb and the song's lyrics about a man marrying Isis and his inability to hold on to her.

In early May 1979, Tackle and Currens were flown into the Ruth Glacier. A short way up the route, a snow ledge collapsed and Currens fell 240 feet, fracturing his femur. Tackle lowered him to a cave, skied out, gathered a rescue team and coolheadedly lowered Currens down off the face and into a helicopter.

Tackle could not get the climb off his mind. He came back in 1980 with Jim Kansler. Tackle felt they had erred in 1979, that their packs had been too heavy for the difficult climbing. So Kansler and he climbed up to sixteen thousand feet on the South Buttress via the Ramp Route and left a cache of food, so that they could get to the summit after the Isis Face. They descended and were shuttled over to the Ruth Glacier in a plane.

Dylan's song tells of the two partners setting out for the cold north, with pyramids that were embedded in ice, howling winds and outrageous snow. The climbers could not get anywhere on the route. Tackle got sick and snow conditions prevented them from making any real progress—they gave up.

Tackle went to China (with Jim Donini) in 1981 and attempted a difficult peak, but failed. Tackle still could not get the Isis Face off his mind. The song's refrain also concerns the man who could not understand his drive for Isis.

So, in 1982, Tackle was back, but with bronchitis. His partner, Dave Stutzman, a ski patroller from Montana, had gotten a staph infection from gashing his wrist and ankles while adjusting his crampons.

Above their third bivouac, at 11,500 feet, they encountered three to four feet of depth-hoar snow over fifty- to sixty-degree water ice. This continued for a long way on a fluted ridge, to a rock band. They spent all of the next day fixing their two climbing ropes just 300 feet. There was little hope of making the climb.

The song played in Tackle's head like a needle stuck on a record: one verse refers to chopping through the night and chopping through the dawn.

Stutzman wanted to give up. His infected ankle was so badly swollen he would be forced to cut a hole in his inner boot. But Tackle would not give up. He saw an opening to the left: a thin, blue ice runnel cut up to the rock band, avoiding the fluted ridge. He talked Stutzman into it.

The next day, Tackle led the traverse to the runnel. He prom-

ised Stutzman all of the leading, while he hauled packs—anything to continue. They found it fun and straightforward, but it proved to be the psychological crux of the climb.

The first rock band had some 5.8 rock climbing and some easy aid climbing, although Tackle felt they could have avoided the aid with better route-finding. The technical crux proved to be getting around a chockstone in a chimney on the second rock band, where they found a pitch of overhanging ice.

Once they got to the snowfield above the rock band, they climbed unroped to the South Buttress, walked along it, and found the cache from 1980. They had spent eight days on the face, belaying seventy-eight pitches, not counting the first fifteen hundred feet which they had also soloed.

However, Tackle's longstanding infatuation was never consummated. Although his bronchitis had disappeared and he felt strong, Stutzman's ankle and wrist were badly swollen, so they were forced to descend the South Buttress Ramp route—without the summit.

And the man in the Dylan song also felt cheated, for when he finally entered the tomb of the icy pyramid, there were no jewels.

Stutzman climbed a new route on Jiazi Peak in China later that same year, but, tragically, was buried and killed in a ski patrolling accident on Christmas Eve.

As a startling epilogue, the man in the Dylan song hopes his partner's death will not be contagious, then makes up his mind that he has to continue; Tackle came back in 1985 and made yet another attempt to get to the summit from the cache above the Ramp route. Storms forced him down. After resting in Talkeetna, he flew back in and climbed a difficult route on Mount Hunter (see the Diamond Arête route).

Dave Stutzman taking down a tent on a knife-edge on the Isis Face ▲

▲

Ridge of No Return

THE MOST DIFFICULT AND EXTENSIVELY CORNICED RIDGE on Denali begins on the West Fork of the Ruth Glacier. Halfway along, the Ridge of No Return doglegs and begins to climb more steeply, until the cornices end and it merges into a face. After some rock bands and icefields, the route has a very

appealing finish on a fifteen-thousand-foot summit of the South Buttress.

It was first attempted by Glenn Randall and Peter Metcalf in 1983. They decided that the ridge was a trap because of its difficult and unstable cornices. Their name stuck because of the committing nature of the climb.

In 1984, the Italian climber Renato Casarotto came to Talkeetna, fresh from waterfall climbing in Canada. At the ranger station, Roger Robinson showed him a photograph of the ridge that Metcalf and Randall had named. Casarotto knew he must try it.

He wrote in his book, *Winds of the North,* "It is the wind now which is in charge of this land which surrounds us with its ice. The wind and the silence, broken only by the noise of avalanches."

On April 29, Casarotto spoke in nervous monosyllables to his wife, Goretta, on the Ruth Glacier, then kissed her good-bye.

He set out alone in a whiteout, with no radio. When he reached the foot of the route that evening, he climbed eight hundred feet up a snowy slope, to the start of the technical difficulties, and bivouacked.

At dawn the next morning, he followed the left side of the face. The sense of scale took Casarotto some getting used to. He used a pair of sliding knots, attached to the climbing rope on his harness. With gentle movements against the rope, he was able to move upward. With this time-consuming method, he moved up the wall, climbing each pitch three times.

He used no fixed ropes and moved alpine style. His sparse rack consisted of five rock pitons, six ice screws and one deadman.

That first day, he climbed a sixty- to seventy-degree ice wall, then muscled up an overhanging, unstable cornice. On top, he set his tent in a small depression. The next two days, bad weather hampered his progress.

By May 3, he encountered the route's difficulties. For starters, the ridge had rotten ice and holes, which all had to be probed. Each step had to be considered.

He found that the ridge crest had perfectly cylindrical cornices. Casarotto would spend a lot of time pondering the cornices. They preyed on his mind, scaring him to death. He wrote that they were "built over one another in a great unstable, chaotic architecture."

Indeed, one wonders how he could justify the risk not only of climbing beneath the cornices, but pitching his tent under them. When Glenn Randall met Casarotto after the climb, he repeatedly asked, "How did you succeed?"

He found that the easiest way to avoid the unstable cornices was to descend beneath them, effecting long traverses. There were moments when he was surprised to find himself talking aloud: "What's that, a windslab?" "Is this going to fall down?" "That's an ice castle, I don't like it."

His camps were incredible affairs, his red tent roosted on the razored edge like a bird ready to take flight–or tucked beneath the dubious shelter of huge overhanging cornices. On his fourth bivouac, he was so tired he fell asleep before he could set up the tent.

On May 4, he encountered difficult mixed climbing, then a rock tower. On May 5, he left in the afternoon and climbed until 2 A.M. before he could find a tent site during a hailstorm.

On May 6, he woke up and saw two suns in the sky and wondered if he was going mad. He photographed it. Fifteen minutes later, it was normal again and he realized it was a sundog, a strange, dual reflection of the sun.

At one of the cruxes of the ridge, immersed in the fog, he stopped to think below overhanging cornices. He wrote: "It's frightful in silence. Silence has a destructive power all its own."

He gathered his nerve, then slung a rock horn. Balancing on his ice ax, at the limit of his concentration, he tension-traversed to the left. At 8 P.M., after twelve hours of continuous climbing, he realized that he had only gained three hundred vertical feet.

His struggles paralleled those of another soloist, John Mallon Waterman (not related to the author), who was a natural and speedy climber. While soloing Mount Hunter, Waterman would climb hard all day, only to find that he had made scant progress because of the time-consuming nature of self-belaying across cornices.

Casarotto wrote: "Every step I can clearly feel danger from each of the cornices hanging over me. At 1 A.M. I discover a wonderful tent site."

As he continued along the crest the next day, he fell ninety feet off the ridge. He thought it a miracle that his anchor held. He regained the crest and doggedly continued, finding more of the same cornice dangers.

On May 9, the exit from the route seemed very far away to him. He reached the most difficult and most dangerous climbing of his career, which included solos on Broad Peak, Fitzroy, Huascarán, and Mont Blanc in winter.

Grappling with the inexplicable voices within his psyche, Casarotto writes of "having to liberate all contradictions" within himself. And, near the end of the route's difficulties, "I have reached the end of a cruel difficult story. I fall asleep."

On the next day, he climbed with a "mysterious sensation upon my shoulders." In apparent contradiction to *The American*

Alpine Journal 1985, where he would report leaving nothing on the mountain, Casarotto would write in his book that he abandoned his two ropes. Then, without stopping, he soloed three thousand feet of steep mixed ground.

Near the crest of the South Buttress, he was hit by strong winds. Claiming an ambient air temperature of −45°C and a windchill factor of −90°C, the big mountain veteran kept going without putting on his down jacket. Once on the fifteen-thousand-foot crest, he was blown to the ground.

He searched for shelter in vain, finally erecting his tent on top of the ridge, wondering if he would be blown off. It took him a long time to warm up.

When the winds quieted in the morning, he took down what was left of the tent and descended to the col. Then, apparently lost, trying to figure out where he was on the map, he pondered his descent options.

In the midst of his route-finding dilemma, he watched a nearby group of inexperienced climbers on the standard South Buttress route. Suddenly, one unroped climber cried out and fell. Now, with new urgency, Casarotto downclimbed a thousand feet of ice, motivated by the need to get a rescue for the climbers.

On the East Fork of the Kahiltna Glacier, he fell into a crevasse, catching himself by bridging his legs across, and then climbed back out. After walking all night, he arrived at Kahiltna Base Camp and called for the rescue that would save the panic-stricken, helpless trio on the South Buttress. He was reunited with his wife on the Ruth Glacier that afternoon.

The Ridge of No Return was climbed as an entity within itself, regardless of Denali's summit, for Casarotto felt that the natural line culminated on the fifteen-thousand-foot subpeak of the South Buttress. The pioneers of the South Buttress and Southeast Spur, and John Mallon Waterman (who laboriously soloed a route that he had formerly climbed to within two hundred feet of Mount Hunter's summit), all would have found routes without a summit incomplete. Several other recent routes in the Alaska Range have been completed to the end of their technical difficulties and claimed as first ascents. Perhaps this is an option left open to the person making the first ascent, although Belmore Browne (who came within one hundred feet of the summit in 1912) did not claim the first ascent of Denali.

In the summer of 1986, Casarotto attempted one of the greatest solo climbs on earth: K2. After nearly reaching the summit, he descended to the bottom of the mountain, and just as on his descent from the South Buttress, he fell into a crevasse. This time, sadly, he died from internal injuries.

7013

144

DENALI

THE SOUTH BUTTRESS

1   *South Buttress, 1954 Route*

2   *Southeast Spur*

3   *Reality Ridge*

4   *Isis Face*

5   *Ridge of No Return*

6   *Ruth Glacier, Northwest Fork*

Route Guide

Approach: *6 miles west from the 6,700-foot West Fork landing strip on the Ruth Glacier to the 10,000-foot base of the pass.*

Total Time: *14–28 days .*

Climbing Miles: *12.*

Vertical Gain of Route: *10,300 feet.*

Alaska Grade: *3.*

Difficulties, Dangers, Rating: *Up to 60-degree snow and ice from 12,400-13,400 (Lotsa Face); some parties finish route on 50-degree East Face, rather than the long traverse across Thayer Basin to the Northeast Ridge.*

Camps: *11,800 (pass); 12,400; 13,900; 15,000; 15,570; 14,300 (Thayer Basin); 17,200 (Northeast Ridge).*

References: *1955, 1963 (Southeast Spur), 1966 (Ramp route) AAJ.*

Firsts

Ascent: *May 15, 1955; Thayer, Viereck, Wood, Argus.*

Variation: *South Buttress Ramp: July 3, 1965; Kajiura, Nakamura, Nishimae, (Kaburagi, Tsukazaki, Davidson).*

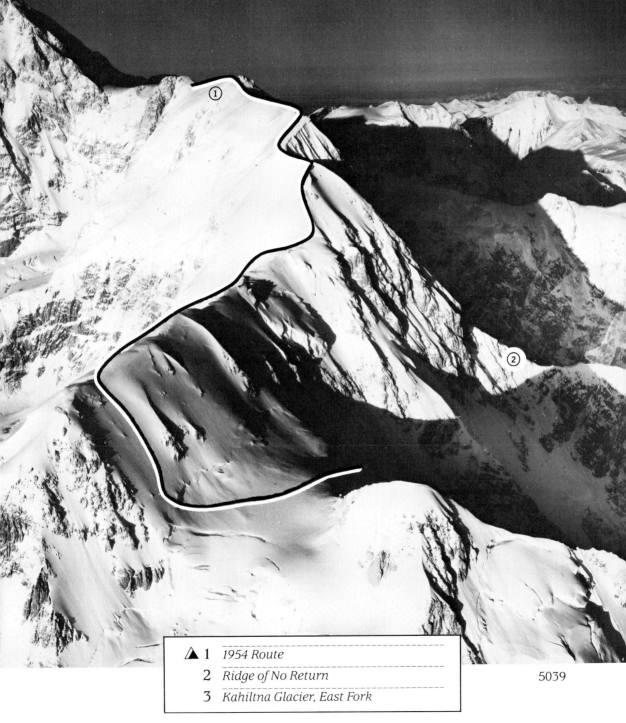

▲ 1   *1954 Route*
   2   *Ridge of No Return*
   3   *Kahiltna Glacier, East Fork*

5039

5158

▲ 1 *1954 Route*

2 *East Buttress*

3 *Southeast Spur Finish*

4 *Harper Glacier*

5 *Thayer Basin*

6 *Unclimbed*

1954 ROUTE

▲ 1   *1954 Route*
  2   *Kahiltna Glacier, Southeast Fork*
  3   *Kahiltna Glacier, East Fork*
  4   *Unclimbed*

5896

7867

Route Guide

Approach: 1 mile from the 7,600-foot Northwest Fork of the Ruth landing strip to the 7,700-foot base.

Total Time: 12–24 days.

Climbing Miles: 8.

Vertical Gain of Route: 12,600 feet.

Alaska Grade: 4.

Difficulties, Dangers, Rating: Up to 65-degree snow and ice climbing and considerable cornicing until 12,000 feet; up to 55-degree snow and ice above 15,700 feet.

Camps: 9,200; 10,200; 10,800; 11,800; 13,000; 15,700; 17,000.

References: 1963 AAJ; October 9, 1962 Look; Expedition Report, Talkeetna Ranger Station.

Firsts

Ascent: June 29, 1962; Everett, Cochrane, (Hollister, Abrons, Wren, Silverstein).

Variation: Reality Ridge: July 24, 1975; Theurmer, (Metcalf, Stoller, Florschutz).

▲1   *Southeast Spur 1962*

2   *Ruth Glacier, Northwest Fork*

SOUTHEAST SPUR

▲ 1	*Southeast Spur Finish 1962*
2	*1954 Route*
3	*Thayer Basin*
4	*Cassin Ridge*

7200

8409

Route Guide

Approach: *10 miles from 7,200-foot Southeast Fork of the Kahiltna landing strip, via East Fork of the Kahiltna to 11,000 feet; move quickly and camp with heed to sérac and avalanche activity on the East Fork of the Kahiltna.*

Total Time: *10–24 days.*

Climbing Miles: *5.*

Vertical Gain of Route: *9,300 feet.*

Alaska Grade: *3.*

Difficulties, Dangers, Rating: *Ramp is avalanche-prone after snowfalls and occasionally swept by séracs from 14,000 and 15,000 feet; there may be short snow and ice walls up to 70 degrees getting over bergschrunds; up to 55-degree snow and ice on East Face finish (16,000–18,960), then a knife-edged ridge.*

Camps: *11,000 (beneath Kahiltna Notch); 12,000; 14,800 (beneath séracs); 15,570 (saddle); 17,800 (East Face).*

References: *1963 (Southeast Spur), 1966 AAJ.*

Firsts

Ascent: *July 3, 1965; Kajiura, Nakamura, Nishimae, (Kaburagi, Tsukazaki, Davidson).*

▲ 1   *Ramp Route*

  2   *1954 Route*

  3   *Unclimbed*

5929

▲ 1	*Reality Ridge*
2	*Ruth Glacier, West Fork*
3	*Southeast Spur*
4	*Isis Face*
5	*Ridge of No Return*
6	*1954 Route*

Route Guide

Approach: 1.5 miles west of the 6,700-foot West Fork of the Ruth landing strip to the 7,900-foot base.

Total Time: 12–24 days.

Climbing Miles: 7.

Vertical Gain of Route: 12,400 feet.

Alaska Grade: 4+.

Difficulties, Dangers, Rating: Double-corniced and knife-edged ridge with rock gendarmes (5.5, A2) until 13,200 feet.

Camps: 10,370; 11,150 (col); 12,190; 15,700; 17,000.

References: 1976 AAJ; October 1976 Summit.

Firsts

Ascent: July 24, 1975; Thuermer, (Metcalf, Stoller, Florschutz).

Alpine Style: May 13, 1982; Randall, Metcalf.

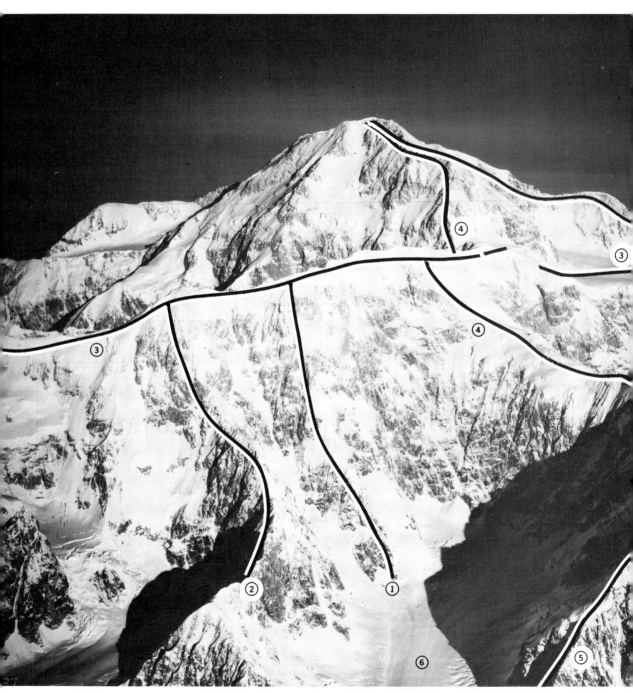

5137

Route Guide

A*pproach:* 5 miles west from 6,700-foot landing strip on the West Fork of the Ruth Glacier to the 8,200-foot base.

T*otal Time:* 10-21 days.

C*limbing Miles:* 6.

V*ertical Gain of Route:* 12,100 feet.

A*laska Grade:* 5+.

D*ifficulties, Dangers, Rating:* 50- to 60-degree snow and ice, with vertical and overhanging sections; 5.8, A1 rock.

C*amps:* There were 6 chopped bivouacs.

R*eferences:* 1955 (South Buttress), 1963 (Southeast Spur), 1966 (Ramp Route), 1983 AAJ; Surviving Denali, Waterman, pp. 95-96.

Firsts

A*scent:* May 1982; (Tackle, Stutzman).

A*lpine Style:* May 1982; (Tackle, Stutzman).

▲ 1   *Isis Face*
  2   *Ridge of No Return*
  3   *1954 Route*
  4   *Southeast Spur*
  5   *Reality Ridge*
  6   *Ruth Glacier, West Fork*

5872

Route Guide

Approach: 2 miles west from 6,700-foot West Fork of the Ruth Glacier landing strip to the 7,800-foot base.

Total Time: 10–21 days.

Climbing Miles: 7.

Vertical Gain of Route: 12,500 feet.

Alaska Grade: 6.

Difficulties, Dangers, Rating: First 3,000 feet are sustained 50- to 70-degree snow and ice, with vertical and overhanging sections, on a double-corniced ridge; last 4,000 feet up a steep mixed face.

Camps: Casarotto had 5 bivouac sites.

References: 1955 (South Buttress), 1963 (Southeast Spur), 1966 (Ramp Route), 1985 AAJ; Oltre i venti del Nord, Casarotto.

Firsts

Ascent: May 10, 1985; (Casarotto).

Alpine Style: May 10, 1985; (Casarotto).

Solo: May 10, 1985; (Casarotto).

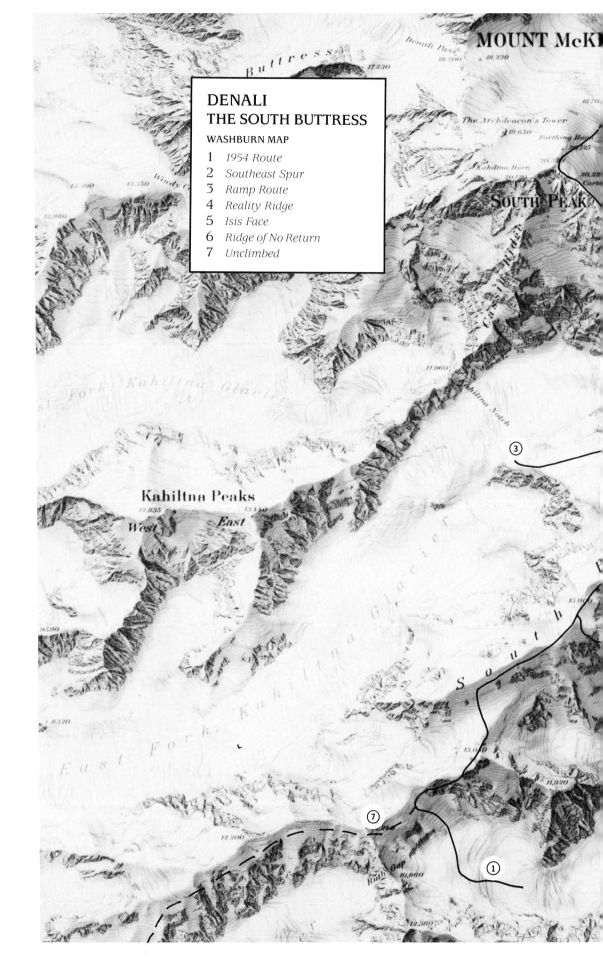

DENALI
THE SOUTH BUTTRESS

WASHBURN MAP

1 *1954 Route*
2 *Southeast Spur*
3 *Ramp Route*
4 *Reality Ridge*
5 *Isis Face*
6 *Ridge of No Return*
7 *Unclimbed*

East Buttress

Northwest Fork, Ruth

Southeast Spur

West Fork, Ruth Glacier

CHAPTER 4

THE SOUTH FACE

Cassin Ridge
American Direct
Milan Krissak Memorial
Southwest Face
Czech Direct

Cassin Ridge

BECAUSE OF ITS INCLUSION IN *FIFTY CLASSIC CLIMBS OF North America* and *Climbing in North America*, and through word of mouth, the Cassin Ridge has become one of the most sought-after climbs. A Washburn photograph tells why: it is a direct, nine-thousand-foot granite ridge to the top of the continent.

In an inspirational article in *The Mountain World*, 1956-57, Bradford Washburn wrote:

> Last and probably the most difficult and dramatic of all potential new routes on Mount McKinley is the great central bulge on the fabulous 10,000-foot South Face of the mountain....this route may be classed as unequivocally excellent climbing from start to finish.

Thus inspired, the Italian Alpine Club invited Riccardo Cassin, fresh from the first ascent of Gasherbrum IV, to lead a team to the South Face in 1961. Cassin had been the first to climb three of Europe's more impressive North Faces. And, like Hudson Stuck in 1913, Cassin had already packed a half century behind him before his Denali climb.

Cassin recruited Giancarlo (Jack) Canali, Luigi Alippi, Romano Perego, Luigi Airoldi, and Annibale Zucchi. All were members of the "spider" climbing club. The team flew to Boston, where Cassin conferred with Bradford Washburn and viewed stereo-photographs of the South Face.

In Anchorage, two other men, Gianni Stocco and Armando Petrecca, who had helped Cassin locate equipment, insisted that they come along; once on the glacier, it proved that they were not prepared for the cold, difficult climbing. Cassin convinced them to fly back out.

At the last minute in mid-June 1961, an American, Bob Goodwin, fresh from a Mount Russell attempt, flew in to join Cassin at the bottom of the route. He became Cassin's tent partner and they got along famously, despite the language barrier. Yet Goodwin (who had limited vacation time) would be forced to fly out before the climb ended.

Goodwin related a story about how Cassin insisted on being dropped near the Northeast Fork of the Kahiltna by Don Sheldon. Sheldon told him that wasn't where he wanted to be. Cassin insisted. Sheldon gave in and it wasn't until after half of the men and equipment were landed that Cassin realized his mistake.

Sheldon picked Cassin up and the team carried their equipment into the East Fork of the Kahiltna. After a long storm, Sheldon finally landed the rest of the climbers where he had originally suggested.

On July 6, the team fixed ropes up a couloir to the ridge. In Cassin's book, *50 Years of Alpinism*, he wrote, "By now I had realized that the couloir we had climbed, was not the one marked on the map by Dr. Washburn [Kahiltna Notch Couloir], but an adjacent one which started 200 meters further up the glacier." This was his second major route-finding error.

Reading Cassin's account, one realizes that he was calling all of the shots: He would regularly ask climbers to go down, or he "bluntly tried to convince…" or "I immediately gave instructions…." However, Cassin's ropemates, or "boys" as he called them, affectionately referred to him as "the bear," an undisputed master and leader. He wrote, "as head of the expedition, I had to act as head of the family and keep everyone's spirits high, be a doctor…."

Following Washburn's detailed route advice, Cassin directed his young "spiders" up difficult granite, on the prow of the ridge above Kahiltna Notch. (In 1984, Washburn would send the Talkeetna Ranger Station enlarged photographs of a route which continued all the way up the prow, which, to date, has never been climbed.)

The team was forced off the prow and around to the Japanese

Approaching the Cassin Ridge in winter ▲

Couloir (see Variations, in the Route Guide). They climbed steep rock beside the ice couloir; in 1961, prior to the ice-climbing revolution, sixty-degree ice was considered more difficult than moderate Class 5 rock. Cassin wrote:

> We were now entering the most committing phase of the expedition, that preceding the final attack. I concentrated on studying the plan of action in great detail so as to create conditions that would guarantee our success. So far the rhythm of work we had adopted allowed us all to give our maximum output with the possibility of recuperating our energies afterwards by taking turns resting.

Thus they went back and forth to lower camps, switching the leaders and load carriers.

In the style of the day, the route was fixed with rope: across the corniced arête and up the hanging glacier, up the chimney at fifteen thousand feet, and up the final icy *dièdre*. Even two decades later, climbers would occasionally find an old Italian rope, a soft iron pin, and various other pieces of Cassin memorabilia.

Their third and final camp was made at 16,700 feet, at the end of the real technical difficulties.

> The boys were truly magnificent in their complete dedication to the ascent, though a certain nervous tension showed on their faces. As a matter of fact, they were all, except for Canali, on their first expedition outside Europe.

At 11 P.M. on July 19, after nearly seventeen hours, they made the top.

> We hugged each other emotionally, barely able to speak.... The boys, wanting to surprise me, had brought a little statue of St. Nicholas, patron of our city, to leave on the summit.

In the final analysis, despite being surrounded by young tigers, it was the fifty-year-old bear who was most magnificent. During an epic descent, in which Canali's feet were frostbitten, Cassin caught Canali's fall in a steep couloir. Cassin hardly slept the next morning in the tent, because he was afraid that the moaning Canali might need something. Cassin wrote:

> I did not move for fear of disturbing my friends, and as a result, suffered slight frostbite under both my big toes.

Then, while descending the next day, two of the climbers fell and the bear interceded.

> Somehow I managed to grab both their ropes and stop them.

And, finally, descending from Camp 1:

> On the rock slabs I lost a crampon and could not catch it. Towards the end of the first couloir I was hit by a big avalanche which

completely buried me but although it had come from high up, it only stunned me a little: I was still holding the fixed rope, and everything ended all right because the snow was extremely light. Unfortunately, however, I had lost the other crampon too, so the descent became even more tiring.

Cassin and his boys flew out. Several of them, including Cassin, were treated at an Anchorage hospital for frostbite. A telegram was sent to them:

I send my warmest congratulations to you and to the other members of the Italian team, who have achieved such a splendid mountaineering feat on Mt. McKinley. This outstanding accomplishment under the most hazardous of conditions is a fine testimonial to your superb skill and fortitude. Our nation is proud to have witnessed within its own borders this conquest which has served to strengthen the ties between the United States and Italy and to earn the admiration of all the world.

—John F. Kennedy

Bradford Washburn said that he would never forget the letter he got from Cassin after the climb. He thanked him for all of his advice, which he had taken, except for one thing: he had not believed it would be so cold at seventeen thousand feet and that their feet would freeze as easily as they did.

In *50 Years of Alpinism*, Cassin humbly entitled the chapter on this climb, "The South Buttress of Mt. McKinley." He concluded that the South Buttress had been one of the greatest satisfactions in his long life as an alpinist. In recognition of the man, mountaineers renamed his route "The Cassin."

Japanese Couloir Variation

In May 1967, a Japanese team made the second ascent of the Cassin Ridge, climbing the couloir to avoid the difficult rock climbing. This was initially named the Hidden Couloir, then came to be known simply as the Japanese Couloir. As ice-climbing standards advanced, all climbers on the Cassin Ridge would use this couloir. The approach to Kahiltna Notch via the East Fork of the Kahiltna would also be abandoned in favor of the Northeast Fork. The latter approach is quicker and involves less climbing, but is also more dangerous due to sérac and hanging-glacier activity.

The Japanese also avoided Cassin's direct rock route above 16,700 feet. Traversing right onto the South Face, then back left, they climbed a long snow couloir which crests at 18,500 feet. This route has now become very popular.

Looking up the East Fork of the Kahiltna Glacier to the South Face ▲

Kahiltna Notch Couloir Variation

The third ascent, with a slight variation, was led by Boyd N. Everett, Jr. in July 1967. The team climbed the Kahiltna Notch Couloir, south of Cassin's couloir. At Kahiltna Notch, they traversed to the top of the Cassin couloir, then rappelled to the Northeast Fork and traversed over to the Japanese Couloir.

French Variant

In 1971, a team of French climbers did a direct variant from 18,500 feet to the summit. Despite the appearance of an article in *The American Alpine Journal 1972*, this is not a significant variant, as the difficulties are not great. However, Danièle Germain became the first woman to climb the Cassin.

Direct Start Variation

In 1983, Wade Henrich and Roger Volkman climbed a difficult start to the Cassin. These climbers mistakenly walked past the Japanese Couloir; thinking they were on the route, they climbed a long fifty-degree ice slope beside the Southwest Face. They then climbed through a 170-foot rock band (5.9, A1). There was no place to bivouac, although they did stop and melt some water. After forty hours of continuous climbing, they intersected the fourteen-thousand-foot level of the Cassin Ridge. Henrich did not recommend the route because of its difficulty and the objective danger involved in climbing underneath a hanging-glacier.

Solo

In summer of 1976, the renowned soloist Charlie Porter made an attempt to solo the route, but came back down when he felt sick. On his second try shortly afterward, he climbed from the top of the Japanese Couloir in a superhuman, thirty-six-hour push, reaching the summit ridge absolutely spent.

As of this writing, several other solos have been completed, but none have trumped Porter's speed. It was a brilliant statement of how far a climber could go, revealing just what the barriers were on Denali; paradoxically, Porter was an extremely private climber and never sought the recognition which he won for this climb.

Second Winter Ascent

Mike Young, Roger Mear, and the author completed the first winter ascent of the Cassin Ridge on March 7, 1982. Standing on the shoulders of Johnston, Genet, and Davidson (West Buttress winter ascent, 1967), we wanted to push the limits by climbing alpine style on a technically difficult route in subzero conditions.

Our theory was basically sound, for we climbed the route in eight days and took full advantage of a long spell of clear weather; pragmatically, it was foolish, for we were unacclimated and I became very sick near the top. With −50°F temperatures and a slight wind, Young and Mear dropped their packs and walked the last two hundred feet to the summit, while I crawled to the summit ridge. We descended via the West Buttress.

▲

American Direct

THE AMERICAN DIRECT IS A MORE SUSTAINED ROUTE than the Cassin and considerably more dangerous, because of avalanches. The ice face and couloirs of the lower half are sheltered by rock bulges to the west; the upper half shoots up mixed granite buttresses, culminating at 19,100 feet on the summit ridge (the route name is misleading, for it does not go directly to the summit).

Another name for this route is the Centennial Wall, as the climbers who made the first ascent were sponsored by the Alaska Centennial Exposition in Fairbanks. Two other major variations, the Japanese Direct and the Haston–Scott, utilize half of the original American route.

The 1967 American Direct team was part of a larger group that also climbed the South Buttress and the Cassin. The three climbs had been organized by Boyd N. Everett, Jr., who led a team to Denali's Southeast Spur in 1962. Everett enjoyed the organization of an expedition as much as the climb itself. In addition to putting in frantic hours as a stock analyst on Wall Street, he had methodically put together the members for the three routes, found equipment and food sponsors, and coordinated the financial aspects of the trip. At that time, Everett's life revolved around an upcoming Himalayan expedition, which would require a massive logistical effort. He saw the organization of a cumbersome expedition to Denali as good training for the Himalaya.

The fourteen-man expedition stopped at the Institute of Arctic Biology in Fairbanks and underwent the administering of EEGs and EKGs, taking of urine and blood specimens, acclimatization tests in a chamber—where they were brought up to eighteen thousand feet—and a cross-country run. The institute had received a large grant to study the effects of altitude upon climbers and each of the climbers was paid four dollars per hour for testing. During the climb, the testing continued. Afterward, the entire expedition was tested again in Fairbanks.

Once they reached advanced base camp on June 30, Everett assigned people to each climb. Everett himself led a group up the Cassin (a third ascent) and dispatched a second team to the South Buttress. Dennis Eberl, Graham Thompson, Roman Laba, and Dave Seidman, all in their early twenties, were chosen for the South Face.

Eberl, Seidman and Thompson were active Dartmouth climbers. Eberl had joined Everett on Mount St. Elias in 1965 and Thompson had done King Peak with Everett in 1966. In 1968, Seidman had been on a difficult first ascent of Mount Kennedy in the St. Elias Range, where one of his partners remarked that "Seidman could [climb] anything he wanted." Laba was also a strong rock climber.

They brought 7,500 feet of Goldline rope (cutting it into 150-foot lengths), thirty-seven rock pitons, eleven ice pitons, and twelve pickets. Both ten-point and twelve-point crampons were used, although some members felt that the frontpoints took up useless space on ice steps and snagged their pants. Although frontpointing had caught on in 1967, steps were still being chopped.

They started climbing on July 5, a wet and late date on which the mountain would be virtually abandoned in the eighties. Four to six pitches of rope were fixed a day. Occasionally, they were hit by avalanches, even in good weather.

Dave Seidman wrote of the route in the May 1968 issue of *Ascent*: "I was slightly shocked because it was obvious that the face was unsafe, but doing anything else would mean descending. I understood, then, the real nature of the climb: that in several places extreme chances had to be taken."

The climbing was continuous fifty- to sixty-degree ice. Their second camp caused a lot of arguments, because no one wanted to sleep next to the outside edge of the tent, overhanging the face.

All activity ceased on July 16. Snow fell and avalanches regularly swept the face. They were confined to their tents for a solid week. At first they perceived the avalanches as dangerous, but after a while, as their tents were continually buried, it simply became a cold monotony to have to go outside and shovel things free. They sat listless. Eberl was worried, for he had read that such lack of external stimulus caused schizophrenic behavior.

Finally, on the seventh day of waiting, the wind stopped and the weather seemed to be clearing. They began climbing; with incredible speed, another storm blew in. They rappelled back to their tents. The storm raged for another six days.

When it was over, the worst tragedy on Denali had struck another team: seven men on the Muldrow Glacier route had died, their bodies scattered from 17,900 feet to the summit.

Eberl, Thompson, Seidman and Laba continued, unaware of the awful events that had taken place above them. One pair would jumar with seventy- to seventy-five-pound packs, while the other pair had the pleasurable task of leading and fixing ropes.

In the March 1968 issue of *Summit* magazine, Thompson wrote:

> To walk or climb where one knows that no man has ever been before is incomparably exhilarating. And now, this feeling was combined with the freedom of moving after having been cooped up for so long and the excitement of making an ascent of an extremely difficult face which had never before been climbed. The sum total was that emotion of unbounded freedom that the mountaineer knows in his best moments.

At their fourth camp, Dartmouth Meadows, they spent four hours chopping out a platform in the ice. It had occurred to them that they could traverse onto easier, avalanche-prone ground to the west (later climbed by Haston and Scott), but their route had been conceived as a direct, straight line up the South Face, rather than a direct line to the summit.

Above, they were confronted by three granite buttresses, all of which offered difficult climbing at altitude. This seemed far more preferable to the avalanche slopes and couloirs beneath them. They pulled up their fixed ropes and committed themselves.

Thompson wrote that the buttresses were

> F7 in places, with some moves requiring direct aid: bare rock, ice-covered rock, and snow-filled cracks...The climbing is very messy, no finesse, just swearing and moaning with anguish. Up a few feet by some miracle, bang in a pin—there's three more feet that we'll never give back.

The awful packs and swearing and heavy breathing in thin air

continued until they pulled over a huge cornice at 19,100 feet. On August 4, they broke trail up to their waists and reached the summit. It was a brief moment with little glory; in fact, it was so cold and windy that they shook hands later, on the way down.

Seidman was a skillful alpinist, thoroughly understanding the risks. Everett had seen the big picture; he knew how to gather climbers with Seidman's talents and unite them toward a common cause. In 1969, the brilliant alpinist and the prolific leader were overwhelmed by an avalanche on Dhaulagiri, the mountain they had dreamed of and prepared for while climbing Denali.

Alpine Style

The American Direct route was repeated in 1983, by two Japanese, Shohei Wada (29) and Koichi Takeuchi (28). After acclimatizing at 14,300 feet on the West Buttress route, they climbed the route in five days.

Haston-Scott Route

In 1976, a variation was added to the South Face by Dougal Haston and Doug Scott, who had recently completed a difficult new route on Mount Everest. They had intended to climb a new route (see Japanese Direct), but upon their arrival at the face, they realized that the Americans had taken the only reasonable line.

They fixed three pitches over the bergschrund on April 29 and started climbing alpine style the next day. Climbing proved to be an incredible strain with their big packs. Bivouacs were miserable affairs, cramped and blasted by avalanches. Like Cassin on Denali in 1961, neither Haston nor Scott could believe that Denali could be so cold.

When they traversed over onto new ground, directly to the summit, they had continual problems with hidden crevasses, windslab snow and small avalanches. In two days of easier climbing, with a spectacular finish up fifty-five-degree ice, they reached the summit and dug a snow hole—an inadvisable bivouac for anyone without their mountain know-how.

In Haston's account in *The American Alpine Journal 1977*, he said that they had climbed the mountain too quickly (fourteen days) and were suffering from the altitude. Two of the best climbers in the world, who had given their all to get up Denali, were awed by its cold and difficulty.

Most importantly, Haston and Scott had "pushed the limits of the envelope," and shown Alaskan climbers that hard routes could be done on Denali alpine style.

The year of 1976 was one of continual rescues on Denali. While descending from their climb, Scott and Haston became involved in the rescue of a badly frostbitten climber on the West Buttress. The article following theirs in *The American Alpine Journal*, "Denali Dilemma," was written by Bob Gerhard, a Park Service ranger. In it, he presented the abysmal record of accidents, rescues and helicopter evacuations, suggesting that climbers take more responsibility for their actions, so that the Park Service would not be forced to further regulate activity on the mountain.

Fortunately, the number of accidents that occurred in 1976 proved to be an all-time high and although many climbers would continue to call for rescues, 1976 would remain the worst year on record. By 1980, the Park Service dropped its requirements of a radio and a physician's certificate of health. Denali climbers were given their freedom.

Solo

In 1982, Mark Hesse (31) would be the first to repeat the Haston–Scott route, solo. He had climbed the Cassin three years previously and had been impressed with his view of the South Face. After attempting the West Buttress with his brother Jon, an amputee, he skied up to the face.

He climbed for eight days, constantly worried about storms, stretched by the continuous climbing difficulties and the cold (−50°F at fifteen thousand feet). Once he traversed onto the upper South Face, he knew that he would make it.

In *The American Alpine Journal 1983*, he concluded:

> Tears welled into my eyes as I scrambled from the top of North America, half frozen by the storm. In that moment, despite a most fleeting return visit to a summit I couldn't even see, I knew that it would be a long time before I would truly descend from the height to which the mountain had once again pushed me.

Although Hesse would later go on to do more technically difficult faces on Kantega and Huascarán, Denali's Haston–Scott route demanded much more, both mentally and physically. As of 1987, he regarded it as the most difficult climb he had ever done.

Japanese Direct

In 1977, a Japanese team, Kichitaka Kimura, Tamae Watanabe, Yuji Tsuneto, Mitsuo Yamaura, and Yushichi Senda added a variation to the American Direct route. They divided into pushing

Dougal Haston in a snow cave at 20,250 feet after ascending the South Face ▲

and pulling teams, then toiled with eleven hundred pounds of gear on two sleds. The roar of avalanches was the only excitement to enliven the monotony of hauling gear. They arrived at their base camp after a week.

On June 25, they began fixing rope over a steep bergschrund and up an avalanche chute, west of the American Direct. Both their approach and the first nine hundred feet of easy-angled climbing lay under the muzzle of Denali's preeminent hanging glacier, Big Bertha.

A thousand feet up, Yamaura led up a crack and cried down happily, "The rock is great. Just like the Alps. The holds are solid."

While finishing the seventh pitch of a long traverse, an avalanche hit them, but they were unhurt. The next day, they pushed the route another few hundred feet.

On June 29, Senda fell into one of four obvious crevasses while carrying to the face. He was unroped and landed on a small ledge with a view into the abyss. His teammates hauled him out and reported him happy to be saved.

In the February 1978 issue of *Iwa to Yuki*, Kimura wrote: "Nobody wanted to continue, so we returned to the tent to talk it out. Lack of safety and lack of time before return was getting to all of us." Drinking their sake seemed the only cure.

Eventually, they set up a two-man site at 13,800 feet, protected from avalanches by a large overhang. Above there, they climbed hard blue ice to their second camp at 14,750 feet, also protected by a 150-foot face.

By July 9, they finished fixing 3,300 feet of rope to their third camp at 16,400 feet, where there route merged with the American Direct. At this point, they thought it would be impossible to make the summit with their limited schedule, but they agreed to try. Before leaving, they fixed ropes on the more difficult sections of a 2,200-foot gully.

On July 13, they left at 6:30 in the morning from Camp 3. After fifteen hours of climbing, the five of them crammed into a three-man tent at 18,200 feet.

They reached the summit at 8 P.M. the next day, July 14. Watanabe became the first woman to climb the face. Kimura wrote:

> Our success was helped greatly by luck: only scratches after a crevasse fall; our cache at the base, spread out by an avalanche, was still usable; we were missed by a one-kilometer-long avalanche across our trail; and we had good weather. Luck and tragedy, our two companions.

Japanese climbers are often willing to justify objective danger, particularly avalanche-prone routes, that other nationalities won't touch. It has been speculated that this emanates from their traditional enlightened view that life has been predetermined and that there is rebirth after death. Also, as there are many climbers in Japan and climbing is more competitive, Japanese climbers must often do outrageous climbs in order to make their names known.

The timeworn joke among Alaskan climbers is that many Japanese routes are "banzai charges." However, Denali has seen many wise and top-flight Japanese climbers: Wada and Takeuchi on the American Direct; Shiro Nishimae on the winter ascent of the West Buttress and the South Buttress Ramp; Naomi Uemura's first West Buttress solo and the first winter solo.

Milan Krissak Memorial

EAST OF THE AMERICAN DIRECT IS AN ICE FACE BROKEN by two rock bands. The route is relatively safe and ends at 18,100 feet on the 1962 Southeast Spur finish.

This route, done by a Slovak team in 1980, was a memorial to their good friend, Milan Krissak, who died in a rescue helicopter crash in the High Tatra. Krissak had pioneered routes in Czechoslovakia, the Alps, the Pamirs, and the Himalaya.

The team was spearheaded by Michal Orolin, who recruited Daniel Bakos, Vladimir Petrik, Ivan Fiala, Miloslav Neumann, Gejza Haak, Juraj Weincziller, Dušan Kovač, František Vernarčík, and Philip Johnson, an Englishman, who arranged equipment support.

The team flew to Canada, rented a van and drove across the continent to sample the culture and countryside. Upon their arrival in Talkeetna, they were beset by a week of bad weather, which they filled with endless soccer matches and socializing in the bar. They were amazed by the warm welcome they received from the people of Talkeetna.

Like the American Direct and the Czech South Face teams, the ten men split into a face team, a South Buttress support team, and two base camp caretakers.

The face team climbed to 15,500 feet on the South Buttress where their tent was promptly blown apart; they then scratched out a snow hole and weathered a terrible storm. Below, in the sunshine, the support team fixed 750 feet of rope on the face. The face team staggered back down.

On June 9, the face team (Orolin, Johnson, Petrik, and Bakoš) jumared the rope; in consideration of the litter problems on Denali, they dropped it to their friends at the bottom of the face. Leading and jumaring were done in alternate pairs. They spent that night and another stormy day on a long traverse ramp, at an icy bivouac ledge, hard won by two hours of chopping.

On their third day, they followed the ramp for six pitches to a broad icefield, where they continued up to a break in the rock cliff. They climbed two pitches of rock, then an ice arête. To their delight, they found a bivouac boulder at the bottom of a large snowfield, at 16,100 feet. This saved them hours of chopping.

In their fourth and final day on the face, they climbed snow and blue ice, heading toward a gendarme which marked their exit onto the South Buttress. The next day, June 13, they walked the spectacular ridge to the summit. Meanwhile, beneath them on the first ascent of the Southwest Face, Simon McCartney felt the beginnings of the altitude sickness which would precede his epic rescue.

How did the Slovaks climb a new route so effortlessly in five days, while McCartney nearly died after nine days on a similar face? It was simple. Like the unknowing Sourdoughs in 1910 and the Japanese on the alpine-style ascent of the American Direct in 1983, the Slovaks had known the value of an acclimatization trip on the South Buttress. This has become a popular formula for successful acclimatization on Denali.

Although the climb had been important to the Englishman and the Slovaks who carried a torch for Milan Krissak, compared to their rich, cultural experiences in Talkeetna and the shared friendships with climbers of many nationalities, it became anticlimactic.

In *The American Alpine Journal 1981,* Johnson mused,

> despite the differences in cultural and political viewpoints, there is only one stance in the last analysis and that is one of contact between human beings. I am naive enough to believe that friendship constitutes the greatest hurdle to dogmatisms. Long may the McKinleys of this world bring together those who think likewise.

Southwest Face

THIS DEMANDING FACE, WHICH HAS BEEN CLIMBED TWICE, is a direct and uncompromising line to the summit. Both ascents were carried out by experienced alpinists, in remarkably fast style, without fixed ropes. However, all parties, including members of an early attempt, have suffered frostbite and altitude sickness.

In 1979, an attempt was made by a Himalayan-seasoned Japanese team, who succeeded in fixing ropes up over all of the technical difficulties. At 16,500 feet, after a continuous sixteen-hour sprint from the glacier, the entire team contracted altitude sickness. One member developed cerebral edema and was rescued in a dramatic winching maneuver by a military Chinook helicopter, thus ending the Japanese siege.

Roberts-McCartney Route

The first ascent of this route is shrouded in controversy because of the rescue of Englishman Simon McCartney, at 19,500 feet. No accounts of the actual climb, other than a letter by McCartney in *Mountain* magazine (September-October 1980) and the story of the rescue in *The American Alpine Journal 1981*, have been published.

In 1975, Californian Jack Roberts climbed in the nearby Kichatna Spires. Three years later, he and Simon McCartney cut their teeth on a very bold alpine-style climb of Mount Huntington's North Face; just before their climb, Charlie Porter had shown them a photograph of Denali's Southwest Face. Fancying themselves as a latter-day version of Haston and Scott, the two saw this as the next logical plum after Huntington. They came to pick it two years later, in 1980.

During their approach up the Northeast Fork of the Kahiltna, the "Valley of Death," they stopped and talked with Cassin-bound climbers Mike Helms (see Denali West Rim, 1977) and Bob Kandiko. Suddenly, an ice avalanche thundered off the North Face of the Kahiltna Peaks. Helms and Kandiko ran. When the snow settled, Roberts and McCartney laughed at their frightened flight. Boxcar-size blocks and a four-foot wall of snow and ice had stopped a stone's throw from their tents.

They started climbing on June 8 and reached an excellent

campsite, where they rested for two days because Roberts felt sick. They could see the Japanese fixed ropes to their right. Above this, Roberts traversed the 5.9 crux. This led them to a crucial couloir. They bivouacked again and Roberts left some food—which would later prove a mistake.

They finally climbed out onto the large snowfield, below the Clod Face–West Rib variation. Since McCartney was beginning to feel sick, they spent two nights there, a very logical plan which should have allowed him to acclimatize. Nonetheless, he felt worse when they moved up to 17,800 feet.

They could have traversed off to the West Rib, but they had done all of the difficult climbing and McCartney felt strong as he led up a couloir. They hit the Cassin Ridge at nineteen thousand feet. It was there, according to McCartney's letter in *Mountain*, that Roberts took over the lead and they began to look for their final campsite.

> It was at this point that I contracted cerebral oedema…the effect that it had was to disorientate me completely, I lost all power of coordination over my legs. The onset was both frightening and rapid, from being normal but tired to being totally helpless.

McCartney's condition deteriorated even more the next night and the following morning, according to his letter; Roberts resolved to leave him and get help. (Roberts later told me that this letter was written by someone impersonating McCartney.) Just as Roberts was leaving, Kandiko and Helms arrived. At this point Roberts and McCartney had been on the climb for nine days, two of them without food.

They decided that Helms and Roberts would go over the summit ridge (20,120 feet) to get a rescue, while Kandiko remained with McCartney. At sea level, one can find fault in almost any decision made by hungry, exhausted climbers undergoing stress. In my opinion, Roberts chose the option that was in the best interests of his partner.

Occasionally in mountaineering, there is a price for boldness—McCartney would pay it. Through no fault of their own, Roberts and Helms ended up having to rescue a member of the rescue team on the West Buttress. McCartney's rescue fizzled out.

Meanwhile, in an effort which epitomized the fraternal spirit of mountaineering, Kandiko singlehandedly began McCartney's evacuation. At first, he tried to get him up and over the summit. When McCartney collapsed and their hoped-for rescue never materialized, they started down the Cassin. Many others, in particular various climbers on the Cassin Ridge, would be involved in McCartney's epic descent.

McCartney's recovery from cerebral edema was a short respite—he had severe trench foot. Then, at the base of the route, Kandiko fell, pulling McCartney into a crevasse; McCartney suffered a concussion and broke his wrist.

It had taken them ten days to descend. Two days later, McCartney was hauled to base camp by a team of volunteers, coordinated by Ranger Dave Buchanan. Approximately thirty climbers from six countries helped with McCartney's rescue. According to McCartney's letter, Roberts and the Park Service abandoned rescue efforts when Kandiko and McCartney had been seen from an airplane descending the Cassin Ridge.

The latter-day Haston and Scott met in Anchorage's Providence Hospital. Roberts was being treated for frostbite, McCartney for his cerebral edema, concussion, trench foot and a broken wrist that, Roberts told me, "would never heal."

It seemed that neither the rescuers, nor McCartney and Roberts themselves, could agree about what had happened. Inaccurate reports appeared in *Climbing* and *Off Belay* magazines. A team, forced to descend the Cassin for undetermined reasons, claimed it was shortchanged by Kandiko and McCartney (particularly by Kandiko's *The American Alpine Journal* article and slideshows), and wrote an angry letter to *Climbing* magazine. Roberts claimed that he lost a guiding job on Denali the next year because of the false reports of his abandonment of McCartney.

And Roberts told me that McCartney thought it was easily the most "gripping" experience he'd ever had. He had come so close to dying, that he didn't want to go through it again. Ever.

Denali Diamond

In 1983, Rolf Graage paid expenses and a small fee to Bryan Becker, so that Becker could guide him up the Southwest Face, east of the Roberts–McCartney line. They were confronted with one overhanging roof, hard Class 5 climbing, storms and spindrift avalanches. Their route gained the Cassin Ridge at 17,500 feet.

Becker had also climbed in the Kichatna Spires and done hard technical and alpine climbs around the world, including the South Face of Aconcagua, which disappointed him because of its lack of challenging terrain. Graage had done a bit of alpine climbing, but never had been in big mountains; according to Becker, Graage was obsessed with becoming a world-class climber.

They trained in Colorado before the climb. After spending most of the day on a three-pitch, vertical ice climb, Graage insisted that they take a six- or seven-mile run. Becker wanted to

Leading the first ascent of the Denali Diamond ▼

drink beer. Graage started off and Becker reluctantly followed, for just a mile, before limping back to the car. Graage returned an hour later.

They started the climb on May 24, 1983. Becker had forgotten the ice screws, so he scraped together enough money to buy two before he left Talkeetna; Graage had forgotten the climbing rope, so they were forced to use their nine-millimeter haul-line.

Their ascent alone was nearly as prolonged an epic as McCartney's. They spent seventeen hungry days on the route, but frequent storms allowed them to climb for only nine days. They bivouacked six times on the lower part of the face.

They were hit by many spindrift avalanches. Becker spent much of his time painfully massaging his feet during their prolonged bivouacs. Graage did not. By May 31, Graage's feet were purple and frostbitten. The option of retreating with only one rope seemed marginal. They continued.

Becker led the twenty-five-foot, A3 roof on June 5. He thought the terrain above it would ease, but when he pulled over the roof, he soon led what he described as "the most difficult-sustained-mixed-aid-ice pitch of my life." At this point they were getting hungry and exhausted. They had over five thousand feet to go.

When the climbing finally eased on the snowfield above the main rock face, the wind whipped at them, wearing apricot-sized holes in their bivouac tent.

On June 7, Becker was standing outside of their tent, at about sixteen thousand feet, putting on his crampons. He wrote in his diary that:

> A gust of wind caught the tent, Rolf and all, and sent it over the edge. For a moment he hung in the bottom of that bivouac sack like a fish in a net, dangling by a single piece of parachute cord that tied the corner of the tent to the rope…The Bimbo wasn't even tied onto the rope himself!!!
>
> I grabbed the sac, passed him a piece of rope to hold onto…He was hollering scared and I was hollering mad that he'd untied the rope. He was looking over a 3,000 foot vertical (no hope) drop …closest I've ever come to losing a partner…Sleepyheaded youth.

Graage also lost a vital piece of equipment: his sleeping pad. The pair began moving like somnambulists. On June 8, Becker wrote in his journal:

> We're much surer of making it off this mountain alive than we were a couple of days ago. Intense experience! An extreme growing one for Rolf. He'll have a lot to ponder upon about himself, his aspirations and future…I'm hoping the price he's paying isn't too dear for the insights this experience is sure to give him…More immediately I'm hoping to get him out to a hospital.

The next day, a thousand feet from the summit, Becker continued:

> Rolf talked openly about trying to find a girlfriend, drinking a beer, doing other things besides trying to be Reinhold Messner II–Progress. The lad's mind opens…I want off this mountain.

Becker made the summit, while Graage slept in the bivouac tent at 20,000 feet. Becker escorted the hobbling Graage down to the 17,200-foot West Buttress camp, where they were met by this writer, who fixed them hot drinks and food.

Since Graage could barely walk, Becker and I lowered him down the "rescue gully," and to the 14,300-foot medical camp. As Dr. Peter Hackett dressed his suppurating toes, Graage commented, "It was worth it." He was flown out that evening to Anchorage's Providence Hospital by pilot Lowell Thomas, Jr. Later, Graage wrote that his toes were fine and that he was still climbing hard.

Becker stayed on the mountain, consuming every available morsel of food at 14,300 feet. He summed it all up in *The American Alpine Journal 1984:* "Denali gave us a thrashing I shall never forget."

Jumaring during the first ascent of the Denali Diamond on the Southwest Face ▲

▲
Czech Direct

SOARING STRAIGHT UP THE SOUTH FACE, JUST BESIDE the Cassin, this route is the most direct climb that has been done on Denali. The route is primarily a difficult ice climb and a fine challenge for an alpine-style ascent by experienced climbers. Like the other South Face routes, the route is swept by powder avalanches after snowstorms. However, it is not swept by Big Bertha's ice avalanches.

The Czechoslovakians had already distinguished themselves on Denali's South Face, in 1980, with the Milan Krissak Memorial route. And in 1986 a strong Czech team would climb another new, but dangerous, route on Mount Foraker's Southeast Ridge.

Thirty-two-year-old Blažej Adam, a High Tatra guide and rescue worker, was inspired to do the Czech Direct when he and his partners saw a photograph of the South Face. His partners were Tono Križo and František Korl, twenty-seven and twenty-nine years old. Ján Špakula, František Adamík and Ervin Velič would simultaneously climb the South Buttress as a support team.

They were all members of the Metropol Kosice Club and this was their first Alaskan climb. When asked if it was his hardest climb, Adam replied that they had done much harder routes in the Alps.

On May 13, 1984, the three climbers began the route. They carried sixty rock pins, thirty ice screws, eight hundred feet of fixed rope and forty-five carabiners. On their first day, they climbed five pitches of thirty- to forty-five-degree ice. They bivouacked beneath a small rock band.

The rock band was passed with a pitch of 5.4 rock climbing. Above an icefield they passed another rock band via a couloir with sixty- to ninety-degree ice climbing. Easy Class 5 climbing brought them to their second bivouac, after five pitches of climbing that day. On their third day, they climbed eight pitches, with one short section of vertical ice. They spent the next three nights at 13,500 feet, just above the first hanging glacier.

At 13,500 and 16,900 feet, they were able to pitch their tent. However, the rest of their bivouac sites were ice ledges, which they spent an hour and a half chopping each night.

They fixed rope for three days, up thirteen more pitches of rock up to 5.6. The ice averaged fifty degrees, although there were two seventy-degree pitches, with one overhanging section. The final pitch of the day was vertical-to-overhanging mixed climbing and Adam took a forty-five-foot leader fall here. They spent their seventh night on a small icefield. Up to this point, they had experienced good weather; yet, conditions would deteriorate during the rest of their climb. Slowed down by the altitude, they climbed six pitches that day, encountering 5.5 difficulties, one mixed pitch, and easy-angled ice.

The following day, they moved up similar terrain, climbing eight pitches and setting up a tent at 16,900 feet, close to a Cassin Ridge campsite. Above here, the technical difficulties ended. Within three days, their route merged with the Haston–Scott route just below the summit. On May 23, one of the support crew ran down and accompanied them to the top. They descended the South Buttress in two days, happy to be reunited with their friends.

Adam felt that future parties should bring a file, as their crampons and axes had gotten very dull from the continuous ice climbing. Because of the lack of flat bivouacs, he recommended not carrying a tent.

5053

DENALI

THE SOUTH FACE

1   *Southwest Face, Roberts–McCartney*
2   *Southwest Face, Denali Diamond*
3   *Cassin Ridge*
4   *Czech Direct*
5   *Japanese Direct*

6   *American Direct*
7   *Haston–Scott*
8   *Milan Kriššak Memorial*
9   *Kahiltna Glacier, East Fork*

Route Guide

Approach: *11.5 miles from 7,200-foot Southeast Fork of the Kahiltna, via Northeast Fork to 11,500-foot bergschrund; move quickly and camp with heed to hanging glaciers.*

Total Time: *10-18 days.*

Climbing Miles: *2.*

Vertical Gain of Route: *8,800 feet.*

Alaska Grade: *5.*

Difficulties, Dangers, Rating: *40- to 65-degree snow and ice climbing in Japanese Couloir (11,500–13,300) and on Corniced Arête (13,500–13,900); up to 5.8 rock on several pitches below 16,400 feet.*

Camps: *13,400 (Cassin Ledge); 13,900; 15,700; 17,000; 18,100.*

References: *1962, 1968, 1972, 1982, 1983* AAJ; *April 1983* Climbing; *April 25, 1962,* Life; Climbing in North America, *Jones;* Fifty Classic Climbs in North America, *Steck and Roper.*

Firsts

Ascent: *July 19, 1961; Cassin, Canali, Alippi, Perego, Airoldi, Zucchi, (Goodwin).*

Alpine Style: *1976; Porter.*

Winter: *March 7, 1982; Mear, Young, (Waterman).*

Solo: *1976; Porter.*

Variations: *Japanese Couloir: May 26, 1967; Kawagoe, Ujiie, (Keira, Shukuin, Akimoto, Hirakawa, Yamanaka, Sasaki). Kahiltna Notch Couloir: August 2, 1967; Langbauer, Everett, Phillips, Serfoss, Underwood. French variant: July 23, 1971; B. & D. Germain, B. & V. Renard, Morin, Berquet. Direct start: 1983; Henrich, Volkman.*

▲ 1	Cassin Ridge
2	West Rib
3	Denali Pass

5102

▲ 1 *American Direct*

2 *Czech Direct*

3 *Japanese Direct*

4 *Haston–Scott*

5 *Milan Krišsak Memorial*

6 *Kahiltna Glacier, East Fork*

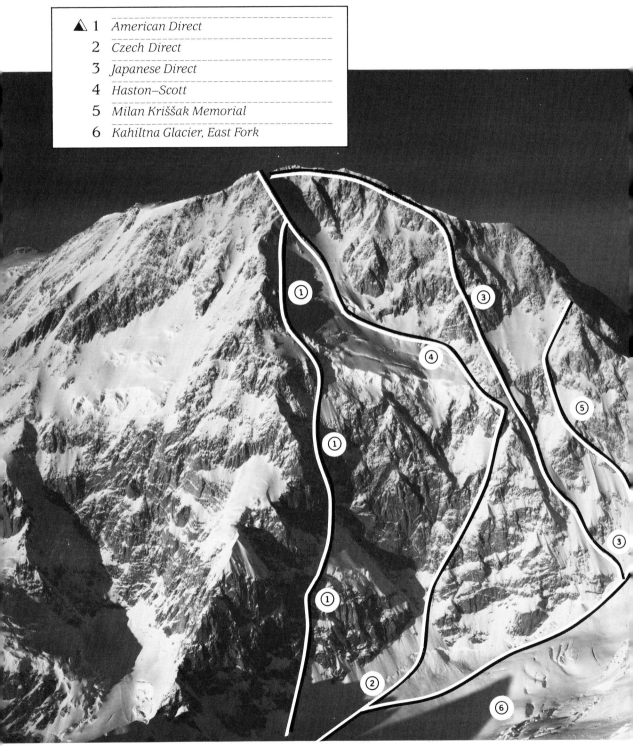

5053

Route Guide

***A**pproach:* 11 miles from 7,200-foot Kahiltna Southeast Fork landing strip, via East Fork of Kahiltna to 11,000 feet; move quickly and camp wisely to minimize avalanche danger in East Fork.

***T**otal Time:* 12-21 days.

***C**limbing Miles:* 2.

***V**ertical Gain of Route:* 8,000 feet.

***A**laska Grade:* 6.

***D**ifficulties, Dangers, Rating:* Approach face with heed to huge hanging glacier (Big Bertha). During snowstorms bivouacs will be swept with avalanches; sustained snow and ice climbing of 50 to 65 degrees from 12,000 to 16,000 feet, then difficult, mixed rock buttresses (5.7, A2) to summit ridge.

***C**amps:* 12,700 (bergschrund); 13,200; 14,000; 15,600 (rock corner); 16,800 (base of buttress).

***R**eferences:* 1968, 1977, 1983 AAJ; 1977 AJ; December 1977 Iwa to Yuki; March 1968 Summit; May 1968 Ascent; Expedition Report (by Everett), Talkeetna Ranger Station.

Firsts

***A**scent:* August 4, 1967; Eberl, Thompson, Laba, Seidman.

***A**lpine Style:* Haston-Scott Route: May 12, 1976; Haston, Scott. American Direct: June 11, 1983; Wada, Takeuchi.

***S**olo:* Haston-Scott Route: May 19, 1982; Hesse.

***V**ariations:* Haston-Scott: May 12, 1976; Haston, Scott. Japanese Direct: July 14, 1977; Kimura, Watanabe, Tsuneto, Yamaura, Senda.

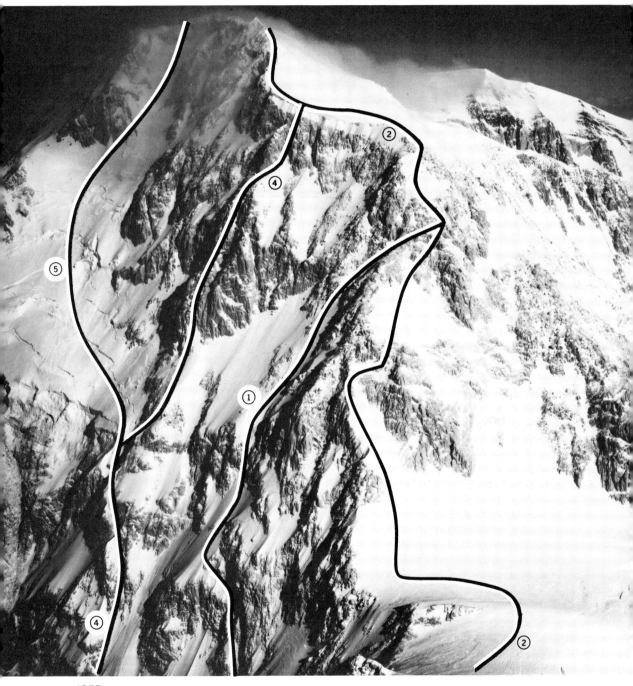

4932

Route Guide

*A*pproach: *11 miles from 7,200-foot Kahiltna Southeast Fork landing strip, via East Fork of Kahiltna to 11,000 feet; move quickly and camp wisely to minimize avalanche danger in East Fork.*

*T*otal Time: *12-21 days.*

*C*limbing Miles: *2.*

*V*ertical Gain of Route: *7,000 feet.*

*A*laska Grade: *5.*

*D*ifficulties, Dangers, Rating: *Up to 65-degree ice climbing and short, difficult rock bands.*

*C*amps: *13,000 feet (bergschrund); 15,000; 16,100; 18,100 (summit ridge).*

*R*eferences: *1981 AAJ; 1981 AJ.*

Firsts

*A*scent: *June 13, 1980; Orolin, Bakoš, Petrik, Johnson. South Buttress support team: June 12, 1980; Fiala, Neumann, Haak, Weincziller.*

▲ 1   *Milan Krišśak Memorial*
2   *Southeast Spur Finish*
3   *Thayer Basin*
4   *American Direct*
5   *Haston–Scott*

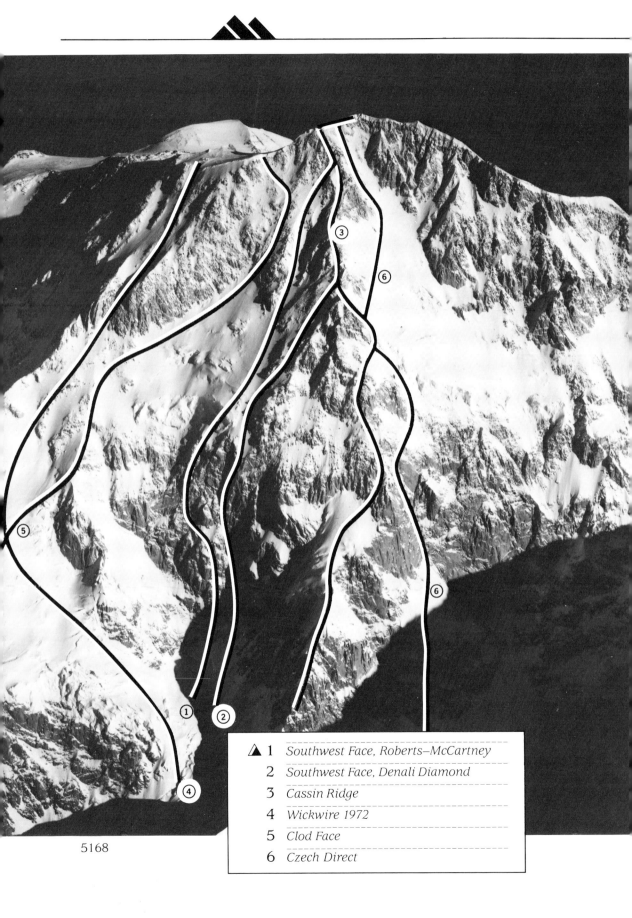

▲	1	*Southwest Face, Roberts–McCartney*
	2	*Southwest Face, Denali Diamond*
	3	*Cassin Ridge*
	4	*Wickwire 1972*
	5	*Clod Face*
	6	*Czech Direct*

Route Guide

Approach: 12 miles from 7,200-foot Southeast Fork of the Kahiltna via Northeast Fork to 12,500-foot bergschrund; travel and camp with heed to numerous hanging glaciers in Northeast Fork.

Total Time: 20-24 days.

Climbing Miles: 1.5.

Vertical Gain of Route: 7,800 feet.

Alaska Grade: 6.

Difficulties, Dangers, Rating: Very difficult mixed climbing (5.9, A3), with short vertical sections of ice.

Camps: Lower rock face offers only hanging bivouacs and occasional ledges; 16,000; 17,800.

References: 1981, 1984 AAJ; September–October 1980 Mountain.

Firsts

Ascent: Roberts-McCartney: June 19, 1980; (Roberts, McCartney). Denali Diamond; June 10, 1983; Becker, (Graage).

Alpine Style: Roberts-McCartney: June 19, 1980; (Roberts, McCartney). Denali Diamond: June 10, 1983; Becker, (Graage).

8413

SOUTHWEST FACE

▲ 1 *Southwest Face, Roberts–McCartney 1980*

2 *Southwest Face, Denali Diamond 1983*

3 *Cassin Ridge, Japanese Couloir Variation 1967*

4 *Henrich–Volkman Variation 1983*

5 *Cassin Ridge 1961*

▲ 1 *Czech Direct*

2 *Cassin Ridge, 1961 Start*

4923

Route Guide

Approach: *11 miles from 7,200-foot Kahiltna Southeast Fork landing strip, via East Fork of Kahiltna to 11,000 feet; move quickly and camp wisely to minimize avalanche danger in East Fork.*

Total Time: *12–21 days.*

Climbing Miles: *1.*

Vertical Gain of Route: *8,500 feet.*

Alaska Grade: *6.*

Difficulties, Dangers, Rating: *5,000 feet of 60- to 100- degree snow and ice climbing, with 5.9 rock.*

Camps: *11,800 (base of first rock); 12,300 (bivouac); 13,400 (tent); 14,500 (bivouac); 15,900 (bivouac); 16,900 (tent); 18,400 (tent).*

References: *1985 AAJ; Route Topo, Talkeetna Ranger Station.*

Firsts

Ascent: *May 23, 1984; Adam, Krizo, Korl; South Buttress support team: May 23, 1984; Špakula, Adamík, Velič.*

DENALI
THE SOUTH FACE

WASHBURN MAP

1 *McCartney–Roberts*
2 *Denali Diamond*
3 *Cassin Ridge:*
   Japanese Couloir
4 *Cassin Couloir*
5 *Kahiltna Notch Couloir*
6 *Direct Start*
7 *American Direct*
8 *Japanese Direct*
9 *Czech Direct*
10 *Haston–Scott*
11 *Milan KrišŠak*

NORTH PEAK

19,470

16,620

18,990

MOUNT McKINLEY

Denali Pass

Buttress

17,230

18,200

18,230

18,705

The Archdeacon's Tower

19,650

Farthing Horn

20,125

Kahiltna Horn

20,120

20,320

20,230
Carter Horn

SOUTH PEAK

18,960

⑩

15,570

①   ②

③

⑥

11,960

④

⑨   ⑧

Kahiltna Notch

⑤

⑦

⑪

15,640

15,895

13,390

15,000

ks

CHAPTER 5

THE EAST BUTTRESS

1963 Route
Catacomb Ridge
Traleika Spur

1963 Route

THE EAST BUTTRESS IS THE WATERSHED BETWEEN THE Yukon and Susitna rivers. As on its larger neighbor, the South Buttress, a myriad of smaller ridges, spurs and faces are connected to it; three of them—the 1963 Route, the Catacomb Ridge, and the Traleika Spur—have been climbed. Although the 1963 Route has been climbed several times, no party has finished on the appealing upper East Face.

A gentle glacial route to the crest of the East Buttress was attempted in 1956 by a four-man team sponsored by Frederick Cook's daughter, Mrs. Helen Vetter. The team assumed that Cook had used the East Buttress on his alleged climb of Denali. *Life* magazine featured a photograph of Bradford Washburn arguing about Cook's claim with the team's leader, Walter Gonnason, in a Talkeetna bar. The team reached 11,400 feet, where they were turned back by elaborate, technical cornice problems. Team member Paul Gerstmann wrote, "Cook didn't make it." Gonnason could never tell Mrs. Vetter this because he didn't want to disappoint her.

Washburn felt that Cook could not possibly have reached the summit. After the copyright on Cook's book had expired, he published elaborate evidence in *The American Alpine Journal 1958* that further proved Cook's claim as false.

The 1963 Route is a snowy spur leading from the Northwest Fork of the Ruth Glacier to Peak 14,630, halfway along the East Buttress. It is a moderately difficult snow-and-ice climb. Because the route meanders around séracs and icefalls, it is exposed to avalanches; the first ascent team was hit by several. A 1982 party remarked that they were quite concerned about avalanches until they got to the crest of the East Buttress.

In Alaska, in the summer of 1962, Warren Bleser ran into a former climbing partner, Jed Williamson. Bleser, who was avalanched off the Wickersham Wall in 1961, had just attempted the Moose's Tooth and Mount Huntington. He asked Williamson if he wanted to join him for a climb of the East Buttress. Soon, Teton guides Al Read, Pete Lev, Fred Wright, and Rod Newcomb joined in the planning.

Bradford Washburn had carefully outlined this route in *The American Alpine Journal 1963,* detailing campsites and strategies. As often happened with Washburn's suggested route articles, the East Buttress team was underway before the article was in print. Washburn wrote that the East Buttress was one of the last major route possibilities, before the more involved gullies, faces, and "Eigerwands" of Denali could be pioneered.

In early April, the Teton contingent was towed up over Teton Pass in a 1948 Dodge, purchased for 125 dollars. They were assured by their tow-truck driver, who had driven to Alaska before, that it was all downhill from the Pass. Fortunately, the ailing, overloaded Dodge made it to Fairbanks with no problems, and they joined Bleser and Williamson.

On April 19, they were flown into the Ruth Glacier by Don Sheldon, who was already a legend among Denali climbers for his accurate and unexpected airdrops, his unflagging support, and his boundless enthusiasm. Sheldon bombarded them with mail, fresh fruit and newspaper clippings with progress reports on both their expedition and the American team on Everest. At one point, Sheldon even dropped recent photos from Washburn, showing that the actual ridge would be too difficult to climb; the team then opted for gullies and the face alongside it.

Williamson wrote in the June 1964 *Appalachia* (while Read echoed similar remarks in *The American Alpine Journal*) that their success was due in large part to the team's cooperative leadership. They were of equal ability, they inspired one another, and they were able to resolve their problems together. In 1963, this represented a relatively new direction in mountaineering expedition hierarchy, particularly since National Park regulations "required" one leader.

They began climbing on April 30. The first difficulty was a three-hundred-foot, sixty-five-degree sugar-ice section called the Bulge. They secured it with the beginning of their three thousand feet of fixed rope.

In *The American Alpine Journal 1964,* Read wrote about the next day:

> As the lower party was climbing the Bulge, it avalanched. A two-foot slab, 300 feet wide and 200 feet long, broke off immediately in front of Lev and plunged over Williamson's back. The fixed ropes were effective, however, and no one came off. As we climbed higher in the beautiful, but all too warm day, huge walls of ice, hundreds of feet thick, began peeling off the Southeast Spur and East Face. These unnerving avalanches fell from three to seven thousand feet, and their gigantic explosions triggered other avalanches. The whole northwest fork of the Ruth was alive and roaring. At such times we felt our own slope split, shake, and settle. By now we were hotly descending, convinced that our buttress would be next to go. When nearly down, a great wall separated from the Southeast Spur and began a roaring descent toward our

Above Camp III on the East Buttress ▲

Climbing the crux section of the East Buttress, 1963 ▲

"safe" Base Camp. We sickened as the mass fell 5,000 feet and began advancing across the glacier toward Base Camp and Wright, who had remained there throughout the day. Both disappeared in the cloud. We waited anxiously as the cloud dissipated. Fortunately the blocks stopped slightly short of camp and no serious damage was done.

The next day, they moved their base camp to a safer site, advanced base camp. Williamson wrote that advanced base camp was usually a euphemism for: "We put base camp in the wrong place to begin with, men."

As they moved higher up the ridge, the crux of the climb, allegedly vertical ice for a hundred and fifty feet, was led by Bleser and Newcomb above Camp 1. Meanwhile, Lev and Williamson were nearly swept away again. A snowstorm brought more powder avalanches down their route.

Above Camp 2, another exciting pitch over an ice cliff was solved by climbing up an ice block, detached from the cliff. Otherwise, snow slopes and ice ramps of up to sixty-five degrees were climbed, fixed, and then carried over.

After three weeks of climbing, they carried their last loads up onto the gentle slopes of the East Buttress proper. A day later, May 21, they were on the 1954 Thayer Ridge finish, poised for the summit at 17,450 feet.

Their first summit attempt, via a long traverse out onto the Muldrow and up from Denali Pass, was foiled fifty yards below the summit. Fred Wright contracted subacute pulmonary edema, then bad weather prevented Newcomb, Williamson, and Bleser from reaching the top. Two days later, taking the shorter and more direct Northeast Ridge (Thayer's route), Lev, Newcomb and Read reached the summit.

They descended the entire route in two days, then descended upon their advanced base camp food supply with great ardor. Half of the team was flown out, while Lev, Bleser and Wright were stranded on the Ruth Glacier for ten days in a snowstorm.

Bleser would return to the range six years later and make a first ascent of the elegant Talkeetna Ridge on Mount Foraker. Lev, Read and Newcomb, the successful summit team, all clung to their Teton roots and became co-owners of the prestigious Exum Mountain Guide Service, Inc. Expanding upon some of their many experiences with avalanches on the East Buttress, Lev and Newcomb both became nationally recognized avalanche forecasters. Williamson, who would become active as a safety consultant for various mountaineering organizations, returned to climb Denali twenty-two years after he had climbed the East Buttress.

Alpine Style

The route was repeated, with fixed ropes, in 1977 and 1981. In 1982, Bill Krause, Ted Waltman and Mike Danaher spent nine days climbing the buttress alpine style. Although they had intended to finish via the unclimbed upper East Face, a bad storm convinced them to follow the footsteps of Thayer and the 1963 team.

Another week-long storm forced them to traverse from the Northeast Ridge to the Harper Glacier, then to Denali Pass. They finally reached the summit on June 8, but a cold bivouac resulted in frostbitten feet for Waltman and Danaher. They descended via the West Buttress, completing the first East Buttress traverse.

Catacomb Ridge

THIS LONG ROUTE IS ONE MILE EAST OF THE 1963 ROUTE on the East Buttress, they merge at the 14,300-foot level. Avalanche problems are minimized, as the climbing is almost entirely upon a ridge. The route was named for its unusual crevasse formations.

Joe Davidson did research on this unclimbed route with Ken Jones in 1968. Davidson quickly enlisted a partner from an earlier climb on Mount St. Elias, Gordon Benner; Neils-Henrik Andersen, Pete Reagan, Jim Given, and Bob Fries rounded out the team.

In all probability, the lower East Buttress had been attempted by Frederick A. Cook and Benner felt that their expedition was taking care of Cook's unfinished business from 1906.

They carried 10,500 feet of fixed rope, an all-time record for Denali. Their hardware consisted of seventy-four pickets, three rock pitons, six ice screws and two ice pitons. Davidson's expedition was unusual in that, although they had intended to climb the less technically difficult route pioneered by Gonnason in 1956, via an icefall and basin, avalanche hazards forced them onto a more difficult ridge.

Until recent years, many parties, such as Davidson's, started climbing in June, a month renowned for its warmer temperatures, heavy snow storms, increased avalanche hazard and collapsing crevasse bridges. Not surprisingly then, several scary crevasse falls occurred as the Catacomb team approached their ridge.

On June 22, 1969, they began climbing up a gully with forty-five-degree black ice, overlaid with deep snow. For the next week, they dealt with delicate meringue and marble snow, a creaking ridge they called the Haunted Traverse (the creaking was caused by walking above a cornice fracture line), a huge snow gendarme they dubbed the Matterhorn, and continuous, intricate crevassing that created an entire network of catacombs.

Jones and the up-and-coming ice climber, Andersen, led a steep (sixty to ninety degrees) ice step and they finished the bottom part of the ridge. They moved into their camp, at 11,920 feet on the crest of the East Buttress, on July 3.

After crossing a broad plain, they climbed over cornices and an ice step. Then they traversed more cornices, huge and strangely alternated on either side of the ridge. The cornices were overhung and involved spectacular shoveling; the climbers perched astride exhilarating drops of several thousand feet, the Susitna River drainage under their left feet, the Yukon drainage under their right.

While descending from the climb, Davidson remembered a lesson learned from Boyd N. Everett, Jr. on Mount St. Elias when cornices broke above their fracture line. As Davidson felt and heard a cornice release with a great *wumph!* he stood still, thinking he was safe below the fracture line. However, a picket holding the fixed line fell with the cornice; Davidson saw the light of the Traleika Glacier thousands of feet below and was yanked off the ridge. He was held, unhurt. He immediately began chopping steps back up, as the cornice thundered down to the glacier.

Above their sixth camp at 12,400 feet, they fixed over 2,500 feet of rope up a forty-five-degree snow- and ice-slope. By July 8, they finished the unclimbed section of the buttress and moved into another camp, close to the junction with the 1963 route.

After occupying two more camps, they climbed to the summit on July 13. Davidson would write much later in a letter that

> There really weren't any personality problems, there was so much leading to do that no competiton ever got going. We rotated those in the lead in a reasonable way, giving everyone plenty to do.

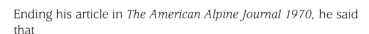
Ending his article in *The American Alpine Journal 1970,* he said that

> problems brought out the best in people. Certainly the most satisfying thing to me was the good companionship and enduring enthusiasm of the expedition members that arose from Mount McKinley's challenges. Everyone thrived on the abundant adversity for the entire thirty-six days on the mountain. And we all reached the summit together.

Andersen returned to the range in 1971, and again in 1972, to complete a new route on nearby Mount Huntington. In 1973, he and Warren Bleser (East Buttress, 1963) both died on a mountain whose name had been used for a scary feature on the Catacomb Ridge, the Matterhorn. In 1974, Davidson, Reagan, Given, and Fries climbed a variation on Mount Foraker's Southeast Ridge.

Benner would later return to Denali's West Rib, full of two-decade-old memories.

> I was struck by the different ethical standards. In 1969 we left 10,000 feet of fixed line on the mountain, plus all our garbage in crevasses, etc. This year [1986], we spent one full climbing day and much planning to remove everything but personal wastes from the mountain, retrieving all fixed line.

Alternating cornices on the Catacomb Ridge of the East Buttress ▼

Traleika Spur

THE NORTHEASTERLY TRALEIKA (COOK INLET INDIAN name for Denali) Spur rises from the junction of the West and Main forks of the Traleika Glacier. There are two twelve-thousand-foot peaks along its four-mile length and it merges with the East Buttress a mile east of Thayer Basin.

The route involves travel through two icefalls, a long ridge walk on an isolated spur that branches off the East Buttress onto the Traleika Glacier and a finish via the Northeast Ridge (Thayer's route) to the summit. Occasional short ice pitches have been encountered, although most of the route is technically easy and straightforward. The objective dangers are considerable in the two icefalls. The route has never been repeated, probably because of the icefalls and its arduous ten-mile length and twenty-nine-mile approach.

Dave Pettigrew attempted this route in June 1971; that fall, he began recruiting another team. Jock Jacober, Pat Stewart, Johnny Johnson, Bill Ruth and Craig Schmidt were assembled and, by early April 1972, the team set off.

Pettigrew was adamant that the climb be repeated in pioneer style: walking in ninety-five miles, then walking out. Many Alaskan climbers seem to prefer such an approach, often referred to as "Alaskan alpine style." Although the esthetics of such an approach are the guiding force, for local climbers the economics—walking versus airplane costs—seem to play an important role. Last-minute complications, however, forced half of the team to fly into Kantishna, while Pettigrew, Stewart and Ruth marched. On April 24, they all met at the seven-thousand-foot base camp on the Traleika Glacier.

Alaskans have embraced a long-standing tradition of climbing "their mountain," Denali, regardless of previous climbing experience. The supposition is that time spent in Alaska's hardy, cold environment constitutes a qualification in itself; witness the Sourdoughs in 1910 and Karstens in 1913. Alaska residents Johnson and Ruth were climbing neophytes, but had spent a lot of time in the wilderness; Schmidt, who also lived in Alaska, had only moderate climbing experience. Pettigrew, Stewart and Jacober, who were excellent climbers, all hailed from outside of Alaska.

Although airdrops had been discontinued within park boundaries in 1964, except for expeditions with scientific objectives, the team received an airdrop at base camp. In their case, the Park Service rules were waived because of the projected length of their climb (forty-five days).

Included in their one-thousand-pound airdrop were a thousand feet of fixed manila rope and an incredible twenty-eight gallons of gasoline. After a month of endless load hauling, Pettigrew and company would break the silence of Denali's east side by braying like donkeys as they staggered along under huge packs.

They forced a route through an icefall just above the Traleika Glacier. From April 23 to 27, every day they were in the icefall, they either witnessed avalanches coming down their route, or were hit by them.

According to Ruth's journal-style Park Service report, their culinary experiences left a lot to be desired. These included skimpy lunches, purplish noodles and kipper snack soup *à la cayenne* that sent everyone sprinting to the latrine. Oatmeal seemed to rule the menu and, at one point, Johnson dropped a boiling pot of it and scalded his face. Tobacco was popular and when they ran out, they began smoking used tea bags, apparently the only thing there was no shortage of.

Toward the end of the expedition, they ate half-rations. When they had run completely out of food, some friends flew by in a private plane and airdropped hamburgers, french fries, fruit, and chocolate chip cookies. Two days later, they received drops of roast beef sandwiches, fruit, candy bars, and three half-gallons of ice cream. So much for Alaskan alpine style.

On May 7, after a four-day storm which nearly blew their tents apart, they crossed an exciting, mile-long knife-edge ridge, then dropped to the second icefall. A six-foot-wide crevasse barred the way and they all steeled themselves for a long running jump; ten days later, it had enlarged to ten feet, and they were forced to climb into it, then up the other side.

They climbed up into Thayer Basin. Ruth's account mentions his and Johnson's crampons falling off three times. By May 20, they began climbing up fifty-degree ice to the Northeast Ridge. Pettigrew took a twenty-foot fall on the ice. Then, just below the ridge, Jacober fell over a hundred feet, pulling off Schmidt. They crashed into one another and were held by a single screw, miraculously unhurt.

On May 24, they made an attempt on the summit from an 18,400-foot camp, but were turned back by bad weather. The next day, they had better luck.

Ruth wrote in his diary:

> The summit was much closer than it originally looked, up one final steep but small ridge, then Grew was there, and we were too.

> I tried to speed up the last 100, my emotions overcame my lungs, I was finally there.
>
> We all embraced each other and then Johnny arrived and I embraced him. The sun was out and it was almost calm. The lowlands below about 8,000 were clouded. All the major peaks stuck up above the clouds and were bathed in sunlight.

They made the long slog out, wallowing through wet snow in their snowshoes. On June 2, they flagged down a Park Service vehicle, caught a ride, and were treated to heaps of eggs and beer.

Most of the team members eventually moved to Alaska, where they resided in the Denali Park area. There, in the shadow of their climb, Johnson became a successful wildlife photographer; Ruth was killed in an auto accident on the Parks Highway. In 1975, Pettigrew, Stewart, and others did a first ascent on Mount Deborah, after being foiled in 1974. Mimicking their Denali climb, done in inimitable Alaskan alpine style, Pettigrew and Stewart walked 240 miles, round trip, to climb Mount Deborah.

DENALI

THE EAST BUTTRESS

1	*East Buttress, 1963 Route*
2	*Catacomb Ridge*
3	*Traleika Spur*
4	*South Buttress*
5	*Don Sheldon Amphitheater*
6	*Ruth Glacier, Northwest Fork*
7	*Unclimbed*

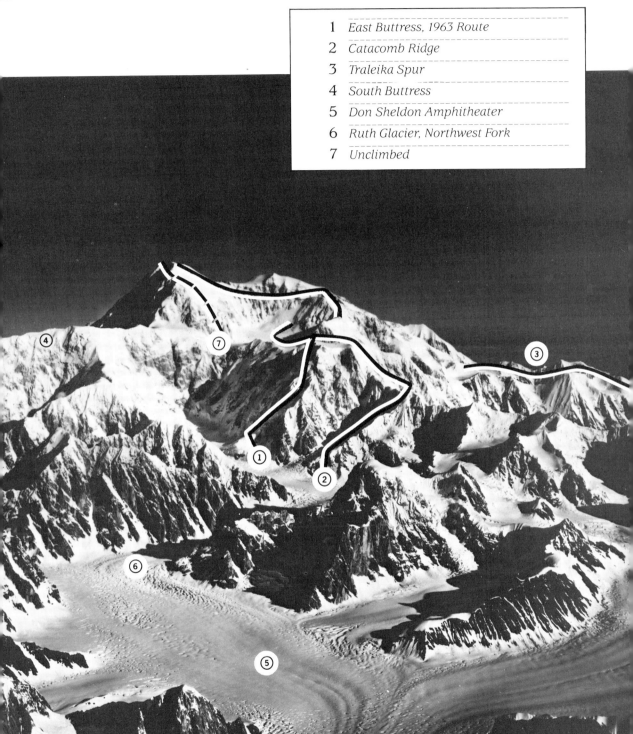

3057

213

▲ 1	*1963 Route*
2	*Catacomb Ridge*

5208

Route Guide

*A*pproach: *2 miles from the 7,600-foot Northwest Fork of the Ruth landing strip to the 8,300-foot base.*

*T*otal Time: *12-26 days.*

*C*limbing Miles: *7.*

*V*ertical Gain of Route: *12,000 feet.*

*A*laska Grade: *4.*

*D*ifficulties, Dangers, Rating: *The route meanders through séracs and avalanche-prone slopes; short sections up to 80-degree snow and ice until 11,100 feet.*

*C*amps: *9,000; 11,100; 12,400; 13,700 (bergschrund); 14,100; 17,450 (Northeast Ridge).*

*R*eferences: *1964 AAJ; June 1964 Appalachia; September 1965 Summit; Expedition Report, Talkeetna Ranger Station.*

Firsts

*A*scent: *May 25, 1963; Lev, Newcomb, Read, (Williamson, Bleser, Wright).*

*A*lpine Style: *June 8, 1982; Krause, Waltman, Danaher.*

*V*ariations: *Catacomb Ridge: July 13, 1969; Davidson, Benner, Andersen, Reagan, Given, Fries, Jones.*

▲1 *Catacomb Ridge*

2 *14,400 Feet*

3654

Route Guide

Approach: 0.5 mile north from 7,600-foot Northwest Fork of the Ruth landing strip via an icefall to the 7,600-foot base.

Total Time: 14-28 days.

Climbing Miles: 9.

Vertical Gain of Route: 12,700 feet.

Alaska Grade: 4.

Difficulties, Dangers, Rating: Several pitches of snow and ice up to 70 degrees; large cornices.

Camps: 9,200; 9,600; 10,600, 11,920; 12,400; 14,300; 14,600; 17,400 (Northeast Ridge).

References: 1970 AAJ; Expedition Report, Talkeetna Ranger Station.

Firsts

Ascent: July 13, 1969; Davidson, Benner, Andersen, Reagan, Given, Fries, Jones.

Route Guide

Approach: *29 miles from Wonder Lake, via McGonagall Pass, up the Traleika Glacier to the 7,000-foot base on the Main Fork.*

Total Time: *16-30 days.*

Climbing Miles: *11.*

Vertical Gain of Route: *13,300 feet.*

Alaska Grade: *3.*

Difficulties, Dangers, Rating: *Two major avalanche-prone ice-falls must be crossed; several short sections up to 60 degrees were encountered.*

Camps: *8,300; 10,400; 11,000; 11,500 (col on ridge); 11,500 (beneath icefall); 13,900; 14,700; 16,500; 18,400 (NE Ridge).*

References: *1973 (1971 attempt is in Climbs and Expeditions section), 1980 (approach map) AAJ; August 1973 Alaska; Expedition Report, Talkeetna Ranger Station.*

Firsts

Ascent: *May 25, 1973; Pettigrew, Jacober, Stewart, Johnson, Ruth, Schmidt.*

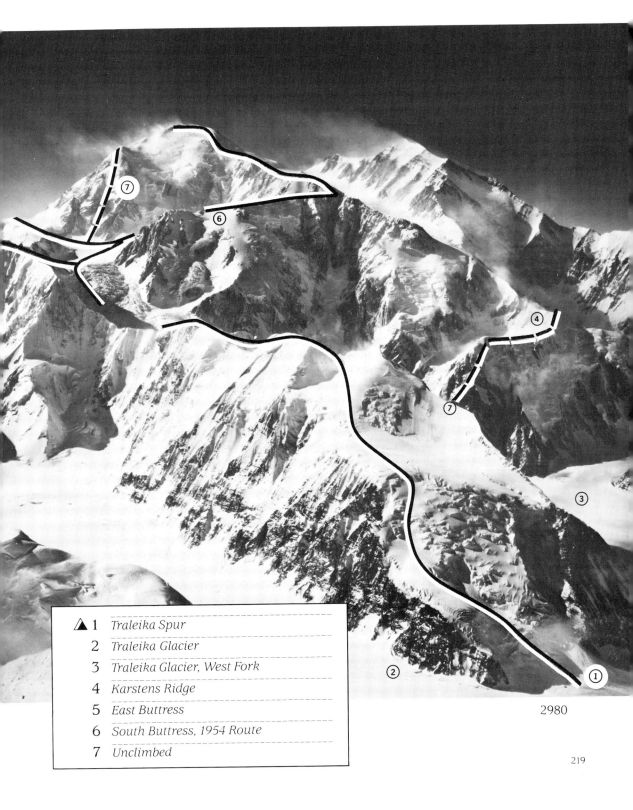

▲ 1	*Traleika Spur*
2	*Traleika Glacier*
3	*Traleika Glacier, West Fork*
4	*Karstens Ridge*
5	*East Buttress*
6	*South Buttress, 1954 Route*
7	*Unclimbed*

2980

TRALEIKA SPUR

▲ 1   *Traleika Spur*
2   *Thayer Basin*
3   *East Buttress*
4   *South Buttress*

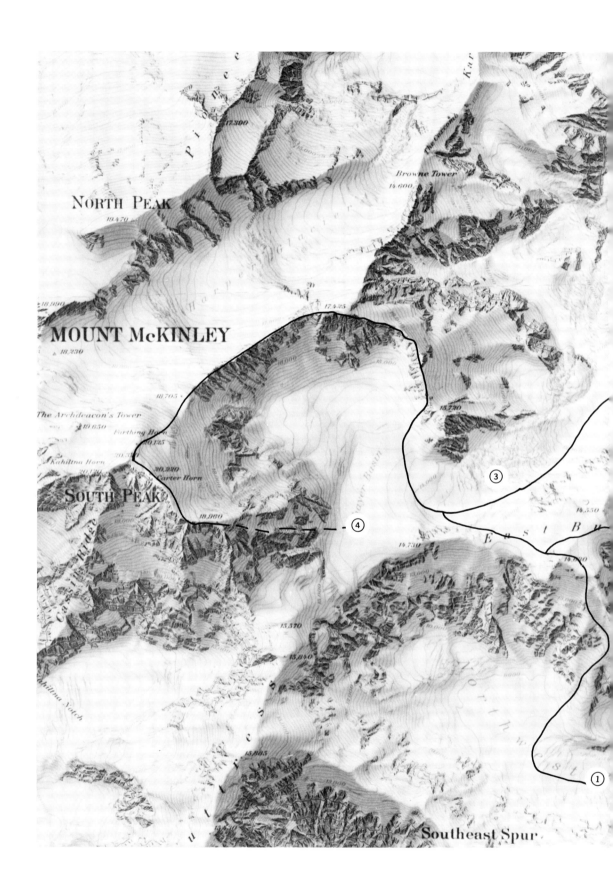

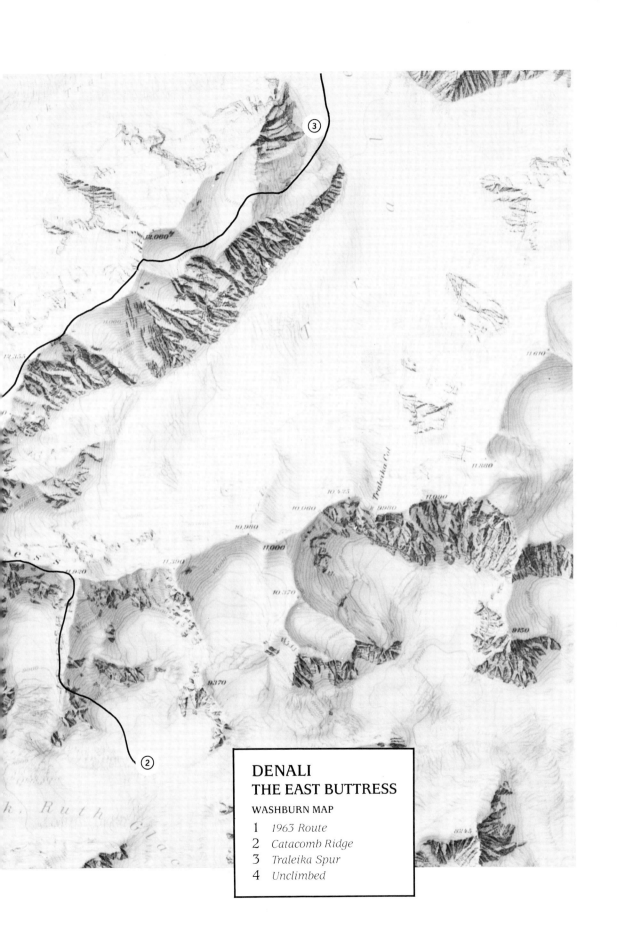

DENALI
THE EAST BUTTRESS

WASHBURN MAP

1   *1963 Route*
2   *Catacomb Ridge*
3   *Traleika Spur*
4   *Unclimbed*

Leaping a crevasse on the Sultana Ridge of Mount Foraker.
BRIAN OKONEK

Aurora over the Alaska Range.
DAVE PARKHURST

Denali aurora with valleys and peaks illuminated by moonlight.
DAVE PARKHURST

Mount Foraker at sunset, as seen from the Susitna River.
ROGER ROBINSON

Moonset over Mount Foraker.
ROGER ROBINSON

Mount Foraker, Mount Hunter, and Denali at sunset.
ROGER ROBINSON

New moon over Mount Hunter.
ROGER ROBINSON

Avalanche on Mount Hunter.
CHARLIE SASSARA

The Kennedy–Lowe Route on Mount Hunter in winter.
GARY BOCARDE

MOUNT FORAKER

SULTANA

PART·2

MOUNT FORAKER, 17,004 feet in altitude, is the sixth highest peak in North America. Like Denali and Mount Hunter, it has a north and a south summit, separated by a half-mile-wide plateau. The smaller, seldom-climbed South Summit is 16,812 feet high.

The mountain stands ten miles west of Mount Hunter and fifteen miles southwest of Denali; it lies almost entirely within the wilderness boundaries of Denali National Park.

The original Tanaina (Indian) name for the mountain was *Sultana,* which meant "woman," or "wife," of Denali. In 1899, Lieutenant Joseph S. Herron saw this mountain and renamed it Mount Foraker, after Joseph B. Foraker,

a senator from (and former governor of) Ohio. Senator Foraker was eventually driven from public office for accepting fees and loans from an oil company.

The average number of climbers on Mount Foraker each year has been under thirty, as on Mount Hunter, or one thirtieth of the traffic on Denali. However, the failure rate on this peak is much higher than on its neighbors. The easily approached Southeast Ridge accounts for most of the attempts on Mount Foraker, but the Sultana Ridge is a safer, easier climb. There are many routes that have not been ascended alpine style, but they all involve either long approaches, or very committing and long ridge climbs.

CHAPTER 6

THE NORTHERN ROUTES

Northwest Ridge
Archangel Ridge
Highway of Diamonds

Northwest Ridge

A N ISOLATED TUNDRA APPROACH FROM WONDER LAKE (or by airplane from the Swift Fork River, outside the boundaries of Denali National Park) makes this route a true wilderness endeavor. Climbers on the north side of Mount Foraker have to rely completely on their own resources. Only single-side band radios will work on this side and quick, alpine-style ascents could be tempting fate.

The climb itself provides the easiest way up the mountain, skirting icefalls, then going up a knife-edge ridge and across a mile-wide plateau to the summit. The first ascent is described in *The American Alpine Journal 1935* by Charles Houston in an article entitled, "Denali's Wife."

Oscar Houston and his son Charles became interested in Mount Foraker after reading Hudson Stuck's *The Ascent of Denali* and Belmore Browne's *The Conquest of Mount McKinley*. An article in the 1928 issue of *Harvard Mountaineering* entitled "Unclimbed Peaks in the Alaska Range," by W. Osgood Field, detailed Mount Foraker's potential. No attempts had been made on the mountain and the entire area had only been crudely mapped.

Charles Houston did the planning and food packing for Mount Foraker, based on what he had learned from Bradford Washburn on Mount Crillon in 1932. He recruited fellow Harvard Mountaineering Club member Charles Storey; his mentor, T. Graham Brown (with whom he had climbed in the Alps); and Chychele Waterston. The five-man team met horse packer Carl Anderson at McKinley Park on July 3, 1934.

Fifty-two years later, Houston wrote in a letter:

> Our park trip in was quite an experience: the mosquitoes were ravenous, the day never ended except in a sort of twilight. The horses were hobbled when we made camp each "night" but when we woke at 0500 each day, they were gone and it took many hours to find them. Meanwhile we sat on the packs and scratched and swatted, until, usually about 1500, the horses were rounded up and packed and we set off. Then they insisted on swimming the deepest part of the several rivers, or sliding down the steepest cliffs, or slipping into deep boggy muskeg pools. It wasn't a great trip except it was so exciting to be in new country.

After reconnoitering the impassable Herron Glacier (which had probably surged a year or two before), the team slogged up the

Foraker Glacier and camped at its head. The routes on the North Face were imposingly steep, but they found what appeared to be a navigable ridge on the side of the face. After a false start up the northern fork on their ridge, they climbed up a branch of the southern fork and set up camp at 9,800 feet on July 30.

It was decided that they could not possibly carry enough food up the mountain to support six people, so Oscar Houston, Anderson and Storey became the low-altitude support team. They went down the glacier to haul up more loads.

Houston, Brown and Waterston passed several "interesting" sections on the narrow ridge above 9,800 feet, hauling their packs behind them. They fixed no ropes and, except for carrying more than once to some camps, it was a pseudo alpine-style ascent.

By August 5, they set up a cramped bivouac at 13,700 feet, just below the large plateau. They reached the North Peak on August 6. Houston, who would become world-renowned for diagnosing and classifying high altitude illnesses, had his first encounter with it, perhaps not even recognizing it, on Foraker's summit. He wrote in his diary:

> I felt curiously unsteady, drunk almost, but not with exultation. It was rather a feeling of finality, conclusiveness, but not of victory.

In describing the surroundings, Houston wrote that

> The whole area south and east of Foraker and McKinley is a wilderness of snow and ice and rock, and I've never seen a more inhospitable land. There is obviously much more snow than on the north side of the range because even the small peaks are eternally white, and most of the glaciers seem to be covered deep with snow but very much crevassed. It looks an impossible country to explore, or at least a difficult and dangerous one.

They had been the first climbing team to gaze up close at the unexplored ocean of peaks along the Kahiltna Glacier.

Several days later, the three men climbed the lower South Peak, just to make sure they had gotten to the highest summit.

They descended their ridge in two days, and all six were reunited at base camp three days later. It was Charles' twenty-first birthday. That night they celebrated with a banquet of fresh caribou and a quart of whiskey. The next morning a large earth-quake shook down their tent and woke them all up. Staggering from an unsteady ground and head, Houston vowed he would never drink again.

Although Charles Houston would never return to the Alaska Range, his contribution to mountaineering and medicine is immense. As a mountaineer, he would go to Nanda Devi in 1936

*Charles S. Houston, Chychele
Waterston, and T. Graham
Brown during the first ascent
of Mount Foraker in 1934* ▶

and K2 in 1938 and 1953. Together with his father, and others, he would explore the approach to Mount Everest through Nepal in 1950. As a doctor, he will be remembered for making artificial hearts in 1959, for his detailed investigations into pulmonary edema beginning in 1960, and for his learned book, *Going Higher*.

Comparing thirty years of significant expeditions, Houston said that Mount Everest was the most exotic, Nanda Devi the most beautiful, K2 the most challenging, and Mount Foraker the coldest.

Oscar Houston died in 1970. But the father-and-son legacy lives on. In 1981, the sixty-eight-year-old Charles accompanied his son, Robin, an accomplished mountaineer, back to Mount Everest.

Western Spur Variation

The Houstons' route was repeated, with fixed rope, in 1977 and again in 1986. Both parties approached from the western edge of the park boundary via the Herron Glacier, which took as long as two weeks with load carrying. (Horse packing from Wonder Lake is no longer allowed in Denali National Park.)

In 1977, Chip Morgan, Chris Niles, Spencer Fulweiler, Mark Siks and Bruce Underwood climbed a slight variation, starting from five thousand feet on the Herron Glacier and joining the original route at nine thousand feet. They reached the summit on July 24, 1977.

Archangel Ridge

IN 1975, THIS ROUTE WAS CLIMBED ONCE. IT HAS NOT BEEN attempted since. It still awaits a second ascent, or a first alpine-style ascent. The walk-in has potentially difficult stream crossings, bear encounters and trailbreaking. The overall difficulty of the route is accentuated because of its remote position and the long approach. The glacial approach to the ridge is exposed to a hanging glacier, which could be avoided. It is an elegant and surprisingly moderate climb, considering its direct line to the summit. Acclimatization can be facilitated by carrying a load up to the plateau on the easier Northwest Ridge.

While Gerry Roach was climbing Denali in 1963, he looked west and saw a ridge arcing straight to Foraker's summit, which became his dream climb; this took twelve years to come true. In the meantime, he climbed Mounts Lucania and Steele. Then, accompanied by his wife Barbara, he did Mounts Logan and Silverthrone.

On June 15, 1975, the Roaches left Wonder Lake with younger climbers Stewart Krebs, Dave Wright, Brad Johnson, and Charlie Campbell. They started horse packing through vast mosquito breeding grounds and made a contest out of how many mosquitoes they could kill in one swat. (Wright won easily, forty-eight to seventeen, on the back of Campbell's head, nearly knocking his eyeballs out.) The team hit it off like a family during the two-week trip in. They agreed that if they couldn't all make the summit, no one would go. By the time they arrived at base camp, they had covered sixty miles and crossed sixteen rivers and creeks.

On the first two thousand feet of their route, as Wright was leading a steep, rotten thirty-foot ice pitch, the whole wall cracked and settled. They decided to climb at night, when the snow was more stable. That night they became soaked in a sudden violent storm and their tents were ripped.

They experienced unusually warm and wet weather, which melted out their igloos and tent platforms, forcing them to sleep outside. Consequently, the snow-and-ice climbing conditions were abysmal until they got above 11,800 feet. It is also interesting to note that the narrow sections of the ridge, like the nearby Highway of Diamonds route, had no cornices.

The crux of the climb was a knife-edge ridge between nine thousand and ten thousand feet, dubbed the Angel's Way. Roach, who went on to climb the highest summit on each of the seven continents, felt that this ridge was the most spectacular place he had ever been on in the mountains.

While load-carrying on the Angel's Way, Campbell fell, somersaulting backward and ripping open the flesh on his arm with a crampon. The fixed line held him and he realized there was blood all over the snow. Wright sutured his arm.

The next day, they moved to their 11,800-foot high camp and built an igloo. The following two days of storm provided needed time for rest and acclimatization. On July 14, they wove their way up and around crevasses on the long snow slope. After twelve and one half hours, they all reached the summit and congratulated one another, particularly Barbara, the first woman to reach Foraker's summit.

They descended their route in a day and basked in the meadows below the eleven-thousand-foot route. This tight-knit family felt that the trip was unique because of its wilderness setting. They had been completely self-sufficient, unconnected by airplanes or radios to the rest of the world. At Slippery Creek Mine, thirty miles from Wonder Lake, however, they gratefully accepted dinner and a flight out from the miners.

On the Highway of Diamonds ▲

Highway of Diamonds

AFTER ITS CLASSIC KNIFE-EDGE BEGINNING, THIS RIDGE climbs more steeply through sérac barriers, then flattens into a nondescript face at two-thirds height. The final ice gullies give access to the 14,600-foot summit plateau, one and one half miles from the North Peak.

This route was admired by T. Graham Brown and Charles Houston in 1934. They called it the Sporting Ridge and talked of "rushing it" after their ascent of the Northwest Ridge.

The climbing is not overly difficult or sustained and the route is curiously devoid of cornices, a common phenomenon of Foraker's north side. The crux ice sérac and key passage of the route may have shifted since it was climbed in 1983. The overall difficulty of the route is accentuated, however, because of its remote position and long approach. Climbers on the north side of Foraker have to rely completely on their own resources (see Northwest Ridge and Archangel Ridge).

The Highway of Diamonds would be difficult to descend and its remote position almost demands a descent to the Kahiltna side. It would be possible to descend the Northwest Ridge to a well-stocked base camp, then walk back out for a prearranged airplane pickup at the western park boundary. The approach from Wonder Lake or Kantishna is not recommended.

Glenn Randall and Peter Metcalf left Kantishna on April 17, 1983. They slogged for nine tiring days to the base of their route. They had planned a five-day approach, and had not expected rotten snow and willows. With only sixteen days of food, they began to worry. They went on half rations.

Metcalf and Randall were no strangers to epics in the Alaska Range. Together they had done the first alpine-style ascents of Hunter's Southeast Spur and Denali's Reality Ridge. They had even climbed Foraker's Southeast Ridge alpine style in 1982, so they knew their descent route. And they were strong technical climbers, experienced on waterfall ice and steep rock. More important, they knew their limits and they knew one another. Everything they had done pointed toward putting up a new, alpine-style route on Mount Foraker. It was the logical step for two climbers who had served a long apprenticeship.

They started climbing on April 26 from 7,700 feet. Ironically, it may have been the lack of technical difficulties which proved their undoing; they moved very quickly. By the first evening they had climbed the crux pitch and put 3,600 feet beneath them. The next day they cruised up easy ground to 1,400 feet, a 2,700-foot gain. They would have gone even higher, but they became concerned about getting altitude sickness.

The following day, they moved up steeper ground, finding few belays, but moving rapidly. They pitched their tent at fifteen thousand feet in gale winds. Metcalf was suffering from a bad headache.

In only three days, they had climbed over 7,300 feet. As Metcalf's head stopped hurting, Randall's began throbbing. He lost his appetite. The next day, his lungs were gurgling—pulmonary edema. Randall and Metcalf opted to get up and over the summit, quickly. They could have descended the Northwest Ridge, but that was unknown territory compared to the familiarity of the Southeast Ridge.

Randall staggered up to the summit, grimly determined, while Metcalf carried both packs. The gurgling in Randall's lungs got worse, but he thought he could make it. By afternoon, they sat on the summit. Because they had climbed unroped the previous year in this same place, they started down unroped.

In *The American Alpine Journal 1984,* Metcalf wrote:

> I rapidly headed down and waited and then headed down again. At the second rest I turned and saw no sign of Glenn, only slide marks below a small crevasse that headed the abyss on the ridge's north side....
>
> It was the ease with which I accepted the realization, not the realization itself, which perturbed me so. Was it the altitude? The numbed, tired state of my body? Or was it the need to concentrate on immediate survival that prompted my passive acceptance of the notion of Glenn's death? Or had I become so cold and stoic after a dozen years of climbing that my best friend's death elicited no more than a mechanical response?... The late hour and worsening weather required descent, and my futile searching had convinced me that Glenn had slid down the north face of the southeast ridge. I headed down....
>
> I saw a packless figure crawl back onto the ridge. As the distance between us narrowed, I was shocked at what I saw. Where his face was not caked with blood, it was sickly white. Glenn had broken through a crevasse, extricated himself and then fallen. I got him into my sleeping bag. Both shock and hypothermia were setting in....
>
> I tried to assess his injuries. The gurgling in his lungs and spewing of blood heightened my anxiety. He was suffering from life-threatening pulmonary and cerebral edema, along with a myriad of fall-related injuries: cracked ribs, a broken leg, badly twisted ankles, an array of contusions.

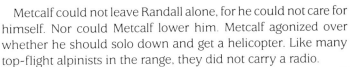

Metcalf could not leave Randall alone, for he could not care for himself. Nor could Metcalf lower him. Metcalf agonized over whether he should solo down and get a helicopter. Like many top-flight alpinists in the range, they did not carry a radio.

Meanwhile, the Talkeetna Rangers grew concerned. Metcalf and Randall were due down and no one had seen them. From an earlier conversation with Randall, I knew their food would be running out.

Pilot Jim Okonek and I flew up to look for them in a Cessna 185. Okonek spotted them at 15,500 feet: Metcalf, who had waited for four and a half days, stood outside the tent, just getting ready to descend for help, while Randall crawled to the tent door. I radioed for an Anchorage helicopter to meet us in Talkeetna.

We made three air drops: the radio missed and bounced down the awful void to the south, the food landed on the far side of a crevasse, and the white gas landed right on target. Unfortunately, they had only a butane stove.

Two hours later, I came back in an Alouette III helicopter with pilot Jim Porter. Okonek flew cover in his Cessna 185. We made three passes over their tent and Porter said that the visibility was not right and if a gust of wind hit us we were in trouble. I told him it was likely that Randall would die if we couldn't pick him up.

Porter boldly landed between wisps of cloud on the tiny site. I ran to the tent. Metcalf and I carried Randall to the chopper and loaded him in, and within seconds we were airborne.

From Talkeetna, Randall was flown to Providence Hospital in Anchorage. The doctors were amazed that his edemas had not worsened and brought death while he remained high on the mountain.

Three years later, Randall wrote:

> That Foraker debacle did affect my desire to push really hard in the Alaska Range, or on any other big mountain. I went there really psyched, with fewer qualms than before any other major expedition. It seemed like absolutely the right thing to do. Now I guess I'm just acutely aware of how far from perfect my mountaineering ability is, and how even a pretty small mistake can be disastrous in the Alaska Range.

Mount Foraker

THE NORTHERN ROUTES

▲

1	Northeast Ridge	6	North Peak
2	Archangel Ridge	7	South Peak
3	Highway of Diamonds	8	The Fin
4	Northwest Ridge	9	Southwest Ridge
5	Foraker Glacier	10	Unclimbed

3231

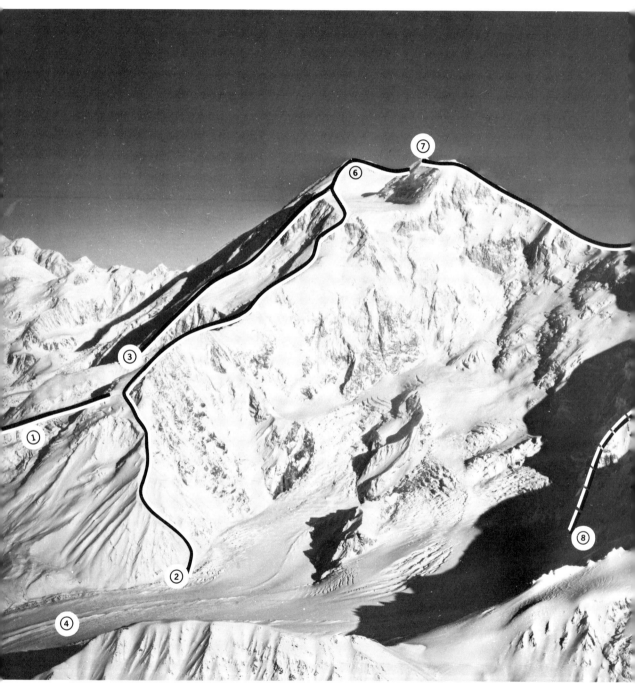

7510

Route Guide

A*pproach:* 25 miles from the 2,400-foot floatplane lake (W of park boundary), up Somber Creek, then up the Herron Glacier to the 5,000-foot base of West Spur.

T*otal Time:* 21-30 days.

C*limbing Miles:* 6.

V*ertical Gain of Route:* 12,400 feet.

A*laska Grade:* 3.

D*ifficulties, Dangers, Rating:* There are no real technical difficulties aside from a knife-edged ridge.

C*amps:* 7,400 (notch in ridge); 8,900 (junction of west and north forks of ridge); 11,700 (after cornicing); 14,200 (above icefall).

R*eferences:* 1935 AAJ; 1935, 1936 AJ; *Maps:* Mt. McKinley A-5, A-4, A-3; Talkeetna D-3, D-4.

Firsts

A*scent:* August 6, 1934; Houston, Waterston, Brown, (Houston, Storey, Anderson).

V*ariation:* Herron Glacier start: July 24, 1977; Morgan, Niles, Fulweiler, Siks, (Underwood, Gamirian).

▲ 1 *Northwest Ridge, 1934 Start*
  2 *Northwest Ridge, 1977 Start*
  3 *Highway of Diamonds*
  4 *Herron Glacier*

  5 *Southwest Ridge*
  6 *North Peak*
  7 *South Peak*
  8 *Unclimbed*

Route Guide

Approach: *25 miles from the 2,400-foot floatplane lake (W of park boundary), up Somber Creek, then up the Herron Glacier to a 3,800-foot side valley; follow it over a 6,300-foot pass, which leads to the Foraker Glacier.*

Total Time: *21–30 days.*

Climbing Miles: *3.*

Vertical Gain of Route: *11,000 feet.*

Alaska Grade: *4.*

Difficulties, Dangers, Rating: *Average angle of climb is 35 degrees; bottom of route has a 30-foot section of near-vertical ice and the crux is a knife-edge at 9,000 to 10,000 feet; slopes above 11,000 feet are avalanche-prone after snowstorms.*

Camps: *8,300; 10,000; 11,800 (basin).*

References: *1976 AAJ; February 1976* Climbing. *Maps: Mt. McKinley A-5, A-4, A-3; Talkeetna D-3.*

Firsts

Ascent: *July 14, 1975; G. & B. Roach, Wright, Johnson, Campbell, Krebs.*

4403

▲ 1	*Archangel Ridge*	
2	*Highway of Diamonds*	
3	*Northwest Ridge*	
4	*Foraker Glacier*	
5	*Northeast Ridge*	
6	*Unclimbed*	

① 1 Highway of Diamonds
2 Northwest Ridge, 1934 Start
3 Northwest Ridge, 1977 Variation
4 Foraker Glacier
5 Herron Glacier

7500

Route Guide

A*pproach:* 24 miles from the 2,400-foot floatplane lake (W of park boundary), up Somber Creek and across the Herron Glacier to a 3,800-foot side valley; follow it southeast to a 6,300-foot pass, which leads to the Foraker Glacier.

T*otal Time:* 21–30 days.

C*limbing Miles:* 4.

V*ertical Gain of Route:* 11,000 feet.

A*laska Grade:* 4+.

D*ifficulties, Dangers, Rating:* Route starts on western fork of ridge as a knife-edge; crux was a 75-foot, 60-degree ice pitch, with a vertical bulge; end of route involves 1,000 feet of 50- to 60-degree snow and ice to 15,000-foot plateau.

C*amps:* 7,700 (col); 11,300 (chopped-out ledge); 14,000 (séracs); 15,000 (plateau).

R*eferences:* 1984 AAJ. Maps: Mt. McKinley A–5, A–4, A–3; Talkeetna D–3.

Firsts

A*scent:* April 29, 1983; Metcalf, Randall.

A*lpine Style:* April 29, 1983; Metcalf, Randall.

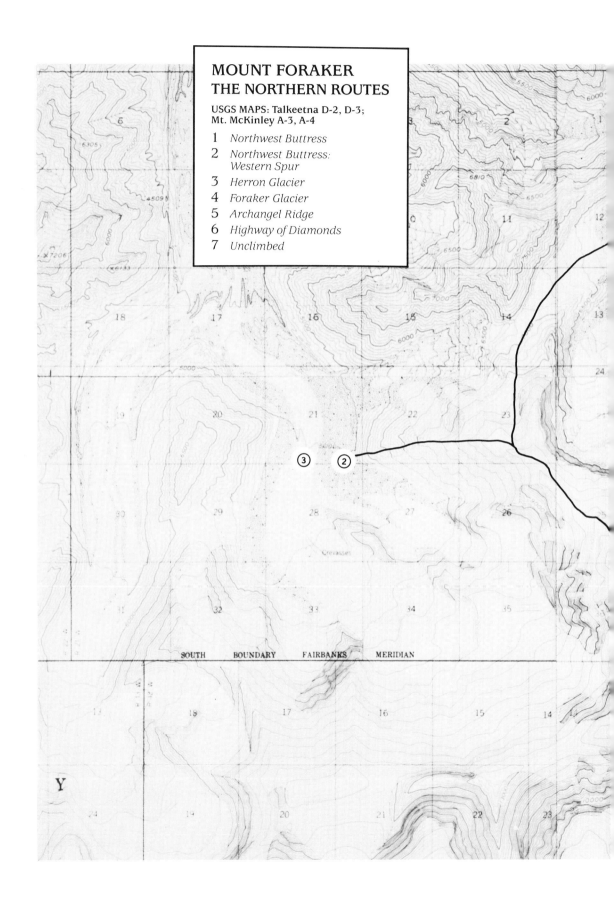

MOUNT FORAKER
THE NORTHERN ROUTES

USGS MAPS: Talkeetna D-2, D-3;
Mt. McKinley A-3, A-4

1 *Northwest Buttress*
2 *Northwest Buttress:*
  Western Spur
3 *Herron Glacier*
4 *Foraker Glacier*
5 *Archangel Ridge*
6 *Highway of Diamonds*
7 *Unclimbed*

SOUTH   BOUNDARY   FAIRBANKS   MERIDIAN

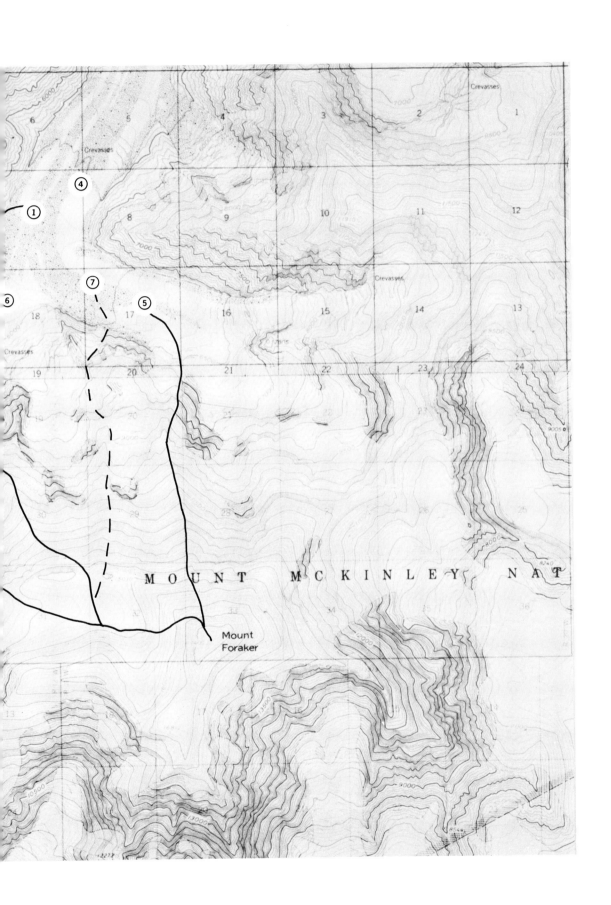

CHAPTER 7

THE EASTERN ROUTES

Southeast Ridge
Northeast Ridge
East Face

Southeast Ridge

THE INITIAL TWO TOES OF THE RIDGE LEAVE THE SOUTH-west Fork of the Kahiltna Glacier and merge into an ill-defined face, replete with small hanging glaciers, until it meets the ridge proper at eleven thousand feet. From here, the ridge narrows into knife-edges and the cornices, until it lays back and broadens into the final three-thousand-foot climb.

Because of its easy access, this popular route sees more traffic than any other route on the mountain. However, there have been numerous accidents on the lower part of the route; poor snow conditions and avalanche slopes are usually to blame. The route cannot be recommended unless the snow is firm; general-ly, after mid-May, snow conditions deteriorate.

In 1963, H. Adams Carter was led to this route by Charles Houston and Bradford Washburn. Houston had gazed down the ridge twenty-nine years earlier during the first ascent of Mount Foraker; Washburn showed Carter the prerequisite photographs.

The forty-eight-year-old Carter was no stranger to Alaskan expeditions. In 1932, also in the company of Washburn and Houston, he had attempted Mount Crillon, finally succeeding in 1933. In 1935, he and Washburn traversed the largest blank spot on the North American map: the St. Elias Range. Carter also climbed on Nanda Devi in 1936, the highest mountain anyone had ever climbed at that date. In 1957, 1958 and 1960, Carter carried out scientific work to the east of Denali, accomplishing several first ascents on eight- to eleven-thousand-foot peaks.

Following the Houstons' father-and-son tradition on Mount Foraker, Carter brought his sons, Larry and Peter, aged fifteen and sixteen. Jim Richardson, Jeff Duenwald, Harry Eldridge, Jerry Halpern, Dr. Harry McDade, Jim Sise, and Margaret Young round-ed out the team.

Richardson (24), Young (30), and Duenwald (21) were fresh from an attempt on the Moose's Tooth and had just completed the first traverse from the Ruth to the Kahiltna Glacier. In 1960 Richardson had climbed Denali; he also made the first ascents of Mount Crosson, East Kahiltna Peak and Peak 10,450 (next to the Southeast Fork landing strip); he then walked out the Kahiltna.

Twenty-three years after the climb, Carter wrote:

> I was set on the southeast ridge from the beginning, having stud-ied Brad Washburn's photos... The gigantic east face was nothing I

wanted to get too close under, but Jim and Jeff wanted a close look. They were soon to learn!

They headed out from Base Camp and had a good look. Just then the ice broke away from near the top of the face and brought tens of tons with it. Although the pair was still well away from the base of the face, they were nearly flattened by the wind and covered by several inches of powder. We heard no more of the second route.

Foraker was to prove a quick and easy climb for such a strong team. They carried loads from 6,500 feet up the toe to 8,100 feet and made their first camp on July 1. The now-savvy climbers knew that even a few inches of new snow on the avalanche slopes ahead would prevent them from making the climb. They moved quickly.

Fixing a bit of rope, the team ran loads across a sérac-threatened traverse and established Richardson and Duenwald at 11,000 feet by July 4. On July 5, Richardson and Duenwald moved camp up to 11,650 feet, above blue ice and cornices. A day of storm kept them in their tents.

On July 7, in what Duenwald described as one of the better days of his life, they cut steps and cramponed across magnificent cornices, which they felt was the most objectively dangerous part of the route. After eleven hours they reached the summit.

With a great flourish, Richardson pulled out a can of beer, but it was frozen. He thawed it in his armpit and the second ascent of Mount Foraker was celebrated.

During the descent, a whiteout forced them to their hands and knees, searching for crampon tracks. Seventeen hours after departing, they found their camp. A second summit attempt was foiled because of bad weather.

Southwest Toe Variation

In 1974, Joe Davidson, Peter Reagan, Robert Fries, James Given (all of whom had climbed Denali's Catacomb Ridge in 1969), Pippo Lionni, Eric Morgan, Mark Greenfield, and Frank Uher made a safer variation on the Southeast Ridge. They climbed the southwest toe, joining Carter's route at 9,000 feet. On July 10, the entire team left 13,300 feet and in fourteen hours reached the summit.

First Winter Ascent

The first winter ascent of Mount Foraker was completed in 1975 by Steve and Gary Tandy. These brothers were part of a larger team that labored for weeks on the difficult South-southeast

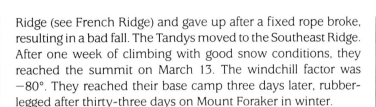

Ridge (see French Ridge) and gave up after a fixed rope broke, resulting in a bad fall. The Tandys moved to the Southeast Ridge. After one week of climbing with good snow conditions, they reached the summit on March 13. The windchill factor was −80°. They reached their base camp three days later, rubber-legged after thirty-three days on Mount Foraker in winter.

The South-southeast Ridge in winter was a bold undertaking, for, until then, no climber had attempted a technically difficult route in the Alaska Range under winter conditions. Nonetheless, the Tandys' tenacity in succeeding on an alpine-style ascent of the Southeast Ridge in winter is inspirational.

Ski Descent

In an incredible feat, the Southeast Ridge was skied in 1981 by the renowned French alpinist Pierre Beghin and a support team (which would later ski Mount Crosson). On Mount Foraker, he skied the route with an occasional belay on the steepest sections below 12,500 feet.

Northeast Ridge

BECAUSE OF ITS EXPOSURE BENEATH TREMENDOUS hanging glaciers, the original approach to this ridge, from the eastern side, cannot be recommended. It is safe to approach the Northeast Ridge by way of Mount Crosson (see Sultana Ridge Variation). The ridge is part broad and crevassed, part knife-edged, with considerable ups and downs between minor peaks. Because it is an exposed divide, balanced between the north and south sides of the entire Alaska Range, winds and storm will have a much more accelerated and debilitating effect upon climbers. The ridge offers superb vistas of both the tundra and the spectacular peaks of the Kahiltna Glacier.

The route had been considered in 1963, when Jeff Duenwald and Jim Richardson insisted upon reconnoitering it (see Southeast Ridge). Two years later, a German team that had made the first ascent of Mount Russell arrived. Its members walked up the icefall and "felt the wind from the avalanches which continually rolled off Mount Foraker." Strangely enough, in their account, they attribute turning back to lack of time, rather than avalanches. A month later, a Japanese team that had climbed the South Buttress variation on Denali moved over to this avalanche-blasted icefall. In its account, however, no reference is made to avalanches. The Japanese Foraker attempt, like the German one, was also in vain.

On June 4, 1966, a Japanese team landed on the Southeast Fork of the Kahiltna Glacier. Yasuhiko Iso, Takeshi Ogawa, Kazuya Murayama, Yasuo Kubota, Yuuzo Samura, and Hideo Nishigori, leader, made the third ascent of Mount Hunter and descended to their base camp on June 25.

Then, without further ado, they moved their camp to a point beneath Mount Foraker's East Face. Three days later (June 30), after crossing the avalanche runout of the huge hanging glacier, 8,000 feet above, they established their first camp at 9,600 feet, on a spur ridge leading to the Northeast Ridge. They made their second camp at the 11,550-foot col.

On July 7, they reached the summit in eight hours, then returned to camp. They descended a very changed icefall in terror of avalanches and falling séracs. They walked out the Kahiltna in a week. Their expedition was a *tour de force*, for few climbers have managed to climb both mountains.

However, their route harbors unjustifiable objective hazards. It was double jeopardy, sneaking through an active icefall, then cringing beneath tons of cocked, hanging glacier, eight thousand feet above their heads.

Traditionally, many Japanese believe in life after death, and courage in the face of great danger, regardless of safety, is often considered a virtue. This philosophy would be exemplified again and again on Mount Foraker, as well as on Denali's Japanese Direct South Face in 1977.

The word was out in Japan and, in 1969, a Japanese team came back to the icefall. On this trip, they placed their first camp directly beneath the hanging glacier. Four members made it safely to the summit in a thirty-hour round-trip (including an eight-hour rest) climb from their 8,500-foot camp. This was the first alpine-style ascent of the route.

The word also was out in the United States. In a prophetic letter to the Chief Ranger at McKinley Park, H. Adams Carter wrote: "Some day these Japanese are going to get buried under a most horrendous avalanche if they persist in using that route. We…

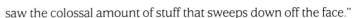

saw the colossal amount of stuff that sweeps down off the face."

A fourth Japanese team returned in 1975. It also succeeded. Then, in 1976, two Japanese teams arrived. Three members of the first team climbed up above the icefall, were separated from their party, and died from fatigue and exposure. As the second team climbed into the arena, a huge avalanche roared from the East Face and three climbers were buried forever, at 7,500 feet. As of this writing, no one has returned to this route.

Sultana Ridge Variation

Between 1974 and 1978, there were eight attempts on Mount Foraker's Northeast Ridge, via Mount Crosson, which avoided the Japanese deathtrap. There was an attempt by a large guided party. There was a solo attempt by Charlie Porter, who was scared off by all the crevasses. Many attempts were foiled by snowstorms. Eventually every section of the ridge was climbed; they now only needed to be linked continuously to the summit.

On March 2, 1979, Brian Okonek, Dave Johnston and Roger Cowles were flown into the Kahiltna by Okonek's close friend, Jim, who had shuttled, dropped care packages, and flight-checked Brian on countless expeditions. For an aspiring Alaska Range climber, it was a dream come true: a guaranteed, dependable pilot and plane to take him anywhere he wanted to climb. Brian, in turn, was a resourceful carpenter for Jim. They enjoyed an extraordinary relationship and loved the Alaskan mountains. They were also father and son.

The twenty-two-year-old Okonek, who had made ascents of Denali and Mount Hunter and made numerous first ascents of the smaller, spectacular Alaska Range peaks, climbed with the sincere and relentless fervor of one who had found his religion in the mountains. His mentor, the kind and gentle giant Johnston, had also left tracks on nearly every Alaskan peak in sight—many with Okonek, and many in winter. With typical generosity, they welcomed Cowles along as a blood brother, although his first Alaska Range climb had only been several weeks earlier on Mount Dickey, with Okonek. It had been the first winter ascent.

It was also typical of Johnston and Okonek (the latter had tried the Sultana Ridge twice), to up the ante with a winter attempt. Although they had both completed technical first ascents in the range, their forte was arduous mountaineering, with long approaches, desperate bushwhacking, endless step-kicking, storm survival, and exposure to the winter's unforgiving cold.

On Mount Foraker, Cowles forgot his sleeping bag. As the trio set up camp at 6,800 feet, Cowles realized, with great delight, that Okonek and Johnston's sleeping bags would zip together. Cowles

squeezed in. They had also forgotten a gallon of fuel. In the dark, Johnston cooked and served a strange, sulphur-flavored glop; his wife had packed the matches in the dinner bag.

The next day, the charmed trio carried a load up the ridge and found a gallon of Blazo at 9,900 feet. On March 4, Johnston pulled out his methodically kept journal and wrote: "…Brian's dad flies out of the murk and throws Roger's sleeping bag at the cache, missing it by only 42 feet! Wild cheers in the wilderness!"

Brian wrote in his journal: "Dancing on ice with V.B.'s [floppy boots], snow crampons, an axe that won't stick, no hammer and 60 lb. packs demands concentration."

As veterans of numerous Alaska Range storms, they carried three snow shovels and no tents. They read books and told stories as storms raged outside of their eleven-thousand-foot snow cave. Johnston was unhappy with his sleeping bag and cut the hood off and sewed it on the top, so he could sleep comfortably on his stomach.

On the sixth storm-bound day, Johnston's journal reads: "10 March… 0 hours climbing. Write five pages to my mother-in-law. Getting desperate."

"Liberation!" was the next day's entry. The weather lifted. They climbed over Mount Crosson, then Peak 12,472. Up and down and up and down. They dug another snow cave at 11,250 feet and ate Dall sheep steaks and salmon that they had caught during the summer.

With Alaskan resourcefulness, they climbed with their sleeping bags tied on their packs to dry, flapping like great capes in the wind. They wore the standard Alaskan footwear: white, floppy and bulbous-toed bunny boots, horrible for climbing, yet essential for preventing frostbite. Much of their gear was home-sewn, miscolored, and hung loosely off their limbs. During their descent, they would eagerly scrounge equipment abandoned on earlier Sultana Ridge attempts, tying it onto their packs.

At 8 A.M. on March 15, they left their third crevasse cave, at 12,300 feet, for the summit. Johnston wrote:

> The slope steepens to 40, slacks back to 35, then tightens up again. Scrunch scrunch. Perfect crampon snow. Scrunch scrunch. On and on. On and on. I get that mechanical feeling. I'm just a slope jumar, camming monotonously upward, forever.

They reached the top at 2 P.M., sat down in the weak sun, ate, and took the obligatory photos. It was thirty degrees below zero. They descended to their crevasse cave in three hours.

Three days later, they arrived at their base camp very hungry. Johnston wrote:

The ravens have cleaned us out. Remnants of wrapping is all that remains of our precious 3 loaves of homemade bread, 4 packages of Philadelphia Cream Cheese, 2 boxes of graham crackers.... Ah...though the dents indicate they tried valiantly, the muthers [*sic*] failed to rob us of our 2 tins of Nabobs! Up goes the tent, out come the spoons and down goes the raspberry jam, spread thickly on our tongues.

Between the lines of their spirited journal entries lies a deep, spiritual respect for the mountains. Indeed, although they flew out like everyone else, they seldom let the Alaska Range out of their sight—no city jobs or stateside careers or more than a stray adventure anywhere but in mountains, usually Alaskan ones.

▲

East Face

MOUNT FORAKER'S EAST FACE RISES TEN THOUSAND feet to the summit. Part of the face ends on top of the Southeast Ridge; the remainder of the face is guarded by séracs and hanging glaciers. The Pink Panther route is the only recommended route, for the Czech Route is unjustifiably dangerous.

Pink Panther Route

This is a steep, mixed climb starting in an S-shaped couloir, linking with a short ridge, then maneuvering through séracs and joining a final icefield. The climb is punctuated with short, steep rock bands, which generally offer the most difficult climbing. The climb connects with the Southeast Ridge at fourteen thousand feet. The route is generally protected from the fall-line of seracs.

The route had been coveted by several active Alaska Range climbers since 1981, but was pounced upon in 1984 by four newcomers: Daniel Vachon, Julien Dery and Jean-François Gagnon from Quebec, and Australian Graham Sanders.

Sanders was sitting on the latrine at the Southeast Fork of the Kahiltna, which looked out on the full splendor of the unclimbed eastern facade of the Southeast Ridge. He ran back to camp and announced, "Guys, we've got to try the east face. If it should turn out to be too tough, then we can go to the southeast ridge as planned."

They started climbing on May 23, 1984. It took them five days to climb the face, although the Quebec trio had already acclimatized by going high on Denali.

Their first bivouac, two thousand feet up the initial couloir, took four hours to chop. Difficulties increased on the second day when they encountered steep ice and 5.7 rock. Their second bivouac was no better than the first.

On the third day, they climbed seventy-degree icefields. A mixed traverse brought them out of the icefields, between two séracs, two thirds of the way up the face. They were euphoric; the climb was growing beneath their feet. They spent their third night in a comfortable crevasse, with an enormous block—a Sword of Damocles—hanging above their heads.

Easier terrain brought them to the most difficult and terrifying part of the climb: a mixture of unstable snow, unprotectable verglassed rock, and vertical ice. The second pitch was even worse: bottomless granular sugar snow at 85°. Then followed a third pitch of crawling across a knife-edge ridge with incredible exposure, the only passageway between two hanging glaciers. They set up the tent under a detached ice block, visibly shaken. Vachon wrote that

> The fourth day had been the most hair-raising of all, but the bivouac that night was devilish. During the day, we had often pulled the Devil by the tail. We had climbed very steep ice walls without protection, and given psychological belays, but the bivouac was the worst I had ever had. All night long the sérac which overhung us creaked, raising our blood pressure.

They climbed easier snow, a section of barely penetrable green ice, a short bit of 5.6; then they scrambled onto the fourteen-thousand-foot level of the Southeast Ridge.

On May 28, the three Québécois reached the summit. In a mood of great celebration, like Jim Richardson pulling out his can of beer twenty-one years earlier, Vachon rejoiced with his stuffed Pink Panther mascot. They descended in two days. Gagnon later soloed the Cassin Ridge.

Czech Route

This climb is a mile north of the obvious S-shaped couloir of the Pink Panther route. The approach to the face was made via the dangerous and badly broken glacier which is subject to avalanches (see the 1966 Northeast Ridge route). This unsafe route has frequent sérac activity.

Jaroslav Jaško (24) and Dušan Becík (30) set out with five days of food, one rope, eight pitons, six ice screws and a set of hex-entrics. They bivouacked in the icefall on May 19, 1986.

After they had completed their climb, Becík, in an interview by Peter Porco of the *Anchorage Daily News* commented: "Alaska, especially this area around McKinley, has so many routes that it is necessary for our young climbers to get here and make some history. Up to now we concentrate on the Himalayas."

The Czechs are renowned for doing difficult climbs in the range; two of them were bold, but relatively safe, routes on Denali's South Face (Ivan Fiala, who stayed in base camp, had led Denali's Milan Krissak route in 1980). The pressures facing Czechs, who are usually government-sactioned, are much different than those of other nationalities. Czechs cannot afford to get stormed off their climbs. Like the Russians, Becík and Jasko had to bring results to the government, their club members, and the West German equipment sponsors who had made their trip possible. Otherwise, they would not be allowed to go on future expeditions.

At the time of the Czech climb, there was a highly publicized Russian team on Denali's Cassin and West Rib routes; no one paid any attention to the competitive Czechs. Their hand had been forced; as they needed equal press coverage, they impulsively set out for an unclimbed, dangerous and illogical line.

After crossing numerous, unnerving crevasse snow bridges, they climbed over the bergschrund. Four pitches up, they were hit by an avalanche. After twelve hours of climbing, having been hit by multiple snowslides, they stopped and bivouacked in a protected snow cave beneath a rock buttress.

On May 21, they climbed quickly up fifty-degree snow; up difficult verglassed rock; up two pitches of eighty-five-degree ice. At midnight they bivouacked on a snow ridge.

The next day, they climbed mixed terrain. At 2 P.M., an overhanging pitch of snow led them onto the Southeast Ridge. They had climbed the difficult face quickly, due in part to their fear of being hit by avalanches. Six hours later, they reached the summit and descended the Sultana Ridge.

Despite their earlier experiences with unstable bridges in the icefall and the heart-stopping sensation of crossing underneath a huge hanging glacier, they cut down the 1966 Japanese route. Both climbers fell into crevasses. But the giant hanging glacier above their heads was quiet that day.

Their remarkable speed—three and one-half days from base camp to the summit and back to base camp—considerably reduced the objective dangers. When they returned to base camp, they got their newspaper interview.

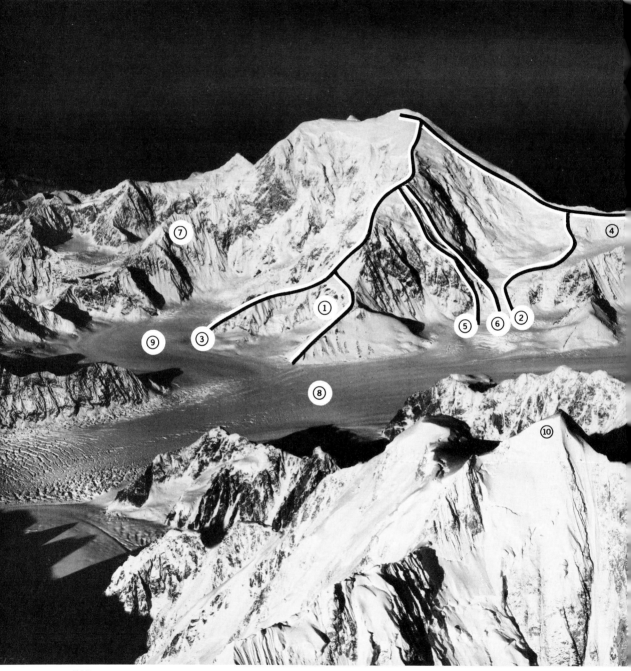

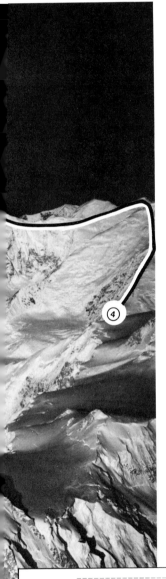

MOUNT FORAKER

THE EASTERN ROUTES

1 Southeast Ridge

2 Northeast Ridge 1966

3 Southeast Ridge Variation 1974

4 Northeast Ridge, Sultana Variation

5 East Face, Pink Panther Route

6 East Face, Czech Route

7 French Ridge

8 Kahiltna Glacier

9 Kahiltna Glacier, Southwest Fork

10 Mount Hunter, South Peak

▲ 1   *Southeast Ridge*

   2   *Southeast Ridge, 1974 Variation*

   3   *Northeast Ridge, 1966 Route*

   4   *East Face, Pink Panther Route*

   5   *East Face, Czech Route*

   6   *Kahiltna Glacier, Southwest Fork*

   7   *Kahiltna Glacier*

   8   *Northeast Ridge, Sultana Variation*

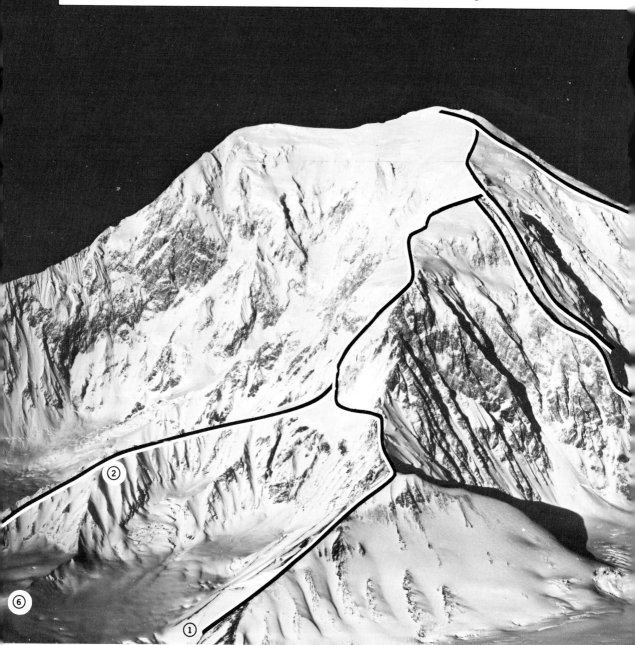

7088

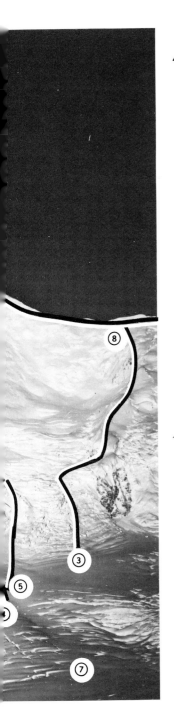

Route Guide

Approach: *0.5 mile from the 6,500-foot Southwest Fork of the Kahiltna landing strip to the 7,000-foot base.*

Total Time: *7-21 days.*

Climbing Miles: *5.*

Vertical Gain of Route: *10,400 feet.*

Alaska Grade: *3.*

Difficulties, Dangers, Rating: *Occasional séracfall from 10,000 feet and avalanche-prone lower slopes can be partially avoided by 1974 Southwest Toe Variation; cornices on ridge from 11,500 to 13,600.*

Camps: *8,100 (southeast toe, or 8,500 on top of southwest toe); 11,650 (above face); 13,200 (before final cornice); 13,900.*

References: *1964, 1975, 1976 AAJ. Map: Talkeetna D-3.*

Firsts

Ascent: *July 7, 1963; Richardson, Duenwald, (L., P. and A. Carter, Young, Eldridge, McDade, Sise, Halpern).*

Alpine Style: *March 13, 1977; G. & S. Tandy.*

Winter: *March 13, 1977; G. & S. Tandy.*

Ski Descent: *May 1981; Beguin.*

Variation: *Southwest Toe: July 10, 1974; Davidson, Fries, Reagan, Given, Greenfield, Lionni, Morgan, Uher.*

2360

▲ 1	*Upper Northeast Ridge, Sultana Variation*
2	*Upper Northeast Ridge, 1966 Route*
3	*Southeast Ridge*

Route Guide

Approach: *3 miles from the 7,200-foot Southeast Fork of the Kahiltna landing strip to the 6,900-foot base of Mount Crosson.*

Total Time: *10–21 days.*

Climbing Miles: *7.*

Vertical Gain of Route: *10,500 feet; (add over 2,000 feet more of elevation gain for ups and downs).*

Alaska Grade: *3.*

Difficulties, Dangers, Rating: *40-degree snow-and-ice sections along a crevassed and knife-edged ridge; exposed to all wind and storms.*

Camps: *11,000 (Southeast Ridge of Crosson); 11,250 (South Ridge of Point 12,472); 12,300 (Northeast Ridge).*

References: *1967, 1980 (photos), 1984 AAJ. Maps: McKinley A-4; Talkeetna D-3.*

Firsts

Ascent: *1966 Route: July 7, 1966; Nishigori, Iso, Samura, (Ogawa, Murayama, Kubota). Sultana Ridge: March 15, 1979; Okonek, Johnston, Cowles.*

Alpine Style: *1966 Route: July 5, 1969; Toda, Nagai, Yamashita, Fukunaga, (Oshima, Tomino, Shimatomi, Miki, Nagae).*

Winter: *Sultana Ridge: March 15, 1979; Okonek, Johnston, Cowles.*

7488

▲ 1	*Southeast Ridge of Mount Crosson, Sultana Variation*
2	*Kahiltna Glacier*

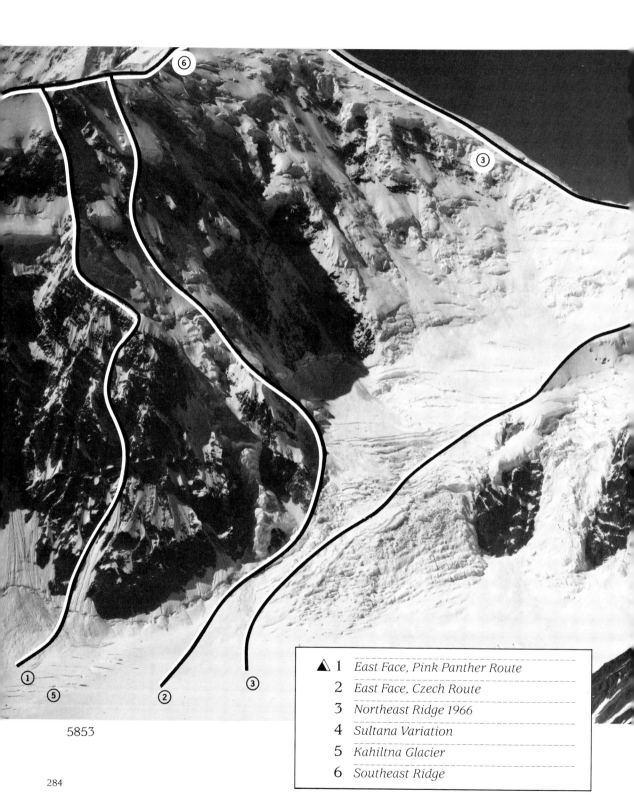

	1	East Face, Pink Panther Route
	2	East Face, Czech Route
	3	Northeast Ridge 1966
	4	Sultana Variation
	5	Kahiltna Glacier
	6	Southeast Ridge

5853

▲

Route Guide

A*pproach:* 3-4 miles from the 6,500-foot Southwest Fork (or Southeast Fork) of the Kahiltna landing strip to a safe spot at 6,500 feet, away from the face.

T*otal Time:* 6-14 days; Czech Route: 3-10 days.

C*limbing Miles:* 2.5-3.

V*ertical Gain of Route:* 10,000 feet; Czech Route: 9,000 feet.

A*laska Grade:* 5+.

D*ifficulties, Dangers, Rating:* Sustained ice climbing of 60 to 75 degrees with short vertical steps; difficult rock climbing (5.7); occasional exposure to hanging séracs. Czech Route: Dangerous icefall crossing with exposure to hanging glacier; sustained ice climbing of 60 to 75 degrees with short vertical steps; steep mixed climbing; much exposure to séracfall.

C*amps:* 9,000 (chopped-ice ledge in S couloir); ca. 9,800 (beneath rock band); ca. 11,000 (crevasse); ca. 12,500 (beneath séracs); 14,000. Czech Route: ca. 8,000 (base); (snowcave beneath a rock buttress); (snow ridge); 14,000.

R*eferences:* 1985, 1987 AAJ. Map: Talkeetna D-3.

Firsts

A*scent: Pink Panther:* May 25, 1984; Vachon, Dery, Gagnon, (Sanders). *Czech Route:* May 22, 1986; Becík, Jásko.

A*lpine Style: Pink Panther:* May 25, 1984; Vachon, Dery, Gagnon, (Sanders). *Czech Route:* May 22, 1986; Becík, Jásko.

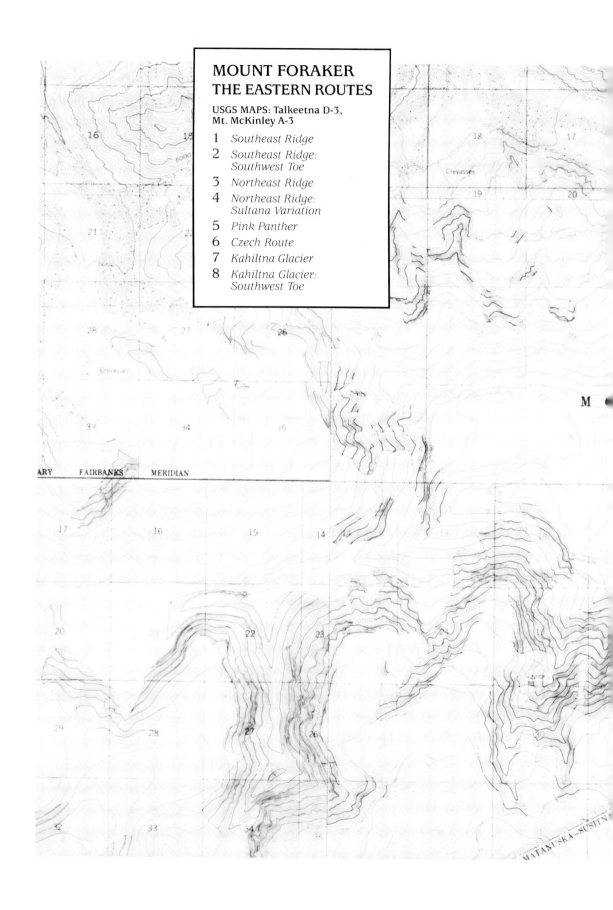

MOUNT FORAKER
THE EASTERN ROUTES

USGS MAPS: Talkeetna D-3,
Mt. McKinley A-3

1 *Southeast Ridge*
2 *Southeast Ridge:
Southwest Toe*
3 *Northeast Ridge*
4 *Northeast Ridge:
Sultana Variation*
5 *Pink Panther*
6 *Czech Route*
7 *Kahiltna Glacier*
8 *Kahiltna Glacier:
Southwest Toe*

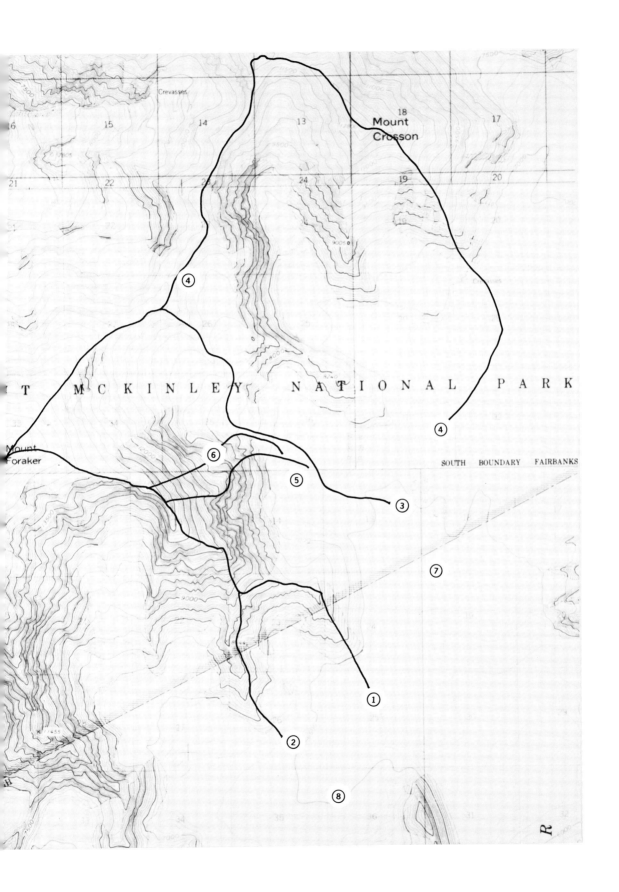

Crevasses

6   15   14   13   18 Mount   17
                                           Crosson

21   22   24   19   20

④

T   McKINLEY   NATIONAL   PARK

④

Mount
Foraker
          ⑥
              ⑤   SOUTH   BOUNDARY   FAIRBANKS

                                  ③

                              ⑦

                      ①

          ②

                  ⑧

                                                      R

CHAPTER 8

THE SOUTHERN ROUTES

Talkeetna Ridge
French Ridge
Infinite Spur
Southwest Ridge

Talkeetna Ridge

LEGANT AND SELDOM-CLIMBED, THE TALKEETNA RIDGE is on the south side of Mount Foraker. There are several bands of Class 4–5 granite on the route and, for 1,500 feet, the ridge merges into a face. At 16,500 feet, just below the South Summit, it joins the more difficult Infinite Spur and French Ridge routes. Most of its difficulties consist of elaborate and continuous cornicing.

This Foraker climb was put together in 1968 by Warren Bleser, a schoolteacher from Washington State, ever hungry for new routes in the Alaska Range (see Denali's East Buttress). Bleser invited Alex Bertulis, who was determined to attempt the South Buttress (Infinite Spur). However, when he arrived on the glacier two weeks late, he discovered that Bleser and Hans Baer had already fixed ropes partway up the South (Talkeetna) Ridge. Bertulis was upset. Three days of debate ensued.

Bertulis had seen the photos of Mount Logan's Hummingbird Ridge; its grandiose cornices looked great, but he would have no part of them. Cornices took perseverance, not skill, Bertulis said. Besides, their original plan was the steep, uncorniced South Buttress (Infinite Spur). Bleser conceded.

Bertulis and Pete Williamson started climbing the South Buttress. Bleser and Baer watched. Four leads up, a huge rock avalanche cascaded over Bertulis' head. The South Buttress was abandoned.

Many routes in Alaska are done in just this manner. The initial itinerary is forged in the comfort of a warm living room over a set of simple photographs. Upon arrival on the mountain, reality sets in: the route is more dangerous than it looked, or snow conditions are abysmal, or the team is not sufficiently psyched. A safer, more practical route is sought out.

The team started up the South Ridge on July 11, 1968. Following the fixed ropes for 1,500 feet up thirty-five-degree slopes, they reached the narrow ridge crest and continued. Bleser put their camp on a huge overhanging cornice, much to Bertulis' dismay. A snowstorm stopped all progress for five days.

Bertulis had designed twelve-inch-wide, one-eighth-inch-thick aluminum discs, to be slung from the center. This was the first Alaska Range use of flukes, which were more effective than pickets, which melted out. They eventually anchored five thousand feet of fixed rope to discs and pickets.

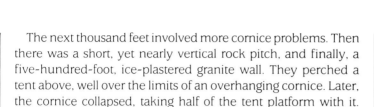
The next thousand feet involved more cornice problems. Then there was a short, yet nearly vertical rock pitch, and finally, a five-hundred-foot, ice-plastered granite wall. They perched a tent above, well over the limits of an overhanging cornice. Later, the cornice collapsed, taking half of the tent platform with it. Bertulis was convinced the route would not be one of his favorites.

The terrain leading to the next camp was more face than ridge. Bleser discovered a key crevasse passageway near the top of a steep ice face. Baer threaded and jumped over crevasses, then finessed up a fifty-degree ice pitch. Finally, a rooster's-tail formation of steep and narrow ice was dispensed with in three demanding leads. Their third camp was placed on a dome, free of objective hazards. Bertulis breathed a sigh of relief.

But 5,000 feet of climbing remained. In *The American Alpine Journal 1969*, Bleser wrote, "The 'Peruvian Way' involved me for the next twelve hours in the most demanding climbing I have ever done." They retreated to the 12,200-foot camp, physically and psychologically fatigued by the climbing.

Bertulis and Baer left Camp 3, hoping to reach the summit in a single push. They found steeper terrain above the Peruvian Way: alternating snow, ice and rock. After twenty-eight hours of trailbreaking and climbing, they rested on a tiny platform at 15,500 feet. Bleser and Williamson caught up in ten hours from Camp 3, greatly aided by Bertulis' trail.

They all plodded up to 16,500 feet and dug a cave. Bertulis and Baer suffered mightily without sleeping bags, while the canny Bleser and Williamson were ensconced in down.

Completely unrested, Bertulis groveled over the South Peak, across a plateau and up to the flat North Peak. It was July 26.

In *The American Alpine Journal,* Bertulis wrote, "To the west there was only a vast plain of velvety tundra, deep green or olive, interrupted by an occasional yellow ribbon winding its way to some sea hidden behind the horizon. A rusty haze and the smell of distant burning forest spiced the cold, clear air."

Williamson and Bleser reached the summit shortly afterward. They descended and caught up to Baer. It was so warm that their fixed rope picket anchors were pulling up—Baer, Bertulis, Bleser and Williamson fell repeatedly. They reached their 12,200-foot camp on the morning of July 27. Bertulis and Baer had climbed without sleep for seventy hours.

After a three-day storm, they descended the ridge in a twenty-hour push. Bleser named it the Talkeetna Ridge, because it pointed in the general direction of the town. They waited for another week of wet, snowy weather before their pilot arrived.

Bleser came back to the range again for an attempt on

Mount Huntington. He was killed in 1973 while descending the Matterhorn. Bertulis returned in 1972 to climb the Cassin Ridge. Mimicking the thwarted South Buttress trip on Mount Foraker, which put him atop the Talkeetna Ridge, Bertulis retreated from the Cassin and added a rapid, alpine-style variation to Denali's West Rib.

Alpine Style

In 1984, some National Outdoor Leadership School instructors were turned back by an avalanche; then again, in 1985, by bad snow conditions.

Dave Auble and Charles Townsend repeated the route, alpine style, in ten days from the base of the route, reaching the summit on May 15, 1986. Conditions were much more stable in early May. They were pinned down by bad weather beneath the Peruvian Traverse for three days and commented that the route could be climbed with eight days of good weather.

Despite the leap in ice-climbing standards since the route was first climbed, Auble and Townsend felt very committed. Auble broke a tooth and suffered frostbitten feet.

French Ridge

WITH MILES OF INTRICATE CORNICING, ROCK TOWers, and very difficult climbing, this is the most spectacular ridge on the mountain. It saw at least three attempts by strong parties, who were turned back by the continuous difficulties, before it finally fell in 1976 to a determined party of six French climbers and one American. Ten thousand feet of fixed rope was carried and reused. An alpine-style ascent of this route would be an audacious undertaking.

A French guide, Henri Agresti, following in the tradition of his countrymen (see Cassin Ridge), wanted to make a statement in Alaska. He put together a team consisting of his wife, Isabelle, Jean–Paul Bouquier, Gérard Créton, Jean Marie Galmiche, Hervé Thivierge, and Werner Landry, an American. (Although Fred

Beckey had been invited, at the last minute, he dropped out because of other Alaskan plans.) None of the group had climbed in Alaska before. Between Landry's limited French and a smattering of English and German, the climbers managed to communicate.

They started climbing on May 5, 1976. Landry felt that the key to their success was the French style of climbing hard, fast, and in every weather condition. Two out of every three days produced wind, whiteouts, or snowfall.

They climbed up a difficult secondary ridge and made their first camp near the juncture of the main ridge, at 8,500 feet. The next section on the main ridge offered interesting mixed climbing. They fixed 10,000 feet of rope and each climber went across ten times.

By May 16, they had stocked a large snow cave at 10,500 feet. The turning point of the climb lay in pulling up all of their fixed rope, plus twenty-four days of food, and starting over again from a comfortable three-bedroom snow cave which served as advance base camp.

They used a small hand-held radio for weather forecasts, which was a tremendous morale booster. Landry called his girlfriend back in California.

Then the real difficulties began. They spent two weeks fixing ropes across a delicate section of lacework cornices, the *dentelles*. All of them would have the heart-stopping sensation of seeing and feeling tons of snow and ice collapse beneath their weight and thunder off to the distant glacier. Much of this terrain was covered with deep snow and the step-kicking proved incredibly arduous. The stable west side seemed to offer the safest climbing.

The giant, two-hundred-pound Landry began asking his tiny French companions about the sparse rations. Volume-wise, he just wasn't getting his share. His six-foot frame was wasting away. Then he would watch in disgust as his teammates mixed ham fat with mayonnaise and crushed garlic. He always traded his share for peanut butter; the French hated peanut butter.

Landry called a meeting in the cave. He was starving, getting weak. They didn't believe him, so he showed them how his pants were falling down. They gave him all of the peanut butter.

By May 31, they had cracked the lacework and made their third camp at 11,300 feet. With most of the difficulties behind them, they moved quickly up to a bivouac at 14,600 feet.

On June 3 and 4, two separate groups climbed a large couloir to the summit, after thirty-five days of climbing. It took them ten days to descend.

As of this writing, their route has not been repeated.

Traversing cornices on the French Ridge ▶

Infinite Spur

SWEEPING NINE THOUSAND FEET DIRECTLY TO MOUNT Foraker's South Peak, with solid granite and steep ice, this climb has all the classic beauty of the Cassin Ridge. The approach is short, but difficult and committing. Bivouac ledges are few and the climbing is sustained, but under the right conditions, there is little objective danger. It is destined to become one of the great test pieces of the Alaska Range and is a tribute to the skills of those who made the first ascent. Strangely enough, the route has not been repeated, perhaps because it can't be seen from the landing strip.

Mike Kennedy and George Lowe came to the Alaska Range in 1977 with this route foremost on their minds. The renowned ice climber, Jeff Lowe, had been a major force behind the route, but he had fallen during their ascent of Mount Hunter and broken his ankle. Kennedy and George Lowe lowered Jeff down, then singlemindedly climbed back up and finished off the dramatic face. Nonetheless, it was only a warm-up climb for Mount Foraker.

Kennedy, an up-and-coming alpine climber and editor of *Climbing* magazine, had been to the Alaska Range only once. The twenty-five-year-old climber was delighted to have the opportunity of climbing with his heroes, the Lowes. The climb on Mount Foraker would open his eyes to his own potential as an alpine climber.

While Kennedy had fanned his desires on unclimbed waterfalls and Colorado peaks, George Lowe had cut his teeth on hard alpine climbs around the country. He was drawn toward the Himalayan giants, but aside from one route on a Himalayan peak, he had never attempted anything on the scale of Foraker's Infinite Spur.

After their new route on Mount Hunter, they had decided to climb the Cassin because the Infinite Spur loomed terribly large, particularly after losing Jeff Lowe. By ten P.M., they had packed and were drinking tea, but the Infinite Spur still preyed on both of their minds.

Suddenly Kennedy said, "Look, we should go over to Foraker. We know we can do the Cassin."

So it was sealed. They would rather fail on the unclimbed Infinite Spur than repeat the Cassin, which was easily within

their abilities. Kennedy repacked, while Lowe—with this new, grand challenge hanging above their heads—wrote a letter home to his children. It was a tremendous psychological leap into the unknown.

They skied from the landing strip to the base of their route on Mount Foraker and spent a day observing the face. It looked safer and easier than in the photos. There was no turning back.

On June 27, they started climbing. For the next eleven days, they would average fourteen hours per day. Their packs were heavy, so they took them off and belayed. They seldom hauled. The second and third days, they climbed in snow and clouds. Spindrift avalanches cascaded over them. Often they couldn't see one another at the end of the rope.

On June 30, Kennedy took a terrifying twenty-foot leader fall. The screw held. After eighteen hours of continuous climbing, they stopped and brewed soup beneath the obvious, rock-capped crux of the route. It was three in the morning, and they talked about bivouacking. They were exhausted.

Nonetheless, Kennedy started up the crux, clearheaded and completely focused. It was the most difficult climbing on the route, but he stepped outside of himself and imagined being on top. Life was reduced to crampons screeching across the rock, burning calf muscles, and choking spindrift avalanches. Time became meaningless.

The next thing he could remember was Lowe jumaring up to him, on top of the third pitch. Kennedy stepped back to reality. In the short span of three pitches, he had discovered his potential as an alpine climber.

On July 1, they traversed all day beneath cornices until the terrain flattened out. They bivouacked under a sérac, relieved that they could sleep unroped. Eighty pitches of climbing yawned beneath them. The following day brought stormy weather and kept them in the tent, acclimatizing.

They dashed to the summit on July 3. They were low on food and sleep, riding the fine, fuzzy edge of exhaustion. The route had stretched their bodies and minds. Lowe raved about the beautiful view and the intense colors.

After the summit, they descended the Southeast Ridge. At first they ran down the easy slopes, gaining energy as they got lower. Kennedy wrote in *The American Alpine Journal 1978:*

> We were very leery of cornices, and moved slowly and carefully around them, well below the fracture line. But we weren't careful enough. Time slowed down: the next few seconds lasted an eternity. George was ahead, 30 feet from the crest of the ridge; he came across what he thought was a small crevasse, probed it and

stepped across. There was a dull cracking sound, and a fracture ran along the ridge for 100 feet. The cornice disappeared, taking George with it, the rope came tight and jerked me off my feet: I flew down one side of the ridge as George plunged down the other in the midst of tons of ice. The rope pulled tighter, arching me up to the crest of the ridge, and I saw myself shooting over the edge and the two of us falling helplessly to the chaotic glacier 8,000 feet below.

But we stopped. I was 20 feet from the edge, and rammed in a deadman within seconds. The rope was still taut. I was sure that George was either dead or very seriously injured. Shouts brought no answers, then the rope slackened. I pulled up a few feet, then another few feet...he was at least in good enough shape to climb! We were soon reunited and set about gathering our shattered wits.

George Lowe at approximately 15,000 feet on the Infinite Spur, 1977 ▼

George was bruised and shaken and had been cut on the nose, but that was it. We had been lucky again.

This was a turning point for two remarkable climbing careers of distinctly different tastes. Lowe would distinguish himself more than once in the Himalaya, most notably putting up many of the hardest pitches on Everest's East Face in two separate years. He reached the summit in 1983.

Kennedy followed through with his initiation, avoiding the Everests and looking for the smaller Himalayan gems. The visualization process that impelled him up Mount Foraker's hardest pitches would see him through a solo of the Cassin, an alpine-style ascent of Thelay Sagar and a new, winter route on Ama Dablam.

Southwest Ridge

N *THE AMERICAN ALPINE JOURNAL 1978*, ERIK LeROY wrote:

> The massive southwest ridge of Foraker is a labyrinthine collection of ribs and buttresses which, with meandering nonchalance, rises out of several different glaciers headed in several different directions. The point of confluence for these subordinate ridges is a 13,800-foot-high spot, essentially a peak itself, known as "The Fin."

The Southwest Ridge had been attempted twice before, in 1976 and 1977. The 1976 team retreated from the South Ridge of The Fin; the 1977 team, which attempted the route in winter, fell and was rescued, after climbing the most difficult part of a steep ridge from the Herron Glacier. There are several unfinished lines left on this ridge. All of these long ridges, particularly the 1977 climb, will involve more miles than any other route on the mountain.

LeRoy, Nancey Goforth, Chris Liddle, and Murray Marvin made up the team. Goforth had been on an all-women expedition before in the Alaska Range and LeRoy had climbed Mount Silverthrone in 1976; Liddle and Marvin had never been in the Alaska Range before.

They had wanted to climb a ridge (Highway of Diamonds) on the north side of the mountain, but the rivers had opened and their pilot would not fly them in. They opted for the Southwest Ridge. They were flown in on May 9, 1977. Their trip would be marked by their flexible attitudes and spontaneity in the face of ever-evolving route plans.

Liddle paraded around in a climbing helmet with wings, which had been split in a fall on Mount Rainier. At first, Goforth (who had never met Liddle) and LeRoy were taken aback. When one of their tents was destroyed in a storm, they were crammed into a two-person box tent for the rest of the trip. It was more sauna than tent. Goforth felt that this closeness broke the barriers of communication and brought them together as a team.

A further concession was made when they could not pass the icefall on the upper part of the Yetna Glacier East Fork. They started up another ridge, wondering if they were taking on a bigger commitment than they had bargained for. Optimism and high spirits buoyed them along the route.

By the time they had climbed five thousand feet higher onto the ridge crest, they realized that the knife-edge ahead of them would not go. They dropped down to a basin, with a two-thousand-foot, granite-sided ice couloir, which avoided the knife-edge. This was the crux of the climb. They fixed the rest of their eighteen hundred feet of rope and painfully ferried loads up the fifty- to fifty-five-degree blue ice.

Once on the ridge, they moved together. The North Peak never seemed to get closer and one of the members began talking as if only "you three" would make the top. Like the Archangel team before them, they decreed "all or none" to the top.

On June 15 they traversed beneath the South Peak. Eight hours from their 16,300-foot camp, they marched arm in arm to the summit, after thirty-six days of climbing. It took them ten days to descend and they cleaned off all of their fixed rope.

Although Goforth would participate in successful all-women ascents of Denali and Bhrigupanth in the Garwahl Himalaya, as well as other attempts on big peaks in the Himalaya, Mount Foraker remains her favorite climb, because of its spirit of spontaneity, exploration and adventure.

8056

1	*Talkeetna Ridge*
2	*French Ridge*
3	*Infinite Spur*
4	*Southwest Ridge*
5	*Lacuna Glacier*
6	*Kahiltna Glacier*
7	*Unclimbed*

MOUNT FORAKER

THE SOUTHERN ROUTES

▲

Route Guide

A*pproach:* 6 miles from 6,500-foot Southwest Fork of the Kahiltna landing site to 7,200-foot base.

T*otal Time:* 15-21 days.

C*limbing Miles:* 4.

V*ertical Gain of Route:* 10,200 feet.

A*laska Grade:* 5.

D*ifficulties, Dangers, Rating:* If unstable snow conditions exist, the cornice climbing will be difficult and dangerous; 5.7 rock climbing on 500-foot granite wall.

C*amps:* ca. 8,900; ca. 10,000; 12,200 (dome); 14,000 (granite outcropping).

R*eferences:* 1969, 1987 AAJ. Map: Talkeetna D-3.

Firsts

A*scent:* July 26, 1968; Bertulis, Bleser, Williamson, (Baer).

A*lpine Style:* May 14, 1986; Auble, Townsend.

▲ 1	*Talkeetna Ridge*
2	*Southwest Ridge*
3	*Lacuna Glacier*
4	*Unclimbed*

5119

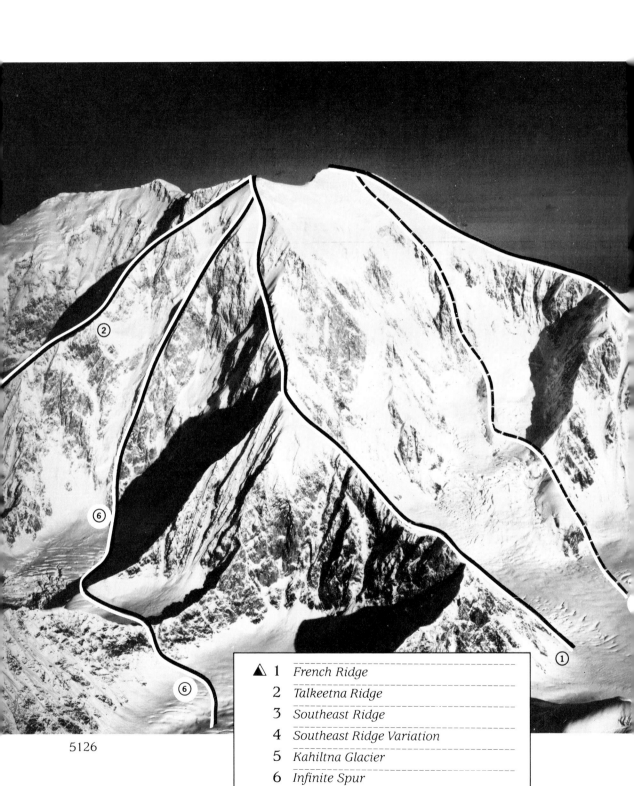

5126

▲ 1 *French Ridge*

2 *Talkeetna Ridge*

3 *Southeast Ridge*

4 *Southeast Ridge Variation*

5 *Kahiltna Glacier*

6 *Infinite Spur*

7 *Unclimbed*

Route Guide

*A*pproach: *1 mile from the 6,400-foot Southwest Fork of the Kahiltna landing strip to the 6,600-foot base.*

*T*otal Time: *15–24 days.*

*C*limbing Miles: *5.*

*V*ertical Gain of Route: *10,800 feet.*

*A*laska Grade: *6.*

*D*ifficulties, Dangers, Rating: *The 1.5 miles of corniced ridge would be very difficult to retreat from; there are near-vertical ice steps and several sections of difficult (5.6) mixed climbing.*

*C*amps: *8,500 (juncture of main ridge); 10,500 (snowdome); 11,300; 15,600.*

*R*eferences: *1977 AAJ; Denali's Wife (expedition account in French), Talkeetna Ranger Station.*

Firsts

*A*scent: *June 3–4, 1976; H. & I. Agresti, Bouquier, Créton, Galmiche, Thivierge, Landry.*

Route Guide

*A*pproach: *6.5 miles west from 6,500-foot Southwest Fork Kahiltna landing strip via 7,200-foot pass, cross crevassed glacier, over difficult 7,700-foot pass; descend and swing north to route.*

*T*otal Time: *13–23 days.*

*C*limbing Miles: *2.*

*V*ertical Gain of Route: *9,000 feet.*

*A*laska Grade: *6.*

*D*ifficulties, Dangers, Rating: *Shattered 5.7 granite and a 5.9 jamcrack pitch on lower third of route; followed by 20 pitches of 50- to 55-degree ice which narrows into the crux: 3 pitches of 85-degree ice with 5.9 rock.*

*C*amps: *7,500 (snow shoulder beneath pass); (rock ledge); (ledge chopped out of ice on rib); (above gully at end of steep climbing, near ridge crest); 15,000 (beneath sérac).*

*R*eferences: *1978 AAJ. Map: Talkeetna D-3.*

Firsts

*A*scent: *July 3, 1977; Kennedy, Lowe.*

*A*lpine Style: *July 3, 1977; Kennedy, Lowe.*

▲ 1	*Infinite Spur*
2	*Lacuna Glacier*
3	*Talkeetna Ridge*
4	*French Ridge*
5	*Unclimbed*

5125

▲ 1 *Southwest Ridge*
  2 *Yetna Glacier*
  3 *The Fin*
  4 *South Peak*

4973

Route Guide

Approach: *4½ miles from 4,300 feet on Yetna Glacier landing area (south of park boundary), to 5,250-foot base.*

Total Time: *21–30 days.*

Climbing Miles: *10½.*

Vertical Gain of Route: *12,200 feet (there is also considerable up and down on ridge).*

Alaska Grade: *4.*

Difficulties, Dangers, Rating: *Ice up to 55 degrees in couloir.*

Camps: *5,250 (base camp); 6,500; 8,100; 9,000; 11,900; 13,000; 16,300.*

References: *1978 AAJ. Map: Talkeetna D-4, D-3.*

Firsts

Ascent: *June 25, 1977; LeRoy, Goforth, Marvin, Liddle.*

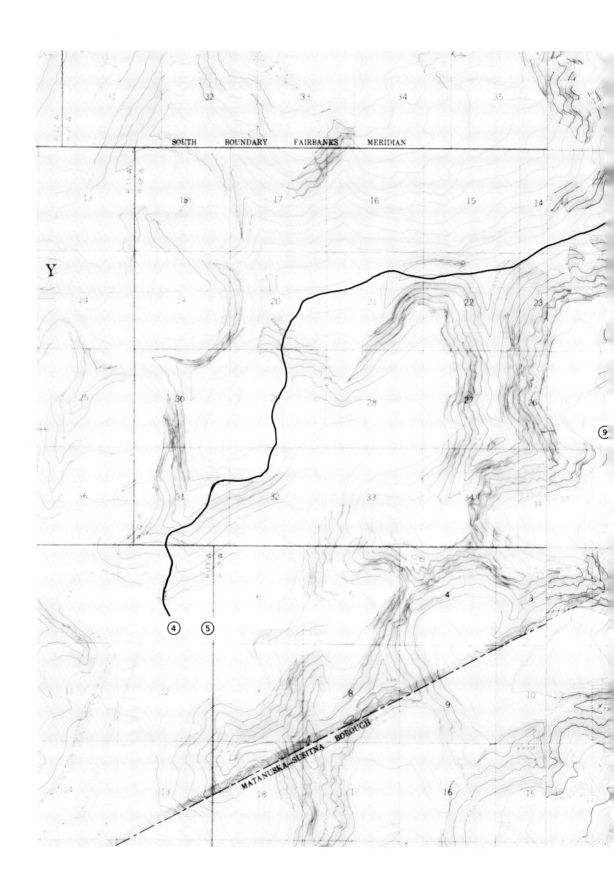

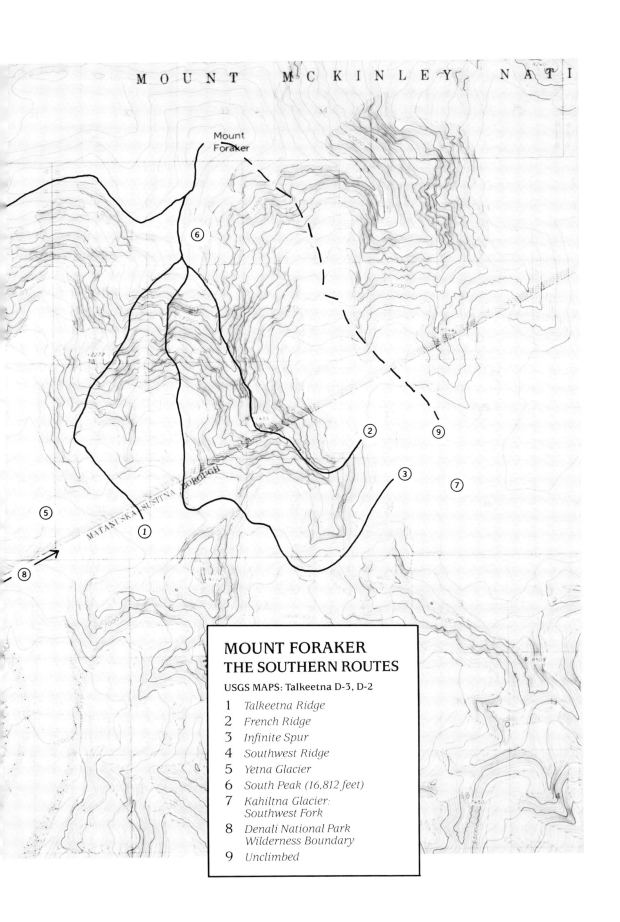

Mount
Foraker

⑥

②

⑨

③

⑦

⑤

①

MATANUSKA–SUSITNA BOROUGH

⑧

MOUNT FORAKER
THE SOUTHERN ROUTES

USGS MAPS: Talkeetna D-3, D-2

1 *Talkeetna Ridge*
2 *French Ridge*
3 *Infinite Spur*
4 *Southwest Ridge*
5 *Yetna Glacier*
6 *South Peak (16,812 feet)*
7 *Kahiltna Glacier:
   Southwest Fork*
8 *Denali National Park
   Wilderness Boundary*
9 *Unclimbed*

PART·3

MOUNT HUNTER

BEGGUYA

PART·3

W HEN SEEN FROM Talkeetna, Mount Hunter appears as a long, broad peak. In reality, it is the steepest and most spectacular of the three great peaks in the Alaska Range and is the most difficult 14,000-foot peak in North America. Hunter's three summits, the North Peak (14,570 feet), the Central Peak (13,450 feet) and the South Peak (13,966 feet), span a three-mile-wide plateau. The mountain is directly south of Denali and stands entirely outside of the Denali National Park wilderness boundaries

The Indian name for the mountain was *Begguya,* which meant "Denali's child." The ever-present prospectors referred to the mountain as Mount Roosevelt. Its present name was awarded in 1903, by Robert Dunn, a reporter for the New York *Commercial Advertiser,* who was with Frederick A. Cook's expedition that attempted to climb Denali via the Northwest Buttress.

As Dunn was leading the way to a high pass, he remarked, "There's the hell of a high mountain over there." He was pointing to the present-day Kahiltna Dome (12,525 feet), which he named after his aunt, Anna Falconett Hunter, of Newport, Rhode Island. Earlier in the expedition, Dunn's aunt had given Frederick A. Cook, the expedition leader, a thousand dollars with the stipulation that Cook's wife leave the party; in an hour she sailed away.

Dunn was not only grateful for this sponsorship, but also very devoted to his aunt. However, it would have been impossible for Dunn to have seen the 14,570-foot peak from his location.

In 1906, a government survey-or mistakenly gave the name to this peak rather than the one Dunn had seen. This error was not discovered until 1950. Dunn was upset. However, Bradford Washburn consoled him by saying that his aunt's name had been bestowed on a more magnificent peak.

Eleven routes have been climbed on Mount Hunter. The West Ridge, lionized in *Fifty Classic Climbs in North America,* is the most popular route, although fewer than half of those who attempt it reach the summit. Most of the other attempts are divided among the easily approached North Buttress, the Kennedy-Lowe route, and the Northeast Ridge. The Southwest Ridge has not been repeated, even though it is the safest, quickest route up the mountain.

It is uncommon for more than six climbers a year to reach the summit of Mount Hunter. Generally, no more than a dozen teams, or fewer than thirty climbers, attempt the mountain per year. Because of the magnetism of Denali's height, this beautiful "little" mountain is overlooked. Solitude is virtually guaranteed on Mount Hunter.

CHAPTER 9

THE NORTHERN ROUTES

West Ridge
East Ridge
Northeast Ridge
Kennedy-Lowe
North Buttress
Diamond Arête–East Face

West Ridge

A CHALLENGING VARIETY OF GRANITE, ICE AND SNOW climbing is offered by this five-mile-long ridge. It is one of the easier routes on the most difficult fourteen-thousand-foot mountain in North America. However, climbers who have started down it, thinking it an easy descent route, are always surprised. The descent is difficult, long, and time consuming.

In *The American Alpine Journal 1953*, Bradford Washburn wrote a painstakingly detailed ten-page proposal. His photographs delineated campsites along the way, and every option, including the approach, was laid bare for a "team of climbers with extended practical experience on both steep ice and rock, as well as a capacity for glacier camping."

Fred Beckey jumped at the opportunity. The first ascent of Mount Hunter by Beckey, Henry Mehbohm and Heinrich Harrer would come at the end of a busy summer which began with Beckey and Meybohm climbing a new route on Denali's Northwest Buttress; Harrer warmed up on the first ascent of Mount Drum. Then the three accidentally met in Fairbanks. They flew in and did one of the most difficult ice climbs and first ascents of the day: Mount Deborah. With hardly a rest, in characteristic fast-paced Beckey style, the three climbers flew to Mount Hunter.

Beckey, who was thirty-one, had already gained experience on climbs of Mount Waddington, Kate's Needle, and the Devil's Thumb. The Austrian, Harrer, was world renowned for his first ascent of the Eiger's North Face in 1936; Meybohm, who had not climbed before that summer, was a German skier living in Fairbanks. "He was strong, a natural snow-and-ice man," said Beckey.

On June 31, 1954, the three men landed on the Kahiltna Glacier, next to the West Ridge. Later that day, they packed light loads and reconnoitered (with help from Washburn's proposal) a route up to the ridge crest. The following day, they made three rappels off a tower and pushed through to a 9,500-foot col. They fixed three ropes up a 500-foot granite wedge before going to sleep.

The next day, above the col, they hauled their packs over cracks and up a Class 5 chimney. Few difficulties were encountered en route to their second camp at 10,600 feet.

As ice climbers, Beckey and Harrer were decades ahead of their time. Although step-chopping was de rigueur in the fifties, it was much faster to climb on the frontpoints of their Stubai crampons. This technique allowed them to climb the entire route, despite fixing three ropes, in five days (faster than most recent repeat ascents). This was the first alpine-style climb of a technical route in the Alaska Range. Beckey said, "If we screwed around ferrying loads like we did on McKinley, the weather would've gotten us." Boldness and vision (which only gained Harrer scorn for his "dangerous" Eiger climb) were vital characteristics of this team.

This was also a landmark climb because few climbers had dealt with such steep ice and extensive cornicing. Beckey concluded his article in *The American Alpine Journal 1955* with a two-page "Word of Caution" which detailed the specific Alaskan issues of night climbing, steep ice, and the objective dangers of cornices.

At 4:30 P.M. on July 4, they set out from their 10,600-foot camp with down jackets and a large lunch, their eyes cast toward the summit. The cornice problems continually scared them. They smashed in ice pitons and chopped bucket-belay seats for thirteen pitches. They frontpointed on hard ice beneath sloppy snow. And their rope froze.

Finally, they arrived at the 13,000-foot ice cliffs that tumbled down from the summit pleateau. A ramp led them through. They postholed for four hours across the plateau and reached the 14,574-foot summit twelve hours after leaving their high camp. In *The American Alpine Journal,* Beckey wrote:

> Hunter had been climbed! It would be difficult to imagine a more beautiful view than that afforded by the summit .... We agreed that the entire region was one with a great mountaineering future, for there are dozens of very intriguing high summits within its scope.

It took them another seven hours of careful downclimbing and rappelling to reach their high camp. They set off several avalanches to clear their route to base camp. In typical adventurous style, they walked out the Kahiltna Glacier, where no one had ever walked before.

Of the three, only Beckey would come back to the Alaska Range. He would pull maps and photographs from his briefcase, making sure no one else was looking, and show potential partners his secret climbs. There was Avalanche Spire, the Tusk, Hayes, Hesperus, Huntington, Dickey, and the Moose's Tooth. Yet, he would never again find the magical combination of good weather and the synergetic vision of his partner Harrer.

On the West Ridge ▲

Mount Hunter as seen from the West Buttress on Denali ▲

Southern Couloir Variation

In 1963, Dave Johnston, Tom Choate, Cliff Ells, and Vin Hoeman did the first north-to-west traverse of Denali, winding up beneath Hunter's West Ridge. Ells flew out. Their original plan had been to climb Mount Foraker, too, but they opted for Mount Hunter first, because a second ascent was more appealing to Hoeman than a third.

Hoeman was busy writing a guidebook about Alaskan mountains. He was famous for keeping climbers' significant ascents on note cards. Most climbers occupied one card; Fred Beckey, Dave Roberts, Dave Johnston, or Art Davidson would take two cards; Hoeman would fill three.

They climbed a variation of the 1954 route, taking a short cut up a couloir to the 9,200-foot col where Beckey first camped. After a near miss, when a cornice collapsed under Hoeman, they continued step-chopping up to the summit plateau.

Johnston, Coate and Hoeman walked the long miles across the plateau and bagged the untrodden Central Peak (13,470 feet) and the South Peak (13,970 feet), before climbing the higher North Peak.

By the time they got back down, time was running out; they turned their backs on Mount Foraker and walked out the Kahiltna.

Johnston would complete Denali's first winter ascent in 1967 and Mount Foraker's Sultana Ridge in the winter of 1979. Hoeman, who would methodically stockpile more obscure Alaskan first ascents than any other climber, was killed in the avalanche on Dhaulagiri in 1969.

Northwest Basin

In April 1978, Jeff Babcock, Gunnar Naslund and Jack Duggan climbed up the northwest-facing snow basin, which joins Beckey's route at 10,200 feet. They reached the summit plateau and retreated when they were hit by a storm. This popular variation avoids the 500-foot granite tower of the original route.

East Ridge

MOUNT HUNTER'S EAST RIDGE DESCENDS TO THE 10,500-foot level, then climbs up and down to Points 11,520 and 11,530, pointing like a crooked finger toward Mount Huntington. It is the longest ridge on the mountain.

The entire northern facade of the ridge is rimmed with hanging glaciers, a formidable and questionable obstacle for climbers shortcutting the ridge. It might be possible to start more safely on the lower part of the ridge, which has never been done, but the long, level sections, and the ups and downs would be time consuming.

In *The American Alpine Journal 1967,* Donald N. Anderson wrote of his and Jeff Duenwald's search for an easier route than the West Ridge. They decided on the East Ridge, for careful inspection showed them that the initial part of the long, tortured ridge could be avoided. Only eighteen hundred vertical feet of steep ice separated the glacier from a straightforward path to the summit. However, the approach and the first several hundred feet of the route above the bergschrund is an obvious avalanche funnel, a shooting gallery for the hanging glacier above. Their strategy was to climb over the bergschrund and then quickly traverse left to a prominent and protected snow rib.

Anderson had seen this route in 1961, while descending the West Buttress and making the first ascents of East Kahiltna Peak and Mount Crosson. Duenwald had spent a lot of time gazing wistfully at Mount Hunter during his successful new route on Mount Foraker in 1963. They invited a third climber, Donald W. Anderson (no relation).

In early June of 1966, they were flown to 8,500 feet on the Tokositna Glacier, miles above the start of the ridge. They moved to 8,800 feet and began fixing their 1,700 feet of rope.

Two days later, Duenwald, plagued with asthma attacks, flew out. Morale dropped. Avalanches thundered down their route. Nonetheless, they pushed higher.

They established their first camp out of the fall line of various hanging glaciers, on the protected snow rib. After fixing all of their rope, they came down to the glacier and waited for safer conditions. It snowed. Avalanches poured down the funnel of

their route. At nightfall on June 19, they reclimbed their ropes. Near the top, they watched an ice avalanche sweep the bottom of the route. They had been lucky. They crested the ridge and set up camp at 11,100 feet.

Just before 9 P.M., on June 20, they set off for the summit. They postholed, but there were no other difficulties until they reached the ice of the final slope. Donald N. Anderson wrote,

> I felt the slope break beneath my feet. Throwing myself into a double somersault, I nearly cleared the path of the avalanche. However, my momentum gave out and I found myself riding amid the ice-blocks toward a cliff. Then a reassuring tug let the blocks rush on to their destruction while I looked back at Don W. who had managed to step free and stop me with a perfect hip belay.

They started up again, straight up, and, at four in the morning, they made the fourth ascent of Mount Hunter. The summit was festooned with Japanese flags from the third ascent of the West Ridge the previous day.

That night, they descended all the way to the glacier, cleaning their ropes behind them. Donald N. had a close call on the last rappel, getting stuck on a knot and nearly choking. After a few minutes, the knot released and he fell twenty-five feet into the bergschrund.

Immediately after the expedition, Donald N. Anderson joined H. Adams Carter, Bob Bates and Eric Shipton for an ill-fated attempt on Mount Russell. And in 1968, the Andersons teamed up with Duenwald again, for an attempt up another objectively dangerous route: Denali's convoluted, icefall-laden Traleika Spur.

Twenty years later, Donald N. Anderson thought that their route on Mount Hunter should only be repeated alpine style, to minimize the exposure to avalanches. His primary recollection was of continually being hit by avalanches. For him, a new route on Mount Hunter was worth a dash underneath a hanging glacier, but he conceded, "We were obviously playing the odds."

Japanese Variation

In 1975, a Japanese team added a variation to the route because, according to its prospectus, the members thought the East Ridge had not been traced completely and successfully. This may be due to the fact that Donald N. Anderson's article in *The American Alpine Journal* was entitled "Mount Hunter from the Northeast." Following the lead of another Japanese party in 1974, they started one mile down the glacier from the Andersons. On June 1, they climbed up to the 10,700-foot col, placing their camp directly beneath a cornice. The cornice collapsed the next day, burying their camp and nearly killing one member of the team.

They continued fixing ropes along a knife-edge, placing two more camps before they joined the section of ridge that the Andersons had climbed. After bivouacking in a snow cave at 13,900 feet, they all reached the summit on June 11, 1975.

Northeast Ridge

ACCESS TO THE NORTHEAST RIDGE, WHICH JOINS HUMBLE Peak (or Kahiltna Queen, 12,380 feet), is from either the Tokositna Glacier (not recommended) or the Southeast Fork of the Kahiltna Glacier. The low point of the ridge is a 9,950-foot col. Above here, the ridge is very knife-edged and most parties have dropped down to the Tokositna Glacier and climbed the snow face (hanging glacier exposure) to regain the ridge. At two different levels, the ridge merges into a low-angled face, dotted with small séracs and hair-trigger avalanche slopes. In addition to witnessing hanging-glacier releases, many parties have set off slab fractures on this route.

On May 15, 1971, K. Takahashi, N. Sasada, S. Kosaka, K. A. Suzuki, and Hirokazu Hamada were flown to the Southeast Fork of the Kahiltna Glacier. (C. Suzuki, who later climbed Kahiltna Dome, was also flown in.) From the landing strip, they moved two miles up the glacier and set up camp at 8,200 feet.

From May 21 to 24, they fixed ropes from 8,600 feet to the 9,950-foot col, climbing back and forth under the fall line of a small sérac. They found sustained ice climbing at fifty to sixty degrees. This was the crux of the route.

They camped on the col. Continuing to fix ropes, they climbed the snow face, then 1,000 feet of knife-edge ridge. They bivouacked for several nights at 12,500 feet. On June 4, they tunneled through a cornice onto the 13,900-foot plateau, reached the summit and returned to their high camp after twenty-four hours.

Tokositna Variation

In June 1977, another Japanese team added a variation to this route, approaching it from the Tokositna Glacier. An American team, which had arrived just ahead of the Japanese, fixed ropes most of the way up the lower part of the climb. (I have camped on the 9,950-foot col and seen a hanging glacier avalanche onto the Tokositna Glacier approach. This variation is not recommended.)

I. Inui, H. Kamuro, K. Tsutagawa, H. Kudo, M. Tanaka, and S. Mori landed on the Tokositna on June 14, 1977. Using the Americans' (Glenn Milner, Guy Toombes and Dick Olmstead) ropes, the Japanese scurried in and out of the fire of the hanging glacier; on June 19, they established a camp at 11,500 feet, near the ridge crest. They fixed ropes all the way to the plateau and reached the summit in bad weather, ahead of the Americans, on June 23.

The Northeast Ridge can only be recommended as a fast, alpine-style climb, to minimize exposure to avalanche hazards. *If* snow conditions are good, this may be the quickest descent from the north side of Mount Hunter; it is somewhat preferable to descendilng the long West Ridge. John Mallon Waterman descended it solo in 1978 during his incredible Mount Hunter traverse. When Jack Tackle and Jim Donini descended the upper part of the route in 1986, they set off multiple avalanches.

Mount Hunter from the northeast ▼

▲

Kennedy-Lowe

MANY ICE CLIMBERS DREAM OF A ROUTE LIKE THE Kennedy-Lowe up the Northwest Face of Mount Hunter. Five thousand feet of moderate-to-steep snow and ice climbing lead to the thirteen-thousand-foot plateau. The route starts with a moderate snow spur, connecting to the steepening Triangle Face, which culminates in one of the wildest sections of corniced ridges in the Alaska Range. The exit is found through an ice cliff onto the plateau.

For quick, alpine-style ascents, this route is relatively safe and also has the quickest access of any route in the range. It has become one of the most talked-about, yet seldom-repeated routes on Mount Hunter. Poor snow conditions turn many of the attempts away.

The route was given serious attention by an Eastern party in the snowstorm-ridden May of 1971. Guy Waterman, one of the strongest climbers of that five-man team, commented, "If I had been the weakest member, we might have had a chance with it." An avalanche swept across their approach route and ended their attempt.

In June 1977, a star-studded trio was flown onto the Kahiltna Glacier. Jeff Lowe was single-handedly responsible for more steep and difficult ice routes than anyone else in North America. George Lowe, his cousin, had made impressive first ascents in the Canadian Rockies, had climbed Alaska's Devil's Thumb, and made impressive winter ascents in the Tetons. Mike Kennedy had done difficult first ascents in Colorado and, in 1975, had retreated from the East Face of the Moose's Tooth after nearly being wiped out by rockfall.

This powerful team embraced the freedom of moving fast and light, shunning the traditional umbilical cord of expedition-style tactics. Questions about the advisability of climbing alpine style—without a radio, should a rescue be needed—were answered by the events of this climb and the unflappable, capable manner in which Kennedy and the Lowes reacted.

At midnight on June 14, they started climbing, moving together over crevasses, then belaying past a sérac. They reached the bottom of the triangle face at 6 A.M. and stopped to eat.

They began belaying up the steeper ice on the face. The solstitial sun burned out of the sky, making them hot, causing dehydration, and rendering the snow wet and unstable. They tried climbing the ridge to the right of the face, three pitches from the triangle's apex, but eventually, they continued on the easier face.

Kennedy led the last pitch of the triangle face to the apex. He wrote in *The American Alpine Journal 1978* that

> ...there was nothing. No decent anchors, no place to sit, let alone set up the tent, and after almost 18 hours of climbing, no energy left to think straight. But the worst has yet to come: the ridge ahead looked impossible, or at best, suicidal. It was not just steep and corniced, but *horribly* steep and corniced. Huge snow mushrooms sat on top of a knife-edge of ice, in places overhanging on both sides. In no condition to make any rational judgment, we left the anchors at the last stance, wrapped the rope around a lump of snow at the apex for additional security and chopped a small ledge for a bivouac.

After waiting for cold midnight conditions to set in, Jeff started across, followed by Kennedy, one rope length behind. Suddenly, America's premier ice climber fell, dragging Kennedy along the ridge. When Jeff stopped, nearly sixty feet later, his ankle was shattered.

Everyone caught his breath. The rope stretched taut from Jeff, dangling above distant ice cliffs, to Kennedy, straddling the knife-edge, to George, holding a tight belay. Jeff was able to hobble back to the belay, where they evaluated their position. They couldn't go up. So they started down the triangle.

Nine years later, Kennedy wrote:

> I remember telling George that I thought he should go first and set up the rappels, since he was so much more experienced. He told me later that this surprised him (I suppose I appeared competent).... .
>
> George went down, set up anchors, then Jeff, then I'd take out all but one anchor and come down last. Once off the triangle, the ground was lower-angled, and I'd generally lower Jeff off various combinations of ice axes, deadmen and body parts buried in the snow.

Jeff flew out and a day of storm confined Kennedy and Lowe to the tent. Depression set in and all signs seemed to point toward safety and home. But they had been given the ultimate test of alpine-style climbing and passed it with flying colors. Their mode of self-sufficient climbing would become the standard to which many Alaska Range climbers would aspire.

Their smooth handling of the accident had given them confi-

*George Lowe at the end of the
awesome mushroom ridge* ▲

dence and brought them close together. They were a well-organized, efficient climbing team. Their minds were set.

On June 20, Kennedy and George Lowe climbed a direct line to the apex, avoiding the ridge on the right, in thirteen hours. The corniced section still looked evil and they felt more afraid than before.

At 2 A.M., George led until he found a good stance with anchors. The ridge couldn't be climbed on its crest, so Kennedy rappelled down its east side and traversed rock-hard ice, barely maintaining contact. Just as he ran out of rope, the difficulties eased. Getting through the ice cliff was a stroll by comparison. They bivouacked on the plateau, a thousand feet from the summit. At three o'clock on the afternoon of June 22, they reached the top.

The epic descent began. They followed the West Ridge in a whiteout, using Lowe's careful compass bearings. Kennedy took his first-ever crevasse fall. Lowe fell twenty feet when a cornice collapsed. Finally, they reached base camp on July 24. But their trip was far from over—two days later they would be on the stunning South Buttress of Mount Foraker.

First Winter Ascent

In the winter of 1980, Alaska residents Gary Bocarde, Paul Denkewalter and Vern Tejas arrived at the base of the route. They had all climbed Denali. Bocarde had done a difficult wall on the Moose's Tooth. Bocarde and Denkewalter had climbed in the Kichatnas and done winter climbs on the Ruth. Tejas had done the second ascent of Mount Mather and would later ski the 350-mile length of the Bagley Icefield.

The domain of dark winter climbs was fast becoming an Alaskan specialty. Witness Johnston, Genet and Davidson on Denali; or the Tandy brothers, then Johnston, Okonek and Cowles on Mount Foraker. Many would agree that Alaskans have psychological advantages over lower-forty-eight climbers—after all, Alaska is their backyard, they are used to the darkness and cold, and the trip is cheaper and quicker.

Bocarde led, Denkewalter cleaned, and Tejas jumared. Denkewalter left their ice screws in every rope length for a quick descent. They all wore plastic ski-mountaineering boots. Tejas wore two pairs of overboots.

They dug a snow cave below the triangle. Their second bivouac, where they shivered all night with their boots on, was most of the way up the triangle. And their third bivouac was beneath a cornice at the apex.

The bivouacking reminded Bocarde of his wall climbs in Yosemite Valley. He felt that the triangle had some technically difficult pitches, but the final mushroom ridge was the crux; it looked impassable, insane. They climbed sugar snow on top of ice, burning it up behind them, rushing to beat a storm.

They reached the summit on a cold, windy day, a bit below zero. The weather had been relatively warm, seldom colder than −15°F., yet they kept looking over their shoulders, wary of a storm.

They descended the route in two days. Bocarde, their ever-confident leader, conceded that he'd never been so happy to get off a climb. Denkewalter, who suffered minor frostbite on his toes, admitted that the weather had really worried him. And Tejas, the quintessential modern-day adventurer, confessed that he had made out a will before the climb.

The animated Tejas became the first person to climb the Cassin with floppy bunny boots. And he did a new route on Mount Deborah. In 1982, Bocarde guided the second ascent of Denali's Northwest Buttress. His experience as a wall climber gave him the experience to do technical routes in the Alaska Range under trying conditions.

▲

North Buttress

A SWEEPING PROW OF GRANITE, THE NORTH BUTTRESS invites comparison with The Nose of El Capitan. It rears up at 8,400 feet, ending in the final rock headwall at 12,000 feet, then merges into the Northeast Ridge. Despite its granitic appearance, the wall is climbed primarily by ice runnels. This route offers the steepest, most sustained climbing on the entire mountain and is, undoubtedly, the hardest ice climb yet completed within the Alaska Range. Prior to the first ascent in 1981, there had been no less than fifteen attempts.

The early attempts often concentrated on the prominent North Buttress Couloir to the east of the prow. Yet huge spindrift avalanches, broken and dropped ice tools, and unrelenting verticality daunted all potential takers.

The 1980 Denali National Park Mountaineering Summary mistakenly reported a moderately-angled snow-and-ice climb (skirting to the west of the North Buttress, beneath the release zone of three consecutively tiered hanging glaciers) as the first ascent of the North Buttress. The climb cannot be recommended under any circumstances. From July 1 to 7, 1980, Ulf Björnberg and Billy Ireland completed the route. As these two climbers were new to the Alaska Range, it is likely that they had not developed a sense for the considerable objective dangers of their route.

In late April 1981, after their successful ascent of the long-sought-after East Face of the Moose's Tooth, Mugs Stump and Jim Bridwell joined the list of climbers attempting the buttress. However, it was a raw April and they flew out. Stump had cracked the Emperor Face on Mount Robson, had a penchant for difficult aid routes in Yosemite Valley, and had flashed the Super Couloir on Fitz Roy. Although climbers are often judged by their successes, Stump's qualifications for Mount Hunter's North Buttress may also be judged by his alpine-style attempt of Mount Logan's prolonged Hummingbird Ridge.

In 1980, Pat and Dan McNerthney, Doug Klewin and Rob Newsome, the self-proclaimed "White Punks on Dope," had been stormed off the route. They had alternated a festive lawnchair-and-stereo lifestyle on the glacier with twelve pitches of climbing. They returned in 1981, with Portaledges; dressed in all black, they renamed themselves "Back in Black" and set to work on the route.

Meanwhile, Stump had recruited a New Zealander, Paul Aubrey, who was eager to climb a good route after failing on Denali's South Face. They started up to the west of Newsome's line, carrying spartan rations, in marked contrast to the Back in Black team, partying up the route, until one of their Portaledges broke and they came down.

After two pitches, Aubrey gave the lead to Stump, conceding that the climb would go much faster. After jumaring up some of the more intimidating pitches, Aubrey would fuel Stump's confidence by telling him, "Mugs, you're Superman."

As the Back in Black crew watched through a telescope, lounging in lawn chairs at the landing strip, Stump joined their line. Newsome observed their progress for four days, commenting, "It's like having your girlfriend stolen from you." They turned up the volume on their stereo and ordered more beer flown in.

Stump spent the nights in a hammock, while Aubrey laboriously chopped ledges on patches of ice. From memory, Stump carefully linked together ice ribbons with pendulums and key traverses, occasionally climbing rock. The crux of the climb was the Shaft, a four-hundred-foot vertical column of ice, which he alternately aided and rock-climbed to its side. Stump wrote:

> As I moved up the arc, I immediately felt my centre of gravity move away from the ice and I was not only pulling up but in with my whole body to keep my front points in contact. I made a few moves like this and realized the ludicrousness of trying to free climb like this way out here.... Never had concentration made so much noise in my head. I was a simple shell of forces and movement. When above the start of the crack to my left I determinedly put in a screw and swung over to it. My body relaxed as I moved upward in my etriers. Above the bulge I swung back onto the seventy-five-degree ice and ran it out. My excitement was explosive as I screamed to release the fullness; I felt I belonged here.

A combination of aid, mixed climbing and ice brought them to the last ice band and their fourth bivouac beneath the final headwall. On their fifth morning they followed iced-over ledges to the last obstacle. Stump fell on some mixed ground, regained his position, then got into the final jam crack.

> With hands and feet stacked in the narrow ice I gazed up to its end, and the top. No place to stop, there was no need to stop. Freedom was my catalyst as I deliberately and methodically made each placement. As I pulled over the top and onto the summit slope I

was envisioning a crack such as this running for days. Where could I find it? I didn't want the feeling to stop.

Stump had no interest in climbing two thousand feet of avalanche terrain to the summit. They had virtually no food left either. When Aubrey joined him, they agreed to rappel the route.

Unlike many other routes on Mount Hunter, the buttress continued to attract other climbers, even after Stump and Aubrey's ascent. This was partly because the second ascent party considered Stump's climb incomplete without the summit. The third and fourth ascents would demonstrate that the North Buttress was a safe, desirable ice-climbing classic and a grand test piece of the Alaska Range.

In 1983, Doug Klewin and Todd Bibler arrived to put the route to rest. Bibler's short account was buried in the back pages of *The American Alpine Journal,* while Stump's was a full-length narrative in the previous year's journal, and a cover story in *Mountain* magazine. It is one of the ironies of climbing that Bibler and Klewin, accomplished, dedicated hard men, received little recognition for finishing Stump's climb, which had been conceived by Klewin and the Back in Black gang to begin with.

The unsung Bibler had climbed the Cassin and Foraker's Southeast Ridge; with Klewin and Pat McNerthney, he had reached the top of the North Buttress' couloir in 1979. After that attempt, Klewin and McNerthney flashed the Kennedy–Lowe route as a consolation prize.

Bibler wrote of the climb:

> We began to the left of Mug Stump's start, climbing eight pitches up to the base of the Prow. We continued to the base of the Shaft for 17 pitches on the first day. Bad weather trapped us there for a day. Then we climbed the Shaft, freeing sections of overhanging ice. This was the only day of the climb when it did not snow. In bad weather we climbed the next rock band and pitched our tent somewhat below Stump's high point, which we think was somewhat lower than he indicated, and little to the right. For the next four days we sat in our tent threatened by constant avalanches and high winds. Once we tried to climb out of the situation but after four pitches we found the spindrift so heavy that I could neither see nor hear Doug only inches away at the belay. We were forced back to our bivouac site after getting to within 40 feet of the top of the last rock band. When the weather cleared, we went for the top. The clearing was brief and soon we were in a storm again, waiting to see which way to go. We bivouacked again before getting to the summit on June 3 and again on the descent of the west ridge. It snowed so much during the eleven days that we lost our well-wanded cache of $2000 worth of equipment at the base of the climb.

Bibler would go on to reach the summit of Cholatse by its impressive North Face, then climb high on Everest and K2.

In May 1984, Newsome and Pat McNerthney, who had renamed themselves "Up the Butt," arrived at the base of the buttress. Based on Bibler's advice, they made a twelve-foot cache marker and finished the line they had started four and five years earlier. This was the second complete ascent and McNerthney brilliantly free-climbed the entire Shaft. The skeletons in Newsome and McNerthney's closets were finally buried.

North Buttress Couloir Variation

On June 24, 1984, after climbing Denali's West Rib and the Rooster Comb's North Face, French climbers Yves Tedeschi and Benoit Grison started up the North Buttress Couloir. They sped up the couloir in a day and bivouacked at its top at 10,500 feet.

On June 26, they traversed up and right toward the center of the face on thin and brittle ice. On their third day of climbing, after difficult mixed pitches, they bivouacked on top of the Northeast Ridge. They reached the summit on June 27, in an incredibly fast four-day ascent. They descended the West Ridge in two days under dangerous storm conditions.

Mugs Stump at the base of the North Buttress ▶

▲

The Diamond Arête—East Face

THE ROUTE WAS NAMED FOR ITS RESEMBLANCE TO THE Diamond on Longs Peak. The first two thousand feet are a steep rock wall and buttress, which merge into an ice ridge at about ten thousand feet, then settle back, near thirteen thousand feet, onto the easier-angled North Summit slope.

While Jack Tackle was on his third attempt of Denali's Isis Face in 1982, his eyes drifted southward and discovered Mount Hunter's East Face. It would be three years before he returned to climb it with Jim Donini, who had never climbed in Alaska, although he had done difficult routes on other big mountains.

On June 11, 1985, Tackle and Donini were flown into the middle of the three eastern branches of Tokositna Glacier. No one had ever been there. That afternoon, they climbed five steep mixed pitches, with the leader hauling his pack and the second jumaring. In *The American Alpine Journal 1986*, Tackle wrote:

> As I pulled vigorously on the sack through my single pulley, I suddenly found myself airborne, scarping down the rock from my stance. The anchors had pulled and I had dropped twenty feet into a chimney. Bewildered, I looked up to see that both of the Friends I had placed had come out. Flaring cracks in the frozen rock had loosened under the pressure of hauling. Fortunately, Jim had yet to start, and I promised him to be a good boy and never do that again.

By the third day, although a snowstorm was unleashing avalanches onto their site every half hour, they managed to fix two pitches. When the thin ice he was climbing collapsed, Tackle fell and slid off the rock, but a shaky Friend stopped him.

The crux came on the fourth day, up a vertical ice-filled chimney and wall. Above this, they climbed many pitches of fifty- to sixty-degree snow-covered ice.

That night, as Tackle was chopping a tent platform, Donini untied himself from the second rope, thinking that Tackle was still tied in—the rope slithered down into the abyss. Donini was shocked. It was a crucial hauling and rappelling rope. He climbed over to his partner, put his hand on his shoulder and broke the bad news, "There's something I have to tell you, Java Man. I dropped the rope."

Mount Hunter as seen during the first ascent of Peak 12380 ▶

Illustrative of climbers who look on the bright side, Tackle replied, "I guess we're going to get *up* this route, because we sure as hell can't go *down*."

The next day, after passing through the ice cliffs, they stopped belaying and dug their first level site. They had climbed thirty-eight difficult pitches. But Hunter was not through with them yet.

The next day was bitter cold as they took turns breaking trail to fourteen thousand feet. Tackle spent his sixth night shivering, curled over a hot-water bottle inside of his useless, wafer-thin down bag. Donini slept soundly in the synthetic bag.

On the seventh day, hurricane winds prevented them from climbing the last several hundred feet to the summit, so they started down the Northeast Ridge. Because of wind-loading, they had close calls with two avalanches before they stopped and dug a cave.

Eventually, they made their way down to 11,500 feet on the knife-edge ridge, but could not proceed to the 9,950-foot col because of the steep snow. In desperation, they started rappelling with a single rope down toward the Kahiltna. After twenty rappels, they came to the edge of a hanging glacier and traversed off a deep snowfield, just in time to watch the entire snowfield avalanche.

Tackle took a hit in the head with a piece of falling ice, which slurred his speech and numbed his arms. But they had to get down, for everything was falling off, avalanching. They threw the last rappel rope down single and it barely cleared the bergschrund; they cut off the remaining rope to insure safe passage down the glacier. They had used every bit of hardware rappelling.

Ten weary days after they had started, they staggered toward the landing strip, breaking through the crust. Bleary-eyed and nursing his concussion, yet somehow inspired, Tackle responded to Mount Foraker looming ahead, just as his eyes had drifted over Hunter's East Face from Denali.

Like the first traverse on Denali's South Buttress in 1954, Tackle and Donini's commitment represents the ultimate alpine-style challenge in the Alaska Range: relying only upon themselves, fired by optimism, they had climbed up and over untrodden territory and down the other side of the mountain.

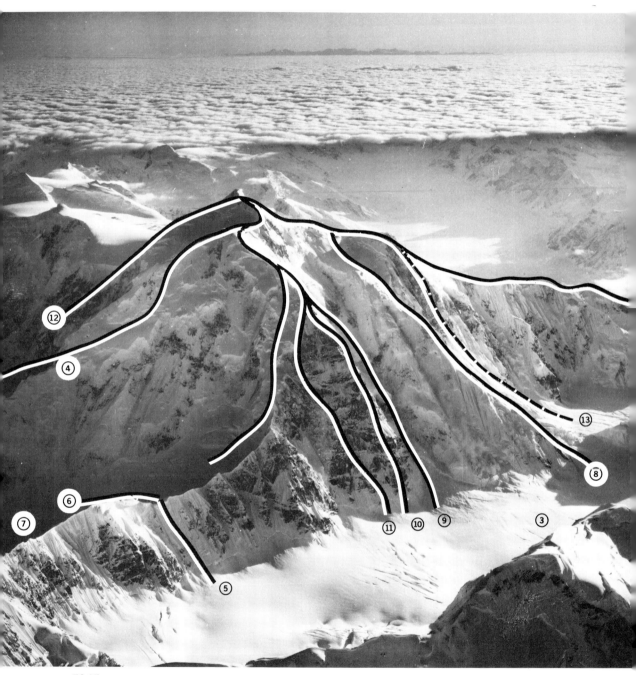

5045

MOUNT HUNTER

THE NORTHERN ROUTES

1   *West Ridge*

2   *Kahiltna Glacier*

3   *Kahiltna Glacier, Southeast Fork*

4   *East Ridge*

5   *Northeast Ridge*

6   *Northeast Ridge, Tokositna Start*

7   *Tokositna Glacier*

8   *Kennedy–Lowe*

9   *North Face*

10   *North Buttress*

11   *North Buttress Couloir*

12   *Diamond Arête*

13   *Unclimbed*

▲ 1 *West Ridge*
   2 *Northwest Basin Variation 1978*
   3 *Kahiltna Glacier*

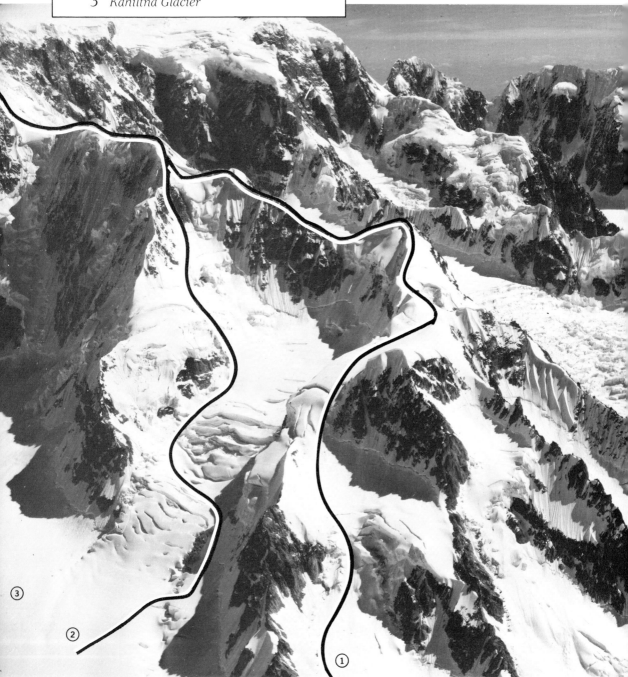

5841

Route Guide

Approach: *0.5 mile from the 6,500-foot Kahiltna Glacier.*

Total Time: *7-14 days.*

Climbing Miles: *5.*

Vertical Gain of Route: *8,000 feet.*

Alaska Grade: *3+.*

Difficulties, Dangers, Rating: *Extensive cornicing and ice climbing up to 70 degrees; 1954 and 1963 routes involve low Class 5 climbing on 500-foot granite tower.*

Camps: *9,200 (col); 10,600; 11,300.*

References: *1955, 1964 AAJ; Fifty Classic Climbs in North America, Steck and Roper; Climbing in North America, Jones. Maps: Talkeetna D-2, D-3.*

Firsts

Ascent: *July 5, 1954; Beckey, Harrer, Meybohm.*

Alpine Style: *July 5, 1954; Beckey, Harrer, Meybohm.*

Variations: *Southern Couloir, South Peak, 13,470; Central Peak, 13,970; and North Peak: July 30, 1963; Choate, Hoeman, Johnston. Northwest basin to summit plateau: April 1978; Babcock, Naslund, Duggan.*

5844

▲ 1 *West Ridge*
2 *Northwest Basin Variation 1978*

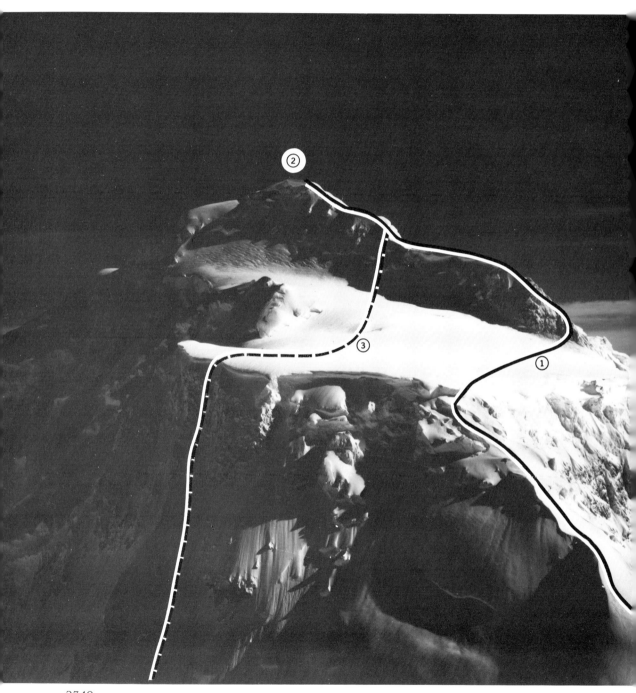

2348

▲ 1 *West Ridge*

2 *North Peak*

3 *Unclimbed*

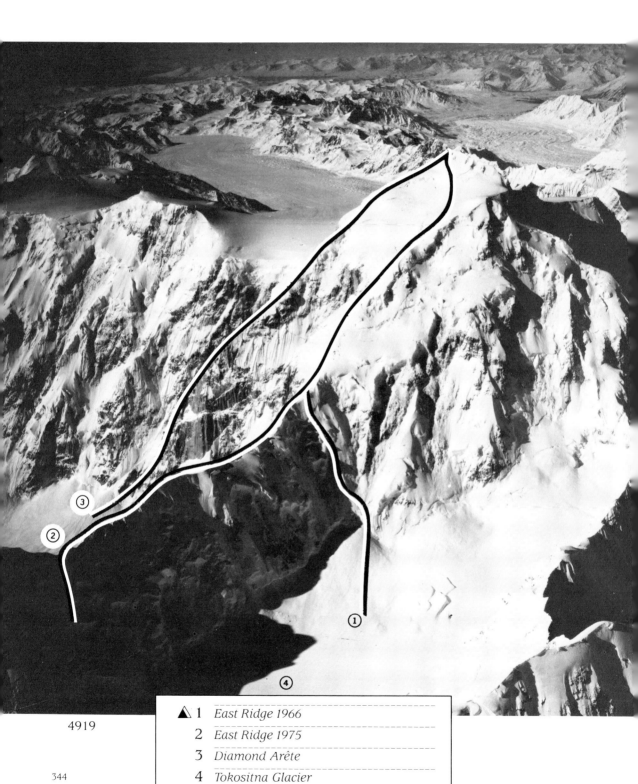

4919

▲ 1	*East Ridge 1966*	
2	*East Ridge 1975*	
3	*Diamond Arête*	
4	*Tokositna Glacier*	

344

Route Guide

A*pproach:* 2 miles from the 8,000-foot landing area on the North Fork of the Tokositna Glacier.

T*otal Time:* 7-21 days.

C*limbing Miles:* 2.5.

V*ertical Gain of Route:* 4,600 feet.

A*laska Grade:* 3.

D*ifficulties, Dangers, Rating:* Ice climbing up to 60 degrees. Initial section from glacier to ridge has dangerous hanging glaciers and is very prone to soft-snow avalanches after snow storms.

C*amps:* ca. 9,000 (snow rib to left of ice cliffs); 11,100 (broad ridge); 13,900 (small plateau).

R*eferences:* 1967, 1972 AAJ. Maps: Talkeetna D-2, D-3.

Firsts

A*scent:* June 21 1966; D.W. Anderson, D.N. Anderson, (Duenwald).

V*ariation:* Via 10,700-foot col: June 11, 1975; Shiro, Yamashita, Sekizuka, Nakai, (Jo).

▲1 *Northeast Ridge 1971* ----------------------

4919   2 *Northeast Ridge 1977* ----------------------

               3 *Kahiltna Glacier, Southeast Fork* ----------------------

          4 *Tokositna Glacier*

Route Guide

*A*pproach: *3 miles from the 7,200-foot Southeast Fork of the Kahiltna landing strip to the 8,600-foot base of the ridge.*

*T*otal Time: *7-14 days.*

*C*limbing Miles: *2.*

*V*ertical Gain of Route: *6,100 feet.*

*A*laska Grade: *3+.*

*D*ifficulties, Dangers, Rating: *Exposure to hanging glaciers and slab avalanche conditions after snowfall or wind; crux is sustained 50- to 60-degree ice climbing from 8,600 feet to 9,950 col.*

*C*amps: *9,950 (col); 11,500; 12,500.*

*R*eferences: *1972, 1979 (photo) AAJ. Map: Talkeetna D-3.*

Firsts

*A*scent: *June 4, 1971; Takahashi, Sasada, Kosaka, Suzuki, Hamada, (C. Suzuki).*

*S*olo: *Descent only: July 26, 1978; J.M. Waterman.*

*V*ariation: *Tokositna approach: June 23, 1977; Inui, Kamuro, Tsutagawa, Kudo, Tanaka, Mori.*

5859

▲ 1	Kennedy–Lowe
2	Unclimbed

Route Guide

Approach: 1.5 miles from 7,200-foot Southeast Fork of Kahiltna landing strip to 7,800-foot base.

Total Time: 5-10 days.

Climbing Miles: 1.75.

Vertical Gain of Route: 6,700 feet.

Alaska Grade: 4.

Difficulties, Dangers, Rating: There is 1.5 hours of exposure to a hanging glacier on the approach; the triangle face is 80 degrees near the apex; the crux is several pitches of steep, exposed ice mushrooms and the lower-angled slopes above the ice cliff are exposed to avalanches.

Camps: 10,200 (beneath triangle face); 11,300 (apex), 13,000 (plateau).

References: 1978, 1981 AAJ.

Firsts

Ascent: June 24, 1977; Kennedy, G. Lowe, (J. Lowe).

Alpine Style: June 24, 1977; Kennedy, G. Lowe, (J. Lowe).

Winter: March 4, 1980; Bocarde, Denkewalter, Tejas.

5859

▲ 1	*North Buttress*	
2	*North Buttress Couloir*	

 # *Route Guide*

A*pproach:* 2 miles from the 7,200-foot Southeast Fork of the Kahiltna landing strip to the 8,400-foot base.

T*otal Time:* 7-16 days.

C*limbing Miles:* 1.5.

V*ertical Gain of Route:* 6,100 feet.

A*laska Grade:* 6.

D*ifficulties, Dangers, Rating:* A-3, 5.9 mixed rock climbing; vertical and overhanging ice is found on the crux (400-foot "shaft"); spindrift avalanches and dangerous exit up avalanche-prone summit slopes.

C*amps:* Hanging bivouacs or small chopped-out ledges until 12,000 feet.

R*eferences:* 1982, 1984, 1985 AAJ; May-June 1982 Mountain; June 1986 Climbing; Route Topo, Talkeetna Ranger Station.

 # *Firsts*

A*scent:* To 12,000 feet: May 1981; Stump, Aubrey. June 3, 1983; Bibler, Klewin.

A*lpine Style:* To 12,000 feet: May 1981; Stump, Aubrey. June 3, 1983; Bibler, Klewin.

V*ariations:* West of North Buttress: July 7, 1980; Björnberg, Ireland. North Buttress Couloir: June 27, 1984; Grison, Tedeschi.

5833

▲ 1	*Diamond Arête*	
2	*East Ridge*	

Route Guide

Approach: *0.5 mile from the 7,900-foot middle-eastern branch of the Tokositna Glacier landing area, to the 8,400-foot base.*

Total Time: *8-14 days.*

Climbing Miles: *1.*

Vertical Gain of Route: *6,100 feet.*

Alaska Grade: *6.*

Difficulties, Dangers, Rating: *Very difficult mixed climbing; crux was vertical ice chimney and wall on 17th pitch.*

Camps: *Chopped bivouacs until 12,000 feet.*

References: *1986 AAJ*

Firsts

Ascent: *To 14,200 feet: June 17, 1985; Donini, Tackle.*

Alpine Style: *To 14,200 feet: June 17, 1985; Donini, Tackle.*

▲ 1	*Diamond Arête*	
2	*East Ridge*	

5831

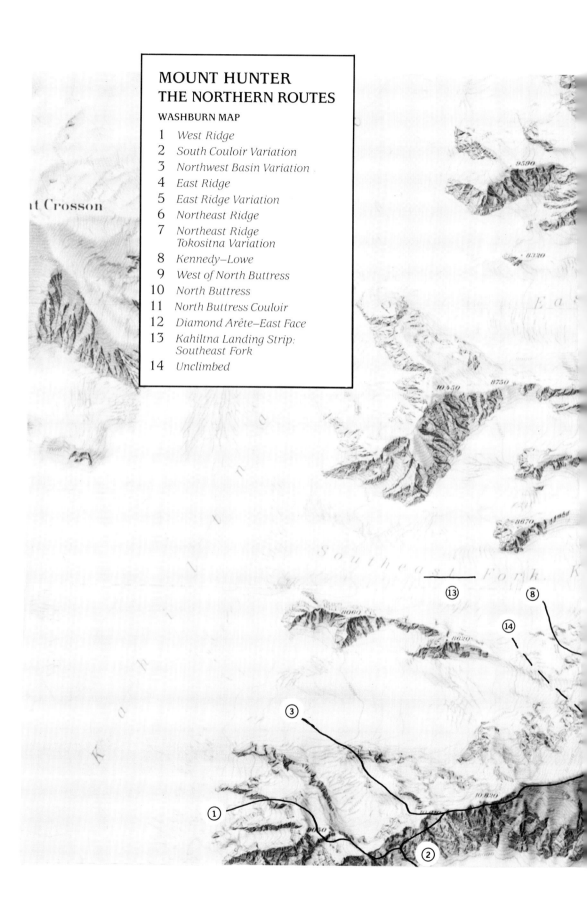

MOUNT HUNTER
THE NORTHERN ROUTES

WASHBURN MAP

1 *West Ridge*
2 *South Couloir Variation*
3 *Northwest Basin Variation*
4 *East Ridge*
5 *East Ridge Variation*
6 *Northeast Ridge*
7 *Northeast Ridge*
   Tokositna Variation
8 *Kennedy–Lowe*
9 *West of North Buttress*
10 *North Buttress*
11 *North Buttress Couloir*
12 *Diamond Arête–East Face*
13 *Kahiltna Landing Strip:*
    Southeast Fork
14 *Unclimbed*

CHAPTER 10

THE SOUTHERN ROUTES

South Ridge
Southeast Ridge
Southeast Spur
Southwest Ridge

South Ridge

MOUNT HUNTER'S SOUTHERNMOST PORTION IS A FAT, short ridge—often referred to as a face—cloven into two ridges: the Southeast Spur and the South Ridge. In some mountaineering circles, these ridges are called the Central Buttress of the South Face and the South Face. Bradford Washburn referred to these routes as having the finest rock in the McKinley area. Indeed, the various climbers classify it as "generally excellent Yosemite-type granite," or "beautiful pink granite." But the ice climbing and cornice traverses, shared by both routes on the upper South Ridge, also proved to be a considerable, time-consuming challenge.

Many people saw Washburn's photograph of the South Ridge in *The American Alpine Journal 1968*. Many people would come, many would grow obsessed, but few would actually reach the South Summit.

Before Washburn's photo had appeared in print, renowned British climbers Tony Smythe and Barry Biven took time out from a Yukon River float to attempt the South Ridge in 1968. Slush and steep rock defeated them at the 10,300-foot South Col. Dean Rau arrived the next year and was also defeated at the South Col. In 1970, Rau, John Mallon Waterman, Paul Harrison, and Duane Soper flew onto the Tokositna Glacier. They climbed most of the difficulties, but were turned back by bad weather.

Rau and Waterman couldn't let go. The route had cast its spell over them. They returned, in 1973, with Dave Carman and Don Black.

Rau had attempted the mountain twice, but his interest was now tempered by a healthy acceptance of his own mortality. This was in direct contrast to Waterman (first ascent of Mount Huntington's East Ridge, 1971), who would not accept defeat. In *The American Alpine Journal 1974*, Rau wrote, "Johnny Waterman is an outstanding climber on all media, but on the mixed ground of Alaska's difficult mountains, his climbing becomes superb." Carman was inexperienced in Alaska, awed by the unpleasantness of Mount Hunter's climbing, but swept up in Waterman's drive for the summit. Black had recently retreated from 16,700 feet on Denali, after a new route up the dangerous Traleika Icefall; he was not about to miss another summit.

They placed three thousand feet of fixed rope with forty anchors on the lower rock ridge. In the middle of their climb, Harrison, who had intended to finish this climb, arrived on the Tokositna. He had not been quick enough. Reluctantly, he and his five partners turned to another route (see Southeast Ridge).

Meanwhile, Rau opted to stay behind, tired of struggling with the South Ridge and being tormented by misconceptions, a feeling of completeness, and obsession.

The South Ridge's upper section proved a hard-to-protect tightrope-walker's nightmare, with a six-thousand-foot drop to the Kahiltna and a five-thousand-foot drop to the Tokositna. One pitch was straddled like a horse and dubbed the "Happy Cowboys."

In a twenty-hour push, ending in the decreasing visibility caused by a storm, Waterman, Black and Carman reached what seemed the highest point, the South Summit, on May 29, 1973.

Two days later, they returned to Rau at the ice cave. They descended and were flown out the following morning.

In *The American Alpine Journal,* Rau wrote:

> For me, Mount Hunter has remained enigmatic. By a twist of fate, my partners have come to share my feeling. After flying out, we hurried to look back at the mountain before the morning clouds obscured it. We oriented ourselves on the twin summits. Then we realized that Dave, Don and John had stopped on a spectacular gendarme a few hundred feet short of the actual south summit of Mount Hunter....Rather than the earthy accomplishment of reaching another summit, we are left with something less tangible, perhaps of greater value. A mountain has become a myth.

With the exception of Waterman, who considered the climb a failure (without the summit, the route was not complete), the climbing world seemed to feel that the South Ridge ascent had been successful. No one returned for thirteen years.

Direct Start Variation

On May 4, 1986, two British climbers, Ed Hart and Simon Richardson, arrived on the Tokositna Glacier. Their inspiration came from *The American Alpine Journal 1981* account of the Southeast Spur's ascent, alpine style. In 1984, Hart had climbed Denali's Cassin Ridge in four days; Richardson had never climbed in Alaska.

From the South Col, they cut west of the 1973 route and avoided much of the difficult rock by climbing a long snow face, with occasional mixed climbing.

They traversed beneath the Happy Cowboys area, on its east, which they found frightening. After two pitches up a steep corniced arête, they traversed underneath and away for ten pitches, for the Happy Cowboys had given them more than their share of ugly cornice problems. They reached the plateau after a week.

On their eighth day, in a whiteout, they followed compass bearings around the South Summit, to the start of the West Ridge; their lightweight snowshoes saved the day. The next day, May 12, they reached the North Summit.

They descended the West Ridge in two and a half days, finishing off their ten-day supply of food. Future parties should consider descending via the Southwest Ridge, which should be considerably easier than the West Ridge.

Although both of them had done more technical climbs, they had felt very committed. Hart said it was more difficult than the Cassin.

The South Peak of Mount Hunter as seen during descent of Peak 10800 ▼

Southeast Ridge

CLIMBING IS PRIMARILY ON SNOW AND ICE ON THE SOUTHeast Ridge, the longest of the three southern ridges. Bradford Washburn first suggested it, in an article in *The American Alpine Journal 1968,* "Challenges in Alaska and the Yukon, 1968." The photograph, with Washburn's dashes superimposed over the serpentine and corniced ridge crest, told the entire story.

Paul Harrison, who had attempted the neighboring South Buttress with John Mallon Waterman in 1970, became intrigued with Mount Hunter's southern side. On May 22, 1973, he returned with John Cleary, Paul Corwin, Dan Crowley, Dave Hawley and Chris Walker. All six climbers were Dartmouth students. (The Dartmouth Mountaineering Club had already carved an impressive legacy of first ascents on Denali's West Rib and the American Direct South Face.)

They had planned on finishing Mount Hunter's South Buttress, but, when they arrived, they found that Waterman, Dean Rau, Don Black and David Carman were already there. They switched to the unclimbed Southeast Ridge.

They put base camp at 8,100 feet and nervously cast about for a safe route up to the ridge. A 1,900-foot gully, with a hanging glacier at the top, seemed the only option; several pitches up, they traversed out of its line of fire. Fixing ropes on the steeper sections of ice, they established a 11,400-foot ridge camp by June 3.

The ridge was both knife-edged and corniced. At one point, Cleary collapsed a house-sized cornice while chopping steps. Another time, in a whiteout, Hawley plunged through and bobbed on the end of the rope.

On June 4, they climbed and fixed rope over steep ice. On the next day, they traversed (sans protection) two pitches beneath cornices on rotten, honeycombed ice. And on June 6, they finished fixing ropes around the last ice-climbing obstacles.

On June 7, Corwin, Crowley, Hawley and Walker started from their 11,400-foot camp for the summit. They crept across a rotten ridge and fixed the last of their ropes in an ice couloir behind a rock buttress. Steep snow followed. After twelve hours of climbing, they were on the knife-edge summit ridge, but the weather closed in. They waited an hour for it to clear, then started back.

Then the clouds lifted. They turned back toward the South Summit and, at midnight, arrived on the top (13,966 feet). They could see Mount Foraker, bright as day in the full moon. Harrison and Cleary's attempt to reach the summit the next day was thwarted by a storm.

On their descent from the 11,400-foot ridge camp, the team found the avalanche-prone 9,300-foot camp (Camp 2) buried beneath debris, but were able to dig out their radio and antenna. Their pilot picked them up the next day.

As of this writing, no one has repeated the Southeast Ridge. A safer, but more difficult alternative would be to climb the entire ridge, avoiding the Dartmouth route's hanging-glacier exposure.

▲

Southeast Spur

MOUNT HUNTER'S MOST ELEGANT AND DIFFICULT ridge is the Southeast Spur. Although it is primarily an ice arête, cut by rock steps, its pink granite is among the finest in the Alaskan Range. After 4,500 feet of sustained difficulties, the route merges with the South Ridge (or South Face) at 12,500 feet and continues horizontally, along an exposed and corniced ice blade for a half mile; it then climbs steeply for 1,000 feet to the South Summit, through a gash in the ice cliffs. Both the first- and second-ascent parties grossly underestimated the amount of time it would take to do the climb.

The route stands as a memorial to John Mallon Waterman, whose perseverance became legendary after his solo of this new route, both the first solo and traverse of the mountain. It took him 145 days.

Waterman was renowned for charging about the University of Fairbanks campus in a cape, carrying only flour and sugar on his climbs, and campaigning as an off-kilter candidate for president of the United States. It was also known that Waterman suffered extreme personal problems. But despite his eccentricities, and despite Glenn Randall's excellent book, *Breaking Point,* few really knew who "Johnny" was, what drove him, or how he got started.

He first roped up with Dave Seidman (see South Face, American Direct) when he was twelve years old. Shortly thereafter, his father, Guy, took him rock climbing. He was hooked; climbing became all he ever wanted. By the time he was fifteen, when teenagers were rare in the Shawangunks, he led his first 5.10 climb. Unlike many rock hotshots, and crucial to his development as an alpinist, he was also absorbed by winter climbing.

At an age when most boys were focusing on girls, cars, or school sports, Johnny was training hard every day for climbing. He would walk to school as fast as he could. At the end of the day, he'd come home, tag the front door, walk back to school, then back home again, all at a brisk pace. Each evening he did four hundred push-ups in ten sets.

His mentors and friends were among the best expedition climbers in North America: Seidman, Boyd N. Everett, Jr., Ed Nester, Tom Frost, Warren Bleser, Niels-Henrik Andersen, Rocky Keeler, and Leif-Norman Patterson.

In 1969, when he was sixteen, Nester invited him to climb Denali, accompanied by Frost; at that time Johnny was the third youngest on the summit.

He later made the first ascent of the North Face of Mount MacDonald, soloed the North Face of the Grand Teton, completed the first north-to-south traverse of the Howser Towers and did the third ascent of Mount Robson's North Face with Bleser.

Finally, he came back to Alaska, anxious to prove himself on Mount Hunter's South Ridge. During the first attempt in 1970, even though they had nearly finished the route, Waterman felt that his team wasn't strong enough. This failure nagged him.

In 1972, with Anderson, Keeler and Frank Zahar, he climbed Mount Huntington's East Ridge. On the summit, while his companions rejoiced at their new route, Waterman stared at his nemesis, Mount Hunter.

In 1973, he was back on the South Ridge with a strong team, determined to succeed. With Waterman leading many of the most difficult pitches, they finally stopped on a summitlike spire, in decreasing visibility, thinking they were on top. After they flew to Talkeetna, they looked back through the parting clouds and discovered they had missed the South Summit by two hundred feet. In Waterman's mind only, the climb became a failure.

Meanwhile, many of Waterman's mentors and friends were killed climbing: Seidman and Everett on Dhaulagiri, Chuck Loucks

John Mallon Waterman on his solo climb of the Southeast Spur (delayed-action shutter used) ▲

in the Tetons, Bleser and Andersen on the Matterhorn, Keeler in Scotland, Nester in the Selkirks, and Patterson in a Canadian avalanche. All of this had an effect on Waterman and his personal problems intensified, leading to his big solos. Dying in the mountains became a stark reality for Waterman.

In 1977, Peter Metcalf and three others attempted the Southeast Spur, but could not pass a 350-foot overhang. Another obsession began.

On March 24, 1978, Waterman arrived on the Tokositna Glacier. He would refer to his climb in *The American Alpine Journal 1979* as "my vendetta with Mount Hunter." He started up the Southeast Spur with seventy-four days of food, thirty-six hundred feet of rope, forty ice pitons, pickets and flukes, and twenty rock anchors. He broke the mountain down into eleven sections, fixed his rope, made a dozen carries, and moved his camp to the beginning of the next section.

He climbed a twelve-hundred-foot gully, broke through a rock step with some Class 5 moves, then moved his camp beneath the crux overhang. In three days, he cracked the overhang. By May 2, he moved his camp and supplies to the top of the overhang, finishing with the second section.

Waterman's *American Alpine Journal 1979* account is filled with painstaking detail about the route. His solo was monotonous, tortuous work. Although the route took a tremendous amount of time, Waterman was not a slow climber; in fact, he excelled on difficult mixed terrain. But he could not have climbed any quicker, because dispensing with his self-belay and load-ferrying system would not have been safe.

He moved across the cornices wearing floppy bunny boots, belaying himself with a Sticht plate attached to a Goldline. He placed his protection a hundred feet apart to save time. At one point, he collapsed a cornice and fell forty feet; like Casarotto soloing Denali's Ridge of No Return, he was surprised that his rope held him.

One can only imagine the profound psychological dimension that Waterman must have entered during his lonely vigil with the mountain. He dubbed three different formations "judges," as if he were being watched. He became miserable with body lice and was forced to ask Cliff Hudson, within hearing range of innumerable listeners on the CB radio, for an airdrop of the appropriate cure.

Once Hudson flew by and Waterman did a handspring on an incredibly exposed and tiny ledge. Over the radio, he asked, "Did you like that, Cliff?"

"Don't do that again!"

Waterman continued. He carried loads in the worst storm of the entire trip. The climb reduced him to tears, frustration, and rage.

After one hundred and two days out, he went to the South Summit with a bad sunburn, seeking any excuse to avoid another day of strenuous load carrying. It took him another forty-three days to cross the plateau, climb the Central and North summits, and descend the Northeast Ridge.

The mountaineering world stood up and took notice. Who was John Mallon Waterman?

Waterman believed that he had belittled the mountain by climbing it alone. In fact, he had deliberately begun fixing ropes down the Northeast Ridge before he climbed the North Peak, not believing that he could actually complete the climb without dying. When he reached the summit, he figured it must not have been a big enough challenge.

A year later, in the winter of 1979, he came back into the range to solo an unclimbed route on Denali's South Face. But this time, the loneliness and overwhelming scale of the mountain belittled him. He turned around. Something changed in Waterman. He felt cut down.

In 1981, he came back again, apparently to solo a new route on Denali. He disappeared, walking with only a day pack up the Northwest Fork of the Ruth Glacier. Despite extensive searches, his body was never recovered. Almost everyone in the mountaineering community thought it was simply another accident. Waterman's father and closest friends believe differently.

Waterman's accomplishments and incredible determination spoke for themselves: he had tasted the worst storms and stood on two of the most difficult summits in the Alaska Range, forging routes where no one had climbed, sometimes alone, otherwise, usually leading. If nothing else, he had learned how to survive.

Dogged by the inexplicable demons of his soul, Johnny had tagged his front door and set out for a walk from which he knew he could never return.

Alpine Style

In 1980, Metcalf, accompanied by Glenn Randall and Peter Athens, returned to settle his own vendetta with the Southeast Spur. They wanted to up the ante and climb the route alpine style. In stark contrast to Waterman, they carried only six days of food, six ice screws, two deadmen and some rock hardware for the overhang.

On the climb, they would extend themselves to the very edge. It took them six days to simply reach the South Ridge. They were

climbing on half rations, through blizzard conditions, irreversibly committed. Metcalf wrote about the Happy Cowboys:

> Pete becomes a human belay anchor as I gingerly hop onto it in straddle position, crampons biting both sides of the hollow crest as if I am spurring a bronco. One axe shaft goes straight down while I chop away at the unconsolidated cornices in front, praying all the time that the fracture line does not cut back under me. For two unprotected hours I repeat this tedious process until I reach the safety of a snug col. With a sigh of relief, I scream, I'm alive, I'm alive!

After nine days out, they still had not reached the plateau. They were growing weak with hunger and they could barely stay warm. Their open bivouacs were miserable affairs. Randall froze his fingers. Athens collapsed a cornice and fell. And Randall broke his crampons while leading.

The ascent became a survival climb and the three gave the mountain everything they had. When the ridge finally let them go, there was no question about trying to reach the summit. They staggered across the plateau, lashed by another blizzard, groping toward the West Ridge. Dexedrine became Athens and Metcalf's sustenance. After thirteen days, they limped into Kahiltna Base Camp, frostbitten and haggard, unrecognized by their friends.

Metcalf touted it as an alpine classic, the finest climb that any of them had done. But in another light, they had been terribly overextended.

Both Waterman and Metcalf's ascents were the products of a vendetta. And both paid steep psychological and physical tolls. The route, understandably, has not been repeated.

▲

Southwest Ridge

THIS RIDGE IS THE SAFEST, MOST STRAIGHTFORWARD route up Mount Hunter. It is a thirty-five- to fifty-degree snow-and-ice climb, with few cornices and little objective danger. It offers the quickest access to the South Summit and would also be an excellent descent from the more difficult southside climbs.

The route was first climbed in 1978 by Jeff Thomas, Malcolm Ulrich, and Alan and Shari Kearney. Thomas, who had climbed Denali's South Buttress in 1975, first saw Mount Hunter's Southwest Ridge the following year, while attempting Mount Foraker's Southwest Ridge. In 1977, Alan Kearney and Ulrich had camped at the base of Mount Hunter's Southwest Ridge, prior to making the first ascents of Thunder Peak and Humble Peak (Kahiltna Queen).

They approached Mount Hunter like pioneers, spending two and one half weeks marching from the Petersville Road to the mountain. By the time they reached the summit, they had gained over thirteen thousand feet. In an era of airplane approaches, their overland approach achieved a distinction that few other first-ascent parties on the south side of the Alaska Range would match.

On April 16, 1978, they started climbing a snow couloir; they had eight days of food in their packs. Shari wrote:

> We all agreed afterwards if we had not skied in and gotten somewhat numbed to heavy loads, we might have stumbled no further than to the foot of the couloir before setting down our packs and abandoning them for base camp. As it was, we went up, cursing, swearing, sweating for 2,500 feet.

The next day saw them on an easy, broad-shouldered section of ridge. But Ulrich went into a crevasse and they spent a lot of time extricating him. They gained only five hundred feet.

Leaving the tent behind on the third day, they teetered up boiler-plate ice covered with two inches of snow. As the sun sank behind their shoulders, with no place for a bivouac, they pushed one more pitch and miraculously found a perfect boulder-alcove. They watched the northern lights, darting green and yellow, curling luminescent colors through the sky. The moon rose. They were the most beautiful mountains Shari had ever slept in.

A camp on the upper Southwest Ridge route ▶

The next day, they finished the ridge in ten pitches and bivou-acked on a snow platform. They were behind schedule and began to chant, "When in Alaska, multiply by four." They had underestimated everything. The next morning, April 20, they rushed to the summit, concerned about the changing weather. Shari described her thoughts.

> I think I was a little drunk on the air up there, but it was beautiful being on top. Vague and indistinct, fabled peaks rose out of the ice and rock below.... We were only a short time on top before turning to head back down. After all, it's not the being on top, but the getting there and back.

On April 21, they rappelled off eleven bollards in the midst of a snowstorm, the flakes coming down thick and evil. They reached their tent.

The next morning, as the snow continued to fall, Shari insisted that they wait for safer conditions, but the male vote prevailed. They started down the couloir.

Ulrich and Thomas downclimbed quickly, disappearing from sight. Then a huge avalanche came down, narrowly missing Shari and Alan. They found Ulrich and Thomas' tracks obliterated in places by the avalanche. Shari optimistically commented that they would probably be setting up the tent at base camp. Alan's reply chilled her blood: "Yes, if they're still alive."

They became more and more anxious as they continued down. Shari wrote:

> A huge avalanche started pouring over me. It had been silent until it hit, and now it roared. It was spilling over my shoulders, but my axe was in and with my nose ducked inside my balaclava, I was standing it out. As it began to subside, I suddenly saw the rope pull tight below me. Alan had been above. I only had a moment of sick disbelief before my axe pulled and I lost it.
>
> So this is it, how stupid to die this way, accept it. You have let a lot of people down and now you are going to die. Any moment everything would stop. I would fly over an edge and slam into nothingness.
>
> But I fought, scrambling for my axe and then realized it was gone. I tumbled and twisted, the rope wrapped around my leg and spun me. I dug with my mittened hands and prayed that if it was lasting this long, maybe we could stop. Finally we did begin slowing down. I would almost get a purchase, only to be swung off by Alan's weight. Slowly we stopped.
>
> I sputtered and dug in. Alan, below, looked dazed, hat and glasses gone, hair wet with snow—screaming my name. I called twice before he heard me. I glanced around once for my axe, then fumbled for my hammer and started down.
>
> He was all right, a couple of cuts above the eye and frantic to get

off. We raced down the slope, my heart pounding so wildly I thought it would burst. We had been dragged 500 feet, over the hourglass and within 250 feet of the schrund.

Relief would not be felt for some time, nor could good clean memories of the climb be revived until some time the next day. For now, at the foot of the avalanche cone, dripping wet, exhausted—I was savoring a few basic human emotions. I dropped my pack and stumbled over to hug Alan. We were alive.

They found Ulrich with Thomas, who was nursing a twisted ankle, at the tent. The first avalanche had only clipped them.

A few weeks later, Thomas and Alan flew to the Kichatnas and climbed more new routes. Alan later took the lessons he had learned from the Alaska Range to wind-lashed Patagonia for several consecutive years, where he made more than a few successful climbs.

Shari, who had been the first woman to climb Mount Hunter, and by a new route as well, would write of the climb in both *The American Alpine Journal 1979* and *Climbing* magazine with unusual honesty, emotion and eloquence.

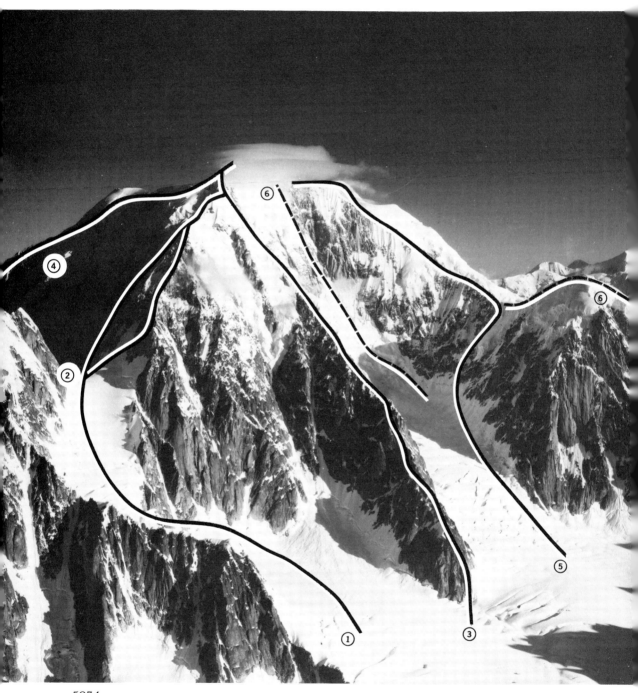

5934

MOUNT HUNTER

THE SOUTHERN ROUTES

1   *South Ridge*

2   *1986 Variation*

3   *Southeast Spur*

4   *Southwest Ridge*

5   *Southeast Ridge*

6   *Unclimbed*

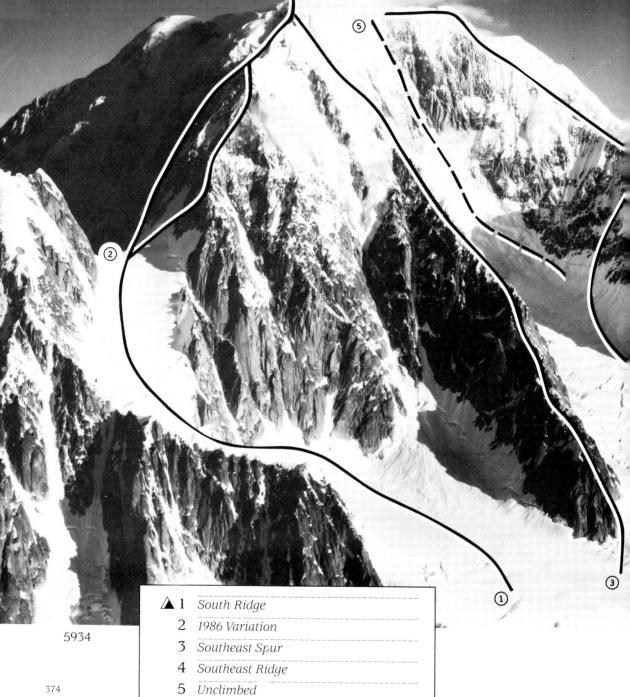

5934

▲ 1	*South Ridge*	
2	*1986 Variation*	
3	*Southeast Spur*	
4	*Southeast Ridge*	
5	*Unclimbed*	

Route Guide

A*pproach:* 0.5 mile from 7,400-foot Tokositna landing area to base of 8,200-foot icefall leading to south col.

T*otal Time:* 10-16 days.

C*limbing Miles:* 2 miles (South Summit).

V*ertical Gain of Route:* 5,700 feet.

A*laska Grade:* 5+.

D*ifficulties, Dangers, Rating:* There is an icefall to be avoided en route to the south col; 5.8 and A2 rock difficulties on first section of rock ridge; ice up to 80 degrees, occasional vertical bulges; exposed and hard-to-protect cornices.

C*amps:* 10,300 (south col); ca. 12,100; ca. 12,800; 13,100 (plateau).

R*eferences:* 1968 (photo), 1974 AAJ; 1987 AJ. Map: Talkeetna D-3.

Firsts

A*scent:* 13,700 feet: May 29, 1973; Black, Carman, Waterman, (Rau).

A*lpine Style:* Direct start: May 12, 1986; Hart, Richardson.

V*ariations:* Direct start: May 12, 1986; Hart, Richardson.

5836

▲ 1	*Southeast Ridge*
2	*Unclimbed*

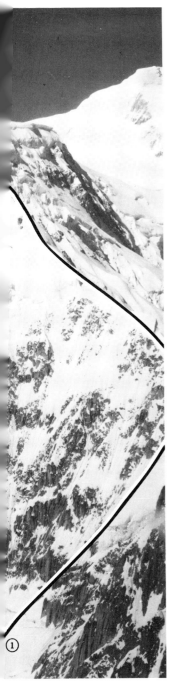

Route Guide

***A**pproach:* 3 miles from 7,400-foot Tokositna landing strip to the 9,300-foot campsite beneath gully; there is exposure to hanging glaciers; or, a lower point of the ridge would entail a shorter and a safer approach.

***T**otal Time:* 7–14 days.

***C**limbing Miles:* 2.

***V**ertical Gain of Route:* 4,500 feet.

***A**laska Grade:* 4.

***D**ifficulties, Dangers, Rating:* 9,000 to 11,000 feet is exposed to a hanging glacier (which could be avoided by a longer and more difficult start lower on the ridge); up to 70-degree ice climbing and cornice traversing.

***C**amps:* 8,100 (base camp); 9,300 (base of gully); 11,400 (low point on ridge).

***R**eferences:* 1968 (photo), 1974 AAJ. Maps: Talkeetna D-2, D-3.

Firsts

***A**scent: South Peak:* June 7, 1973; Corwin, Crowley, Hawley, Walker, (Harrison, Cleary).

5934

▲ 1	*Southeast Spur*
2	*Southeast Ridge*
3	*South Ridge*
4	*1986 Variation*
5	*Unclimbed*

Route Guide

Approach: *0.5 mile from landing area.*

Total Time: *13-21 days.*

Climbing Miles: *2 (South Summit).*

Vertical Gain of Route: *5,800 feet.*

Alaska Grade: *6.*

Difficulties, Dangers, Rating: *Technical crux is a 350-foot over-hang with hard Class 5 climbing and direct aid; Happy Cowboys involve straddling an exposed knife-edge with little or no protection; many unstable cornices and ice, with mixed climbing up to 80 degrees.*

Camps: *Virtually all bivouacs were chopped ledges, 1 cave was possible near top of climb.*

References: *1979, 1981* AAJ; *January-February 1981* Climbing; Breaking Point, *Randall;* Skiing Down Everest and Other Crazy Adventures, *Cranfield.* Map: *Talkeetna D-3.*

Firsts

Ascent: *July 26, 1978; Waterman.*

Alpine Style: *Summit Plateau: May 10, 1980; Athens, Metcalf, Randall.*

Solo: *July 26, 1978; Waterman.*

5836

▲ 1   *Southeast Spur (Upper)*
  2   *South Ridge*

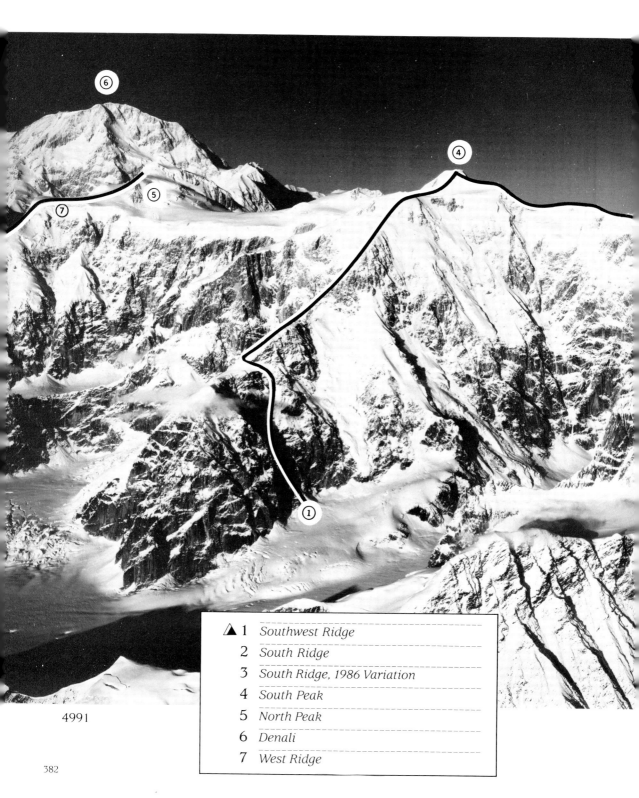

▲ 1	Southwest Ridge
2	South Ridge
3	South Ridge, 1986 Variation
4	South Peak
5	North Peak
6	Denali
7	West Ridge

4991

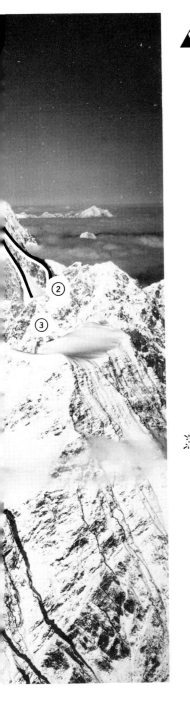

Route Guide

Approach: *Approximately 1 mile from a possible landing area at 6,500 feet beneath the ridge; otherwise, 5 miles from the 7,200-foot Southeast Fork of the Kahiltna landing strip.*

Total Time: *5–12 days.*

Climbing Miles: *2.*

Vertical Gain of Route: *6,500 feet.*

Alaska Grade: *4.*

Difficulties, Dangers, Rating: *30- to 50-degree snow and ice climbing; broad section of ridge from 9,500 to 10,000 feet has crevasses; couloir is avalanche-prone after large snowfalls.*

Camps: *9,500 (above couloir); 10,000; 11,000 (overhanging boulder); 11,600.*

References: *September–October 1978* Climbing; *1979* AAJ. *Map: Talkeetna D-3.*

Firsts

Ascent: *South Peak: April 20, 1978: A. & S. Kearney, Thomas, Ulrich.*

Alpine Style: *South Peak: April 20, 1978; A. & S. Kearney, Thomas, Ulrich.*

| 1 | Southwest Ridge |
| 2 | Kahiltna Glacier |

8435

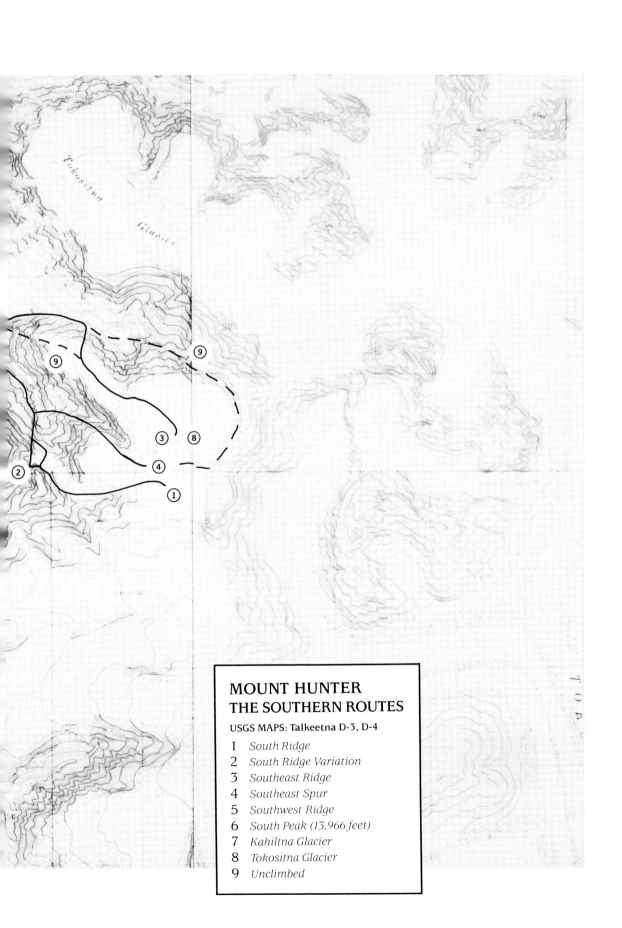

MOUNT HUNTER
THE SOUTHERN ROUTES

USGS MAPS: Talkeetna D-3, D-4

1 *South Ridge*
2 *South Ridge Variation*
3 *Southeast Ridge*
4 *Southeast Spur*
5 *Southwest Ridge*
6 *South Peak (13,966 feet)*
7 *Kahiltna Glacier*
8 *Tokositna Glacier*
9 *Unclimbed*

APPENDIX

REFERENCE MATERIALS

REFERENCE MATERIALS

The journals, magazines, photographs, and maps listed here are invaluable for expedition planning. (For other sources of information, see bibliography.)

Journals, Mazagines, Photographs, and Maps

The American Alpine Journal (The American Alpine Club), *The Canadian Alpine Journal* (The Alpine Club of Canada), *The Mountain World* (Swiss Foundation for Alpine Research; published from 1953 through 1969; collections available for reference in The American Alpine Club Library and several other libraries which have mountaineering collections), and *Ascent* (Sierra Club Books; published infrequently).

There are three independent mountaineering and climbing magazines in the United States: *Climbing, Rock and Ice,* and *Summit.* They publish articles and information on expeditions to the Alaska Range from time to time. *Mountain* magazine, published in England, also carries material on climbing in the Alaska Range.

Photographs by Bradford Washburn, as well as his map covering all routes on Denali and the northern routes on Mount Hunter, are available from the Museum of Science. Maps covering routes on Mount Foraker and Mount Hunter may be obtained from the United States Geographical Survey (USGS).

The Alpine Club of Canada
PO Box 1026
Banff, Alberta T0L 0C0
Canada
403-762-4481

The American Alpine Club, Inc.
113 East 90th Street
New York NY 10128-1589
212-722-1628

Sierra Club Books
730 Polk Street
San Francisco CA 94109-7813
415-923-5601

Climbing Magazine
PO Box E
Aspen CO 81612
303-925-3414

Mountain Magazine
PO Box 184
Sheffield S11 9DL
England

Rock and Ice Magazine
PO Box 3595
Boulder CO 80306
303-499-8410

Summit Magazine
PO Box 1889
Big Bear Lake CA 92315
714-866-3682

ANCHORAGE

Anchorage International Airport is served by several major domestic and foreign airlines. Anchorage is a modern, sprawling city with a population of 250,000. The Chugach Mountains flank the eastern edge of town, and Denali, Mount Foraker, and Mount Hunter are visible 140 miles to the north.

Anchorage is the only dependable place for last-minute shopping needs (common items such as film may not be available in Talkeetna). It is difficult to reach overnight lodging or attend to errands in Anchorage without a car. Rental cars are available at various rates. The airport is eight miles from the Alaska Railroad; taxis are available. Limousine service may be arranged from the airport to downtown hotels, which are closer to the railroad. Several retail stores offer a variety of climbing equipment and sporting goods (including rentals) at reasonable prices.

Most dining and lodging in Anchorage is expensive. Alaska Private Lodging and Anchorage Youth Hostel offer economical lodging alternatives.

TRANSPORTATION

Several means of round-trip transportation are available between Anchorage and Talkeetna. The trip by highway is 115 miles.

Denali Overland will shuttle climbers to and from any Anchorage location in a taxi, limousine, or bus. Advance deposits and reservations are necessary. Drivers are agreeable to groups combining for lower fares. Essential shopping stops or rest stops may be made on the two-and-a-half-hour trip. This service is highly recommended as a dependable, economical means of getting in and out of Anchorage and Talkeetna quickly, without the expense of staying in hotels. The drivers will accommodate any pick-up time and eliminate baggage problems.

Another transportation option for climbers and their gear is the Alaska Railroad. If Anchorage arrivals can be coordinated with train departures, the three-hour trip is renowned for its rural scenery. Talkeetna train service is limited to one or two times per week. Call the Alaska Railroad for current schedules and to make reservations. Although there is daily service in the summer, no baggage off-loading is provided for Talkeetna.

Aleyska Air will fly climbers from the Merrill Field Airport (near downtown Anchorage) or the Anchorage International Airport to Talkeetna, an hour-and-a-half flight. Baggage allowance is fifty pounds per person. Without reservations, flights may be cancelled. Daily service is provided. Most of the Talkeetna air services will also be arranged to shuttle climbers back and forth from Anchorage.

Expedition return dates are variable and there are a number of travel options available upon return to Talkeetna. Hitchhiking from Talkeetna to Anchorage is not too difficult (although hitchhiking from Anchorage to Talkeetna can be an expedition in itself).

TALKEETNA

The town of Talkeetna, with a seasonal population of two hundred to six hundred, is a former goldminers' stop on the railroad. It is a colorful, shopping-mall-sized town, adorned with rustic log cabins, restaurants, hotels, gift shops, a post office, a small general store, and a Laundromat (with showers). There is no bank. Talkeetna prices are slightly inflated. With the exception of fuel and sleds, it is recommended that all food and

Museum of Science
Attention: Bradford Washburn
Science Park
Boston MA 02114
617-589-0229

United States Geological Survey
Denver Federal Center
PO Box 25286
Denver CO 80225
303-236-7477

United States Geological Survey
Federal Building
101 Twelfth Avenue–126
Fairbanks AK 99701
907-456-0244

ANCHORAGE

Alaska Private Lodging
1236 W 10th Avenue
Anchorage AK 99501
907-258-1717

Anchorage Youth Hostel, Inc.
700 H Street–#2
Anchorage AK 99501
907-276-3635

TRANSPORTATION

Denali Overland Transportation
PO Box 330
Talkeetna AK 99676
907-733-2384

Alaska Railroad Corporation
PO Box 107500
Anchorage AK 99510
800-544-0552
907-265-2494, 265-2623

NATIONAL PARK SERVICE

Park Headquarters
Denali National Park and Preserve
PO Box 9
Denali National Park AK 99755
907-683-2294

Ranger Station
Denali National Park and Preserve
PO Box 588
Talkeetna AK 99676
907-733-2231

GUIDE SERVICES

Alaska Denali Guiding
PO Box 566
Talkeetna AK 99676
907-733-2649

Genet Expeditions
PO Box 230861
Anchorage AK 99523
800-334-3638, 907-561-2123

American Alpine Institute
1212 24th Street
Bellingham WA 98225
206-671-1505

Fantasy Ridge Mountain Guides
PO Box 1679
Telluride CO 81435
303-728-3546

Mountain Trip
PO Box 91161
Anchorage AK 99509
907-345-6499

Rainier Mountaineering, Inc.
535 Dock Street–209
Tacoma WA 98402
206-627-6242

National Outdoor Leadership
*   School*
PO Box AA
Lander WY 82520
307-332-6973

equipment be purchased in Anchorage or outside Alaska. Talkeetna ("Three Rivers" in Athapaskan) is fenced by the Susitna, Talkeetna, and Chulitna rivers. Denali is visible from town, twenty thousand feet higher, sixty miles away, looming like a ghost cloud above the silt-laden rivers.

Poor flying weather can maroon expeditions. The most successful expeditions abandon timetables, letting the weather dictate the pace. When the weather is unsuitable for flying, expeditions may have to wait in town (or on the mountain) for a few days. Longer delays are infrequent.

In spring, there are marked and set ski trails in Talkeetna. Volleyball games are popular. In June and July, there are festivals, dances, and bands. There are many running routes, bars, and an excellent public library. Potluck dinners, barbecues, and slide shows become routine for climbers who are stranded in town. And the local salmon runs are legendary.

DENALI NATIONAL PARK AND PRESERVE

Denali and Mount Foraker climbers must submit individual registrations to the Park Service and check in at the Talkeetna Ranger Station before and after their climbs. It is also recommended that one sign in and out for Mount Hunter, although it is not required. This procedure is a simple formality, compensated for by the helpfulness of the rangers, who provide up-to-date route information and perform rescues.

Preregistrations notwithstanding, every group should plan to spend an hour at the ranger station, a prominent log cabin on Talkeetna's main street, taking advantage of the multilingual Denali slideshow, the most extensive Bradford Washburn photo collection outside of Boston, and many volumes of Alaska Range-related books and journals. The rangers have earned a reputation for friendliness and, collectively, possess an unparalleled knowledge of the Alaska Range.

The rangers recommend that all climbers use plastic bags and dispose of feces in crevasses, or, on steeper routes, plan toilet disposal that will not compromise future climbers' drinking water. All trash and food should be carried out; the Park Service has fined parties for littering.

GUIDE SERVICES

Several companies are authorized by Denali National Park and Preserve to guide climbers on Denali and Mount Foraker. They all have well-prepared literature on their services. Climbers requiring guide service should contact the companies well in advance in order to choose the one whose services are best suited to their needs and plans.

APPROACH SERVICES

The Talkeetna pilots are veterans of mountain flying and glacier landings. All are genuinely interested in the welfare of their clients, and routinely check on the progress and well-being of climbing parties. The Talkeetna air services are licensed to fly climbers to Denali, Mount Foraker, and Mount Hunter. Dog sled services and support are available for expeditions on the northern routes of Denali.

BASE CAMP

Base camp lies within Denali National Park and Preserve, just outside of the original boundaries. Nonemergency aircraft landings are prohibited within the original, or old, boundaries of the park, allowing visitors to experience the land in its pristine state and leaving wildlife habitats undisturbed.

A base camp caretaker operates the radio and coordinates flights as a cooperative effort of the Talkeetna air services. Fuel is cached here (for safety and convenience) and can be picked up on climbers' arrival. Expeditions should leave six days of emergency rations in a well-marked, dated, and high-wanded cache. Shallow and unmarked caches have been scavenged by ravens and hungry climbers.

COMMUNICATIONS

Citizens' band (CB) radios are the choice of most Alaska Range expeditions. The Talkeetna air services jointly operate a radio telephone and a CB set at the Southeast Fork of the Kahiltna Glacier (Kahiltna Base) and on the Ruth Glacier. In Talkeetna, the ranger station and four air services are similarly equipped. By carrying a two-and-a-half-pound portable CB, expeditions can contact radio operators at Kahiltna Base and Ruth Glacier. They can also communicate with Talkeetna aircraft, numerous bush dwellers, the Kantishna Roadhouse, Eielson Visitor Center, passing truck drivers, Park Service patrols, and operators in Talkeetna.

Radios are indispensable in emergencies, as long as they are used as a last resort. Many beleaguered parties cannot be helped immediately, or even for days, despite radio contact. Self-sufficiency, common sense, and prudence will weigh less and work longer than any radio.

A portable CB can be rented from various air services and Genet Expeditions, although quantities are limited. A CB can be purchased before the expedition departs, then sold afterward to one of the many needy expeditions. Look for a five-watt, lightweight unit (avoid digital models) set up for Channel 19. If the radio has the capability, carry or install a back-up Channel 19 crystal. An extra set of batteries is recommended.

APPROACH SERVICES

Hudson Air Service, Inc.
PO Box 82
Talkeetna AK 99676
907-733-2321

K2 Aviation
PO Box 545
Talkeetna AK 99676
907-733-2291

Talkeetna Air Taxi
PO Box 73
Talkeetna AK 99676
907-733-2218

Doug Geeting Aviation
PO Box 42
Talkeetna AK 99676
907-733-2366

Denali Dog Tours and
  Wilderness Freighters
PO Box 670
Denali National Park AK 99755
907-683-2314

Other types of radios, such as VHF, single side band, and radio telephone, are available on a limited and more expensive basis. The single side band radio is useful for the northern routes on Denali and Mount Foraker, where line-of-sight radio communication is not possible.

Several expeditions have benefited from K2 Aviation's emergency air-to-ground signals card. Similar air-to-ground signals can be found in the book, *Medicine for Mountaineering*.

WEATHER

It is often said that the weather will make or break a climb in the Alaska Range. This is true. Summer storms emanate almost entirely from the south, when masses of moist ocean air hit the range. Typically, storms last several days, although more unusual storms can rage for a week. June and July, while often warm, tend to have heavier snowfall. An accumulation of several feet is not uncommon. April can have bitterly cold days and strong winds. May tends to be more moderate.

Although there may be slight variations, hours of daylight and temperatures are optimal for Mount Foraker and Denali from late April until early July. August and September are bad months because of significant glacier melt-out and stormy conditions. Temperatures can be −40°F up high and 80°F down low. Mount Hunter climbers should start several weeks earlier, although conditions deteriorate below ten thousand feet in June.

RESCUE

All expeditions should plan for emergency contingencies. On Denali, it is likely that a strong team will be called on to help another team, not an uncommon occurrence on a mountain with more than seven hundred climbers per year.

It has been observed that it is the self-reliant teams, willing to achieve the summit another year if things go wrong, that come back down unscathed.

In instances of life-threatening emergencies, the victims that survived were usually stabilized (warmed up, treated for shock, rehydrated) before evacuation was attempted. Next, if at all possible, it is recommended that climbers evacuate victims to a lower elevation to avoid altitude sickness and exposure to cold and storms. Requesting a helicopter rescue will always be a difficult decision. The Park Service coordinates all rescues and rangers seldom refuse evacuation requests. Rescuers must take into account whether a victim can descend safely by sledding or walking to an airplane landing site, or if the victim's life signs are deteriorating. Many victims have died while waiting for a helicopter in poor weather or at high altitude. Dynamic, immediate descents, particularly in cases of altitude sickness, have saved lives.

In summary, stabilize the victim, then descend. If this is not possible, radio for air evacuation. Helicopters do have limitations—visibility, wind, elevation, and a multitude of other factors must be considered. It is not always possible to evacuate everyone safely by helicopter. Delays in receiving helicopter assistance should be expected—plan accordingly.

Rescue Suggestions

At least half of every team should have emergency medical training (EMT), advanced first aid, nursing, or similar emergency backgrounds. Review literature about the Alaska Range, giving attention to the common accidents or illnesses such as high altitude sickness, frostbite, climbing falls, and crevasse falls.

Carry a copy of the third edition of *Medicine for Mountaineering*. Expeditions have found it invaluable for diagnosing and treating various medical emergencies on Denali.

Carry a well-stocked first-aid kit and be familiar with its contents.

Nearby parties are the best source of assistance if a rescue cannot be self-contained.

EQUIPMENT

The hardware recommendations are based on the number of items climbers have carried in relation to the Alaska Grade of their route. Although some climbers have taken more or less equipment, the following guidelines represent a minimum for two climbers:

GRADE	HARDWARE
2	4 pickets and flukes, 2 ice screws, 1 rope
3	4 pickets and flukes, 4 ice screws, 1 rope
4	4 pickets and flukes, 6 ice screws, 10 nuts (for rock routes), 2 ropes
5	4 pickets and flukes, 10 ice screws, 10 nuts, 3 Friends, 6 pitons, 2 ropes
6	4 pickets and flukes, 12 ice screws, 16 nuts, set of Friends, 12 pitons, 2 ropes

RENTAL EQUIPMENT

Alaska Denali Guiding
PO Box 566
Talkeetna AK 99676
907-733-2649

Genet Expeditions
PO Box 230861
Anchorage AK 99523
800-334-3638, 907-561-2123

Recreational Equipment, Inc.
2710 Spenard Road
Anchorage AK 99503
907-272-4565

Alaska Mountaineering and Hiking
2633 Spenard Road
Anchorage AK 99503
907-272-1811

In addition to carrying the necessary hardware (including carabiners, a set of ascenders, and a pully), each climber should have prior practice, knowledge, and a plan for enacting a crevasse rescue. Crevasse falls have plagued expeditions since 1932.

Snowshoes are invaluable on remote routes with high plateaus, such as Mount Hunter's Southeast Spur and Denali's East Buttress. Although there is other essential gear, mere possession is not a substitute for the necessary experience and knowledge. A comprehensive list of expedition and personal equipment necessary for climbing in the Alaska Range is given in *Surviving Denali,* as well as in other publications.

Prior arrangements should be made to ensure the availability of rental equipment. Boots, skis, bindings, and skins are all suspect rental gear. Expect the best performance (and fewest blisters) from gear that is tested under extreme conditions prior to the expedition. There are several sources for rental equipment in Anchorage and Talkeetna.

There are many retail outlets in the United States that sell climbing equipment. Lists are often published in the climbing magazines. A number of the outlets also advertise in these magazines.

BIBLIOGRAPHY

Browne, Belmore. *The Conquest of Mount McKinley.* 1913. Reprint. Houghton Mifflin, Boston, 1956.

Casarotto, Renato. *Oltre i Vento del Nord.* dall'Oglio, Italy, 1986.

Cassin, Riccardo. *50 Years of Alpinism.* Diadem Books, London; The Mountaineers, Seattle, 1981.

Cook, Frederick A. *To the Top of the Continent.* Hodder & Stoughton, London, 1909.

Cranfield, Ingrid. *Skiing Down Everest and Other Crazy Adventures.* Severn House, London, 1983.

Davidson, Art. *Minus 148°: The Winter Ascent of Mt. McKinley.* Cloudcap Press, Seattle, 1986.

Dunn, Robert. *The Shameless Diary of an Explorer.* The Outing Publishing Co., New York, 1907.

Everett, Boyd N. *The Organization of an Alaskan Expedition.* Gorak Books, Pasadena, 1984.

Hackett, Peter H. *Mountain Sickness: Prevention, Recognition & Treatment.* The American Alpine Club, New York, 1980.

Houston, Charles S. *Going Higher: The Story of Man and Altitude.* Little, Brown and Company, Boston, 1987.

Jones, Chris. *Climbing in North America.* University of California Press, Berkeley and The American Alpine Club, New York, 1976.

Moore, Terris. *Mt. McKinley: The Pioneer Climbs.* The Mountaineers, Seattle, 1981.

Morrow, Patrick. *Beyond Everest.* Camden House Publishing Ltd., Toronto, 1986.

Mountaineering: Denali National Park and Preserve, Alaska. National Park Service, U.S. Department of the Interior, 1987.

Randall, Frances. *Denali Diary: Letters from McKinley.* Cloudcap Press, Seattle, 1987.

Randall, Glenn. *Breaking Point.* Chockstone Press, Denver, 1983.

Randall, Glenn. *Mt. McKinley Climber's Handbook.* Genet Expeditions, Talkeetna, 1984.

Roper, Steve and Allen Steck. *Fifty Classic Climbs of North America.* Sierra Club Books, San Francisco, 1979.

Snyder, Howard H. *The Hall of the Mountain King.* Charles Scribner's Sons, New York, 1973.

Stuck, Hudson. *The Ascent of Denali (Mount McKinley): A Narrative of the First Complete Ascent of the Highest Peak in North America.* Charles Scribner's Sons, New York, 1914.

Waterman, Jonathan. *Surviving Denali: A Study of Accidents on Mount McKinley.* The American Alpine Club, New York, 1983.

Wilcox, Joe. *White Winds.* Hwong Publishing Company, Los Alamitos, 1981.

Wilkerson, James A., editor. *Medicine for Mountaineering.* The Mountaineers, Seattle, 1985.